PELICAN BOOKS

A 771

THE MISEDUCATION
OF
AMERICAN TEACHERS

JAMES D. KOERNER

The Miseducation
of
American Teachers

James D. Koerner

THE MISEDUCATION
OF
AMERICAN TEACHERS

WITH AN INTRODUCTION BY

STERLING M. McMURRIN

*Former United States Commissioner
of Education*

PENGUIN BOOKS

BALTIMORE • MARYLAND

Penguin Books Inc.
3300 Clipper Mill Road, Baltimore, Maryland 21211

This edition first published 1965 by arrangement with
Houghton Mifflin Company, Boston

Library of Congress Catalog Card Number: 63-9082

Chapter 5 first appeared as an article in the *Saturday
Review* Education Supplement, October 20, 1962, under
the title "Teacher Education: Who Makes the Rules?"
© 1962 by Saturday Review, Inc.

Set in Linotype Caledonia

Printed in the United States of America

Acknowledgments

PORTIONS of this book have appeared in different form in *The Atlantic Monthly, The Saturday Evening Post,* and the *Saturday Review.* These periodicals have generously granted permission for reproduction of the material. The following publishers have also been kind enough to permit me to quote or reproduce material which they hold in copyright: *The Daily Cardinal* of the University of Wisconsin; D. C. Heath and Company; Harcourt, Brace, and World, Inc.; Harper and Row; Oxford University Press; and Prentice-Hall, Inc.

I am greatly indebted to several persons who read and criticized the entire preliminary draft: Jacques Barzun, Lawrence A. Cremin, I. L. Kandel, Jack Mooney, and Mortimer Smith. They saved me from errors both of fact and interpretation, and they made many cogent suggestions from which I profited immeasurably; they are not, obviously, in any way accountable for the deficiencies of the book. For the hundreds of other men and women throughout the nation—administrators, teachers, students, laymen—who helped me along the way, often at considerable inconvenience to themselves, I must rely on this wholly inadequate method of offering my sincere thanks. Without the cooperation and help which they rendered in so many ways, even when my views were strongly incompatible with their own, the book could not have been written.

I would like especially to thank the registrars and other administrators of the 32 colleges and universities that contributed samplings of their transcripts of credit to the study; in addition to them, three other persons were of particular help in this matter and deserve particular thanks: S. A. Nock of the executive committee of the American Association of Collegiate Registrars and Admissions Officers, James S. LeSure of the Connecticut State Department of Education, and Elmer R. Smith of Brown University. To Jen Mooney, who undertook with infinite patience and skill the thoroughly wearisome task of assembling, sorting, and coding the several thousand transcripts of credit involved, and then of recording the dozens, sometimes hundreds, of items of information from each transcript used in the final sample—I can only tender an awestruck vote of thanks. My wife, Marjorie, carried out that other laborious job, typing the manuscript, and helped as always in so many other ways that this expression of gratitude hardly covers the matter.

Lastly, special thanks are due the Relm Foundation of Ann Arbor, Michigan, for its support of the study that produced this book.

Contents

Introduction

STERLING M. McMURRIN

FORMER UNITED STATES COMMISSIONER OF EDUCATION

AMERICAN education has achieved much that merits our pride and deserves our commendation. Those achievements, in both the extent of educational opportunity and the quality of the instructional program, are entirely evident to most of us. It is true, however, that the generality of our schools are not as good as they might have been if over the past few decades we had followed a somewhat different course, or as they promise to be in the future because there is now a movement in new directions.

This is not simply to accuse our educators. Society as a whole is responsible for the character and quality of the educational program. What goes on in the schools both determines and is determined by the large cultural and social contexts within which they function. It seems to me that generally speaking the people of our nation have had the kind of schools they have asked for and have been willing to pay for. Indeed, on the whole the schools are somewhat better than we have been willing to pay for. Now, certainly, there is a large demand for something much better and there are indications of a disposition to pay for it. The future looks quite promising.

At least three large factors in our culture have contributed to the present state of our schools insofar as they are less adequate than they should be or might have been. The first of these is the doctrinaire egalitarianism that is the popular expression of our national ideal of equality. This has all too commonly influenced our schools in the direction of a dead leveling process that fails to respect the differences in intellectual and other abilities that inevitably obtain among individuals. Fortunately there is now a widespread recognition not only that we can no longer afford to waste human talent and ability in the manner encouraged by this policy, but also that a genuinely democratic ideal demands a large measure of individualism in the educational process.

The second factor importantly affecting education is the anti-intellectualistic attitude that has in considerable degree been a pervasive quality of our culture over the past half century. This anti-intellectualism is an expression of the strong pragmatic motivations of our society which have generally subordinated the quest for knowledge to its practical uses and have valued the successful accomplishment of practical ends more than intellectual achievement and the cultivation of reason. Here again there are indications of a new direction in educational thought and policy in response to a rising popular criticism that reflects a growing respect for the worth of knowledge and a new appreciation of the large capacities for learning that can be found among our children and youth.

But it is especially at the point of the third factor that James Koerner's book is so pertinent — the issue of the commitment of our resources to education. I refer here not primarily to monetary, but rather to human resources. Quite obviously the American people have placed a high value on education. They are sensitive to the worth of education for the individual and, perhaps in a lesser degree, to its importance for the strength of our nation and the quality of our culture. But whatever his conception of the value of education, our average citizen has taken it for granted that teaching, especially in the secondary and elementary schools, is a profession entirely appropriate for persons of second- or third-rate ability. We have all too commonly, therefore, proceeded to provide them with second- or third-rate educations and pay them third- or fourth-rate salaries.

Now if there is anything that Amercan education needs it is a radical revision of this attitude, which unfortunately pervades even the educational profession itself, and a strengthening and upgrading of the entire complex of policies and procedures that determine who will instruct in the classroom and laboratory and what their talents and intellectual equipment will be.

The revision is not easily effected, as the educational profession is shot through with a basic conservatism and taken in general it is remarkably defensive in the presence of criticism, whether from within or from without. But, as Mr. Koerner indicates, important things are happening even here, as outstanding individuals and institutions come to grips with the difficult problem of attracting persons of high ability to the teaching vocation and the equally difficult task of giving them the kind of education that the first-rate teacher must have. Those who are the real leaders in this movement are often working against large odds and in the face of much inertia and opposition. They deserve strong support and encouragement, for their task is not only difficult, it is one that has unlimited implications for the well-being of our society.

I do not mean to suggest that our schools are without teachers of high ability and good education. We have them in considerable numbers and the nation owes them a great debt of gratitude, for it is they who are the underwriters of the quality that our schools have achieved. Without these first-rate teachers, who with a full dedication and commitment serve their society for a compensation that, being tied to a fixed salary scale wherein the least able are paid as well as the most able, is usually disgracefully low, our schools would be in a condition not pleasant to contemplate. But our problem, and this is the greatest single problem in American education, is that we do not have such people in our schools in adequate numbers.

In this volume Mr. Koerner has concentrated his attention on the character and quality of teacher education. He is frank and blunt and at times, to put it mildly, rough. Many of his readers will applaud. Others, especially some of those who suffer the most direct hits, will be outraged. Nevertheless, I believe his instincts are eminently good. He has taken a hard look at a problem of central importance and has written a highly readable book, a book that deserves to be read, and read widely and intelligently.

In centering his criticism on the quality of teacher preparation in our schools of education and teachers colleges, Mr. Koerner has struck at the nerve center of our entire system of secondary and elementary education, both public and private. Too often it is assumed that solutions to our educational deficiencies lie in buildings, equipment, administration, or salaries. These things are important, and anyone who supposes that American education will achieve the high level of which it is capable and which we now must and do demand of it without a far larger investment of our material resources, especially in teachers' salaries, has his head in the sand. But however important other factors may be, and whatever else may be done to effect improvement, the quality of education in this nation will never be better than the intellectual caliber of our teachers and the education they themselves receive in our colleges and universities.

While recognizing the outstanding work of both individuals and institutions in pointing new directions in teacher education, I must agree with Mr. Koerner that when one views the national scene as a whole the quality of our teacher education schools and colleges is a weak element in our educational complex, a weakness at the point where the most damage can be done — and where all too often it is done. As is well known, for the past several years criticism of the professional education schools has been a favorite academic sport among the faculties of other professional schools and of the sciences and arts. These people, however, have often been more adept as critics of education than in the evaluation of their own operations. All of the deficiencies that Mr. Koerner describes in education can be found in varying degrees and forms in the other schools and departments of most of our colleges and universities. Almost anywhere one looks there is room for a good deal of housecleaning. Fortunately much housecleaning is going on.

But this in no way changes the fact that the health of American education demands a genuine upgrading of the faculties of our teacher preparation institutions, a radical revamping of the curricula of many of them, and frequently some major changes in the entire conception and administration of teacher education. Those who are endowed with high intellectual abilities normally want an education commensurate with their talents. There is every reason to believe that the raising of the admission and retention requirements of our education schools and the stiffening of the scholarly demands that are made upon their students will attract more, not fewer, persons of top talent into the teaching profession. The raising of these standards, of course, would be nothing less than tragic if there were not also a corresponding upgrading of the educational program to which the students are subjected. Teaching is an interesting and exciting way of life and now when it is so entirely clear that nothing less than our national security and well-being depend on the quality of teaching in our schools, we should insist that no task that our society now faces deserves more serious and competent attention than that of securing the best education for prospective teachers that our resources can provide.

It will be a bright day for our schools when the generality of the trustees, administrators, and faculties of our universities show as much interest in their colleges of education as they show in their colleges of medicine, or evidence as much pride in the product of their departments of education as they have in the products of their departments of chemistry or physics. It will be a bright day when all our faculties in education are determined, as some now are, to engage the full resources of their college or university in the education of teachers and are really committed to the elimination of trivia from their curricula and to a full concentration on the large and important educational problems that deserve exacting scholarly attention and excite the interest of the most competent students. It will be a very bright day for the nation when a degree from an education school is a guarantee of a genuine liberal education, a competent mastery of a specialized field, a full grasp of the aims and purposes of education, and effective cultivation in the art of teaching. That day may come — but probably not soon.

The Miseducation
of
American Teachers

CHAPTER I

Findings and Prejudices

For God's sake don't ANSWER these remarks which (as Uncle Howard used to say of father's writings) are but the peristaltic belchings of my own crabbed organism.

— William James in a letter to his brother, Henry

AMERICAN education produces no books that are what everybody says they should be — "objective." Education is as yet far too inexact a phenomenon for meticulous analysis. We are probably no closer now to basing education, that most tormented of subjects, on anything "objective" than mankind has ever been. Aristotle, whose glorious rage for order was occasionally frustrated, sounds reassuringly puzzled and modern as he surveys the education of his time and comments:

> It is clear then that there should be legislation about education and that it should be conducted on a public system. But consideration must be given to the question, what constitutes education and what is the proper way to be educated. At present there are differences of opinion as to the proper tasks to be set; for all peoples do not agree as to the things that the young ought to learn, either with a view to virtue or with a view to the best life, nor is it clear whether their studies should be regulated more with regard to intellect or with regard to character. And confusing questions arise out of the education that actually prevails, and it is not at all clear whether the pupils should practice pursuits that are practically useful, or morally edifying, or higher accomplishments — for all these views have the support of some judges . . .

Perhaps no creation of society as bound up as education is with the emotive ideals and desires of men can hope for any

1

kind of precise discussion. Certainly not contemporary education, whose major characteristic is the imprecision of its stated goals, of its methods for pursuing them, even of its peculiar language.

Despite the uncountable experiments that have been conducted in modern education, the tireless application of scientific method, the endless statistics, and all that which passes for research, educational programs in the United States continue to be constructed, and educational decisions continue to be made, on other than "objective" grounds; they continue to be chiefly acts of faith, hope, or charity. And educational books continue as always to be arguments based more on their authors' personal convictions than on any sort of recognized and accepted data.

This book, dealing with one of the most controversial and most protean areas in education, pretends to no scientific detachment, either in conception or execution. In conception, it grew out of what Albert Jay Nock once termed the first condition of progress, "a lively and peremptory dissatisfaction." Whether, in execution, this book also represents progress is something I can only hope for. My dissatisfaction arose initially, not by the way in which American teachers were educated, but by the way in which Americans were educated. I was led to my subject, that is, through an accumulation of unhappy impressions about the intellectual condition of American youth — before, in, and apart from, college. The signs and portents of miseducation in the United States are a tired though timeless topic: some people point to the low level of our public life and to the abdication of political responsibility by large numbers of citizens; some say the mass media and the persistence of mediocrity therein tell the truest story about American education; some point to the statistics on crime and juvenile delinquency and mental breakdown; some say they can't hire secretaries who can spell, punctuate, or file alphabetically, or workers who can read and comprehend directions or learn a new skill; and some point to the general irrationality and contempt for intellectualism so often evident in American life. The college instructor, for his part, is apt to point out that whatever else his incoming freshmen were doing before they arrived on campus, they were not mastering basic subjects. Nothing is clearer to him than the fact that his freshmen students, and others as well, have no useful grasp of a common body of elementary knowledge of Western culture or their own political or social institutions. They cannot be assumed to have a common acquaintance with any particular books or ideas and certainly not with the fundamentals of their own language. This unhappy condition necessitates the large and expensive remedial programs in basic subjects that most colleges operate; it also depresses standards in the regular classes.

The catalogue of complaint is long. How much justice it contains is the heart of the educational debate. Anyone who believes, as I do, that the complaints are just indeed is inevitably led to consider the education of teachers; for it is obvious that if their preparation is faulty changes must be made in the education of teachers before any substantive ones can be hoped for in public schools. After speculating with growing distress for over a decade about the enormous enterprise known as "teacher education" in our colleges and universities, I undertook a lengthy study of the subject. The study produced this book.

I would again emphasize that most arguments about teacher education no more lend themselves to "proof" than do debates about other educational problems. All the important questions one can ask about educating teachers must be answered on essentially suasive grounds; very few "data" exist on the best way to prepare people to teach in public schools or to administer them. Engineers are fond of referring to the degree of knowledge in technical fields at any given time as "the state of the art." In teacher education, the state of the art is infantile. An examination of the evidence available on the effectiveness of preparing teachers one way as against another leaves one in a familiar cul-de-sac, the only way out of which is through one's reasoned convictions. One can wholeheartedly agree with Mark Van Doren when he says,

> The education of teachers is an education in the liberal arts. When this education is good, and falls on the right ground, it produces persons with usable intellects and imaginations who know both what and why they are teaching. A teacher who can answer neither of those questions is no teacher, for thus he proves himself incapable of the one pleasure reserved for him among the pleasures possible to man: the pleasure of being intelligible.[1]

And one can agree with Sterling M. McMurrin, former United States Commissioner of Education, when he comments on how far short of this goal contemporary teacher education falls:

> The blunt fact is that many of our teachers are not properly qualified to handle the responsibility we have placed on them. This is our basic educational problem. Many of our teachers, for instance, lack native talent for teaching. It is a national scandal, moreover, that large numbers of them are inadequately prepared in the subject matter that they teach, as well as in the elements of a genuinely liberal education. This is, in my view, the major weakness of American Education.[2]

But ultimately one recognizes such comments, as well as the opposing and contrasting ones that fill the educational air today, as statements of position, not subject to scientific verification.

This book is therefore filled with judgments, private evaluations, even prejudices if you like, as are, wittingly or not, all other books on the subject. Having said so much, I should also make clear that I have gone about studying teacher education as dispassionately as possible, have tried to proceed as

---

[1] *Liberal Education*, Beacon, 1959, pp. 175-76.
[2] *Ladies' Home Journal*, March, 1962, p. 6.

undogmatically as I could, have freely modified many opinions with which I began, and have tried to base my assessments of the present state of the art on reasonable and demonstrable grounds. The book contains, in support of at least its main arguments, a considerable body of evidence gathered at first hand over an extended period of time. Whether the evidence is sufficient to justify the conclusions will depend on the reader's own convictions, for what I offer the reader are judgments based on much study and observation but based finally on conviction.

That being so, the reader has a right to ask after my educational principles and the point of view from which I examined the field of teacher education. These principles should not be construed as a "philosophy," a much-abused word in education. Although much is said throughout the field about the importance of one's "philosophy of education," and although training programs always have "courses" in this "subject," probably nobody active in teacher education today, with the doubtful exception of the Jesuits, has developed anything that could properly bear the name. And if he had developed it he would no doubt, as George Santayana once remarked about academic philosophies, have little success in teaching it:

> That philosophers should be professors is an accident, and almost an anomaly. Free reflection about everything is a habit to be imitated, but not a subject to expound; and an original system, if the philosopher has one, is something dark, perilous, untested, and not ripe to be taught, nor is there much danger that any one will learn it.[3]

Even John Dewey, who was a considerable philosopher, could not be said to have formulated his diverse educational ideas around a "philosophy of education." He had his philosophy and he had his educational ideas, but there are few discernible bridges between, perhaps because, as he himself

[3] *Character and Opinion in the United States*, Scribner, 1921, p. 35.

pointed out, philosophies have a kind of poetic and separatist life:

> The material out of which philosophy finally emerges is irrelevant to science and to explanation. It is figurative, symbolic of fears and hopes, made of imaginations and suggestions, not significant of a world of objective fact intellectually confronted. It is poetry and drama, rather than science, and apart from scientific truth and falsity, rationality or absurdity of fact in the same way that poetry is independent of these things.[4]

Yet it is also true that one's educational ideas must presuppose *some* view of man, however undeveloped or unspoken, some view of the nature of reality and of cognition; for education "is obliged from the outset," to use Jacques Maritain's words, "to answer the question, 'What is man?' which the philosophical sphinx is asking." Unfortunately, modern education does not meet this obligation, does not answer the question, does not even ask it. Most educators, in forming their views and certainly in carrying out instructional programs, operate on a less elevated plane. Nevertheless, the programs they do create are implicit evidence of their view of man's purpose and his potential.

I intrude at this point my own educational views, which I cannot dignify as either a philosophy or a theory of education, only because these views may throw some light for any interested reader on the mind-set with which I approached the field of teacher education. Presumably anyone attempting to evaluate the preparation of teachers must do so from some fundamental point of view about educational purpose, else he would have no basis upon which to make judgments. My point of view is this: Whatever our attitude toward the ultimate questions that have always confronted mankind, whether we believe man to be a divinely inspired creature or merely a cosmic accident, we have no choice but to assume that West-

[4] *Reconstruction in Philosophy*, Beacon, 1948, p. 7.

ern civilization is good, at least more good than bad; and that whatever hopes we have for the future will have to be realized through the continuation and improvement of that civilization, building on all that has gone before. Our civilization is the product of a long and painful process of taming, training, and refining the human animal, a process made possible by two characteristics that distinguish man from all other creatures: intelligence and compassion.

These virtues have been the means by which man has raised himself from savagery — his intelligence, by which he has disciplined himself and enabled himself to investigate and in some measure understand and control both himself and his environment; his compassion, by which he has muted his natural selfishness and his continuing capacity for barbarism, and by which he has brought dignity and nobility into his own affairs. If it is true that, as Santayana has suggested, "Perhaps the only true dignity of man is his capacity to despise himself," it is true only because of man's unique capacity to see how far short he still falls of what the ancients called the *summum bonum* — how wide the gulf still is between his achievements and his possibilities, between what is and what might be. The job of education, I believe, is to try to bridge this gulf.

Education can best do this job by training the intellect of each new generation vigorously and systematically in those subjects that are the most fruitful for man's continuing development. At the same time education must seek to awaken the individual's moral faculty and to discipline his will. It follows, then, that young people have far more to unite them educationally than to divide them. They have their humanity itself, their country, and the cultural and intellectual heritage wrought for them, through infinite travail, by those who preceded them. Not merely for the protection and advancement of society, but especially for the individual's own sake, young people desperately need to acquaint themselves with that heritage, with what Matthew Arnold called "the best that has been thought and said in the world"; they need to come to close quarters with great men and great achievements and to sense something of the agony and the joy experienced by those who have moved the world forward.

For most young people these ends are best attained through an education based, not on the development of what, symptomatically, have come to be called "marketable skills" or on vocational training or on ways of adjusting to society, but on the principal areas of human knowledge: *English and foreign languages, history, mathematics, and the natural sciences.* These subjects are not arbitrary divisions of knowledge, as they are so often alleged to be by educationists,[5] but are the divisions, each with its own techniques of research and advancement, that men over long periods have found to produce the most fruitful results. They are the subjects that create other secondary subjects useful in higher education and often important fields in their own right, but which at the public school level are inappropriate. In the common schools of a free society, the question of priorities should be compelling, for there is time only for the essential, generative subjects, which best serve the needs of all men, as citizens and human beings. If our public schools could insure a minimum literacy in these basic areas for most students, while pushing students with the requisite capacity to greater depths, one could hardly ask for more. But this much assumes a view of man's potential that educationists and many others are loath to grant. It assumes that most children are capable of being educated to a sig-

[5] An opprobrious term to many persons who prefer to call themselves "professional educators"; i.e., educational administrators, professors of education, and others whose careers are in the field of Education as such. However, I use the term throughout the book with no unfavorable connotations attached, but merely as a better means of identification than "professional educator," a term which, after all, ought to encompass the liberal arts professor and others whose careers are in education. I take my cue not only from traditional usage (Horace Mann, for example, uses the term many times), but from many contemporary educationists, such as Theodore Brameld, who feels that "the word is a perfectly good one to distinguish those engaged in the practice of teaching teachers." — *Education for the Emerging Nation,* Harper, 1961, p. 195.

nificant degree — at different rates, to be sure — in the basic subjects. There is no body of evidence acceptable to most educationists to support this assumption, and it may well be ill-founded; on the other hand, there is no cogent evidence to support opposing or contrasting views. Until we know immeasurably more than we now know about the mind and heart of man, one's argument for a public education grounded in a few fundamental subjects must remain essentially hortatory.

How this kind of basic education can best be carried on in a classroom is another question. Let us by all means adopt those methods of progressivism that involve the student as actively as possible in the learning process. And let us by all means champion those views, whether coming from a Montaigne, a Rousseau, or a Dewey, that seek to reduce the cruelties or the senseless coercions of the classroom that, it is said, used to constitute education. Let us agree with Dewey when he decries, as he does in a thousand places, the meaningless rigidities of American schools:

> When we think of the docility of the young we first think of the stores of information adults wish to impose and the way of acting they want to reproduce. Then we think of the insolent coercions, the insinuating briberies, the pedagogic solemnities by which the freshness of youth can be faded and its vivid curiosities dulled. Education becomes the art of taking advantage of the helplessness of the young; the forming of habits becomes a guarantee for the maintenance of hedges of custom.[6]

Let us do everything we can to facilitate the learning process, but let the "learning" remain in it. Let us not confuse, as so much of progressivism did, the pleasant with the important, the temporary with the permanent, or "the broad primrose path" which, in Whitehead's words, "leads to a nasty place," with the long and rocky road to genuine education.

It may be that most men are not, after all, capable of such

---

[6] *Human Nature and Conduct*, Henry Holt, 1922, p. 64.

education. It may be that the view of man propounded most eloquently by Albert Jay Nock, and echoed unwittingly by modern educationists, is nearer the truth. It was his conviction that only a tiny minority of men was capable of serious education and that our greatest mistake, from which arose all our insoluble educational problems, was in our failure to heed this fact and in our fruitless attempts to educate everybody. The result, as he saw it, was chaos in which those few persons capable of being educated and serving both themselves and their culture were wasted while the many were exposed to a mishmash of courses in subjects that could not possibly interest them or mean anything to them. Let the majority of citizens be given vocational training so that they can become useful and productive citizens, but let us not squander our resources, said Nock, on futile attempts at anything so absurd as universal education. Surveying our educational history, he found,

> three most serious errors in the theory upon which the mechanics of our educational system were designed. This theory contemplates a fantastic and impracticable idea of equality, a fantastic and impracticable idea of democracy, and a fantastically exaggerated idea of the importance of literacy in assuring the support of a sound and enlightened public order. It is not necessary, I think, to go further in the examination of our educational theory, after finding in it three errors of the first magnitude.[7]

Nock, I believe, was wrong. But I can only appeal likewise to our collective experience, and perhaps to faith as well, to support the idea that the great majority of people can respond well to liberal education when it is conducted well. Universal "education," although we have never given it a trial, and not universal "marketable skills," is a wholly realistic expectation for the United States. But we can go only as far in that direction as the quality of our teachers permits.

*   *   *

[7] *The Theory of Education in the United States,* Harcourt, 1932, p. 44.

It was with these assumptions about educational purpose, and their obvious corollaries for the preparation of teachers and administrators, that I tried to evaluate the field of teacher education. I began with an examination of the vast literature of the field: several hundred books representing extensive surveys of teacher education, yearbooks of various organizations, textbooks, special studies, reports of committees and commissions, and just plain one-author books.[8] I then moved on to the innumerable newsletters, leaflets, monographs, and periodicals that emerge continuously from the educational publishers' cornucopia. Because teacher education is intimately bound up with practically everything that goes on in the larger field of education, the relevant literature, past and present, constitutes

[8] Among the most useful surveys (all of which have been done by educationists) is the *National Survey of the Education of Teachers*, done under the direction of E. S. Evenden and the United States Office of Education, published in 6 volumes by the Government Printing Office in 1933; also the 8 volumes that compose the principal findings of the Commission on Teacher Education, under the direction of Karl W. Bigelow, sponsored and published, between 1944 and 1946, by the American Council on Education; and the one-volume survey based on a study of institutional and visiting-team reports submitted to the American Association of Colleges for Teacher Education, sponsored and published by the Association in 1956, edited by Donald P. Cottrell. The more informative yearbooks proved to be those of the John Dewey Society, the National Society for the Study of Education, the American Association of Colleges for Teacher Education, and the Association for Student Teaching. Of the countless published reports and studies in teacher education, I would mention only a few: Two reports, sponsored and published by the Carnegie Foundation for the Advancement of Teaching, are excellent on the condition of the field at different points in the century: William C. Bagley, and William S. Learned, *The Professional Preparation of Teachers for American Public Schools*, 1920; and William S. Learned and Ben Wood, *The Student and His Knowledge*, 1938. Valuable as a reflection of present conditions are three reports of the National Commission on Teacher Education and Professional Standards, an appendage of the National Education Association, that are based on three national conferences sponsored by the Commission in 1958, 1959, and 1960, all three volumes available from the Commission. A useful summary of these three conferences, somewhat idealized, is G. K. Hodenfield, and T. M. Stinnett, *The Education of Teachers*, Prentice-Hall, 1961. Typical of other informative works are: *The Teacher's Role in American Society*, edited by Lindley J. Stiles, Harper, 1957; *Teacher Education in the United States*, edited by Lindley J. Stiles, *et al.*, Ronald, 1960; and *The Preparation of Teachers*, edited by Seymour Sarason, *et al.*, John Wiley, 1962.

an overwhelming but inescapable obligation for anyone seeking to probe very far into the subject. Unfortunately, it is reading that, however necessary, offers poor rewards for the time spent. "Educational literature," as Nicholas Murray Butler once observed, "is not nutritious as a steady diet."

After my initial survey of these writings, I began visiting institutions. For periods ranging from a day to a week, I visited 63 regionally accredited institutions with programs in teacher education. These institutions represented every type and size of school and every section of the country. I tried particularly to visit those schools that by both general reputation and reputation in training teachers and administrators were widely regarded as the best in the field — institutions like Harvard, Chicago, and Stanford. I visited institutions that, regardless of general repute, had programs in teacher training[9] that educationists themselves thought excellent — for example, the Universities of Wisconsin, Colorado, Minnesota, and Texas, Iowa State Teachers College (now the State College of Iowa), Ball State Teachers College, Western Washington College of Education (now Western Washington State College), and Teachers College (Columbia University); I also went to good liberal arts colleges that had well developed programs, such as Wesleyan University (Connecticut), Carleton, and the Claremont Graduate School; I went to numerous other schools that had programs out of the ordinary, such as those at Brown University, Rice University, Yale, and Johns Hopkins. I went to schools that were generally well regarded in higher education but not notable in teacher education, such as Drake University, George Washington University, Boston College, three campuses of the University of California, and the Universities

[9] Throughout the book I freely interchange the terms "training" and "education" so far as the professional preparation of teachers and administrators is concerned. Educationists dislike the old term, "training," because it carries the stigma of the normal school and because they prefer to think of the work today as more truly professional. But the programs for teachers, and assuredly those for administrators, are still very much training.

of Arizona and Washington; and finally I went to schools that were primarily teachers colleges of no particular reputation, such as Southern Connecticut State College, Keene Teachers College, and Troy State College. For whatever value it may have had, and I think it considerable, I have also had the opportunity over the last few years to visit probably a hundred other institutions that were not part of this study, but involved in teacher education programs of interest to me when I visited them.

Before visiting any school, I did some homework on the institution, its history, faculty, curricula, and programs for teachers and administrators. Thus I often arrived with specific questions to which I hoped to find answers, as well as a desire to see as much of the general program as possible. I limited myself throughout the study to programs for elementary teachers, for secondary teachers of *academic* subjects, and for the various graduate degrees in Education.[10] I have not tried to look at or evaluate the extensive programs in home economics, industrial arts, physical education, and similar ones in operation throughout the country, or programs in those subjects that are legitimately "academic" but that are somewhat special, such as art and music. After getting a reasonable grasp of the training programs in outline, through discussions with the president, dean, or other appropriate individuals, I made a point, whenever time permitted, of (1) visiting Education classes, especially those mandatory and fundamental to all programs; (2) collecting course outlines, syllabi, reading lists, and printed matter of sundry kinds; (3) discussing with the faculty, either in groups or individually, the local program and national scene in teacher education; (4) talking with other administrators and faculty members, especially those in the arts and sciences; and (5) talking with a wide range of students in the Education programs — an activity of great im-

[10] Hereafter I capitalize the word "Education" when referring to the professional field of Education, simply to distinguish it from education in general.

portance. Often, I talked also with the admissions officer of the school and the placement officer. I spent time in the library and the campus bookstore. Through all these means I tried to grasp the intellectual tone of the establishment, an elusive but very real quality about educational institutions.

I made use, with considerable misgiving, of several kinds of questionnaires. However, only in those cases where I was seeking specific factual information, such as the number of secondary teachers of a given subject graduated by an institution or the textbooks used in certain courses, have I regarded information from the questionnaires as reliable enough to use without qualification. A lengthy questionnaire which I left with a number of individuals, educationists and academicians, yielded much interesting information but did not lend itself to the usual tabulation and classification; I therefore make no particular use of it in the book. Another questionnaire, which went to 827 recent graduates of a variety of teacher-training programs, I do use, with appropriate limitations, in Chapter IV.

Still another instrument, curiously overlooked, for gathering data about teacher education programs, is the transcript of credit for the graduates of these programs. As I reviewed the literature of the field, I realized with considerable surprise that nobody, despite the long-standing and embittered controversies involved, had ever bothered to gather any kind of useful information about the quantitative questions surrounding course work in Education. Several individuals had sat down with a selection of college catalogues and toted up the semester hours listed in Education and in liberal arts for the various programs, but such data were hardly reliable. Because these old but still current controversies seemed to me important, I undertook to gather an extensive sample of transcripts of credit from 32 institutions that in the aggregate could be considered representative of the field of teacher education. Every item of information from each transcript was tabulated; the results are discussed in Chapters V and VI, and in Appendix A.

These then were the principal means by which I conducted my study. If some are imperfect and yield ultimately only subjective conclusions, one might take comfort in the fact that more precise instruments have not yet been developed.

There follows a brief summary of the findings, as such things are commonly called, of my inquiry. They represent what seem to me the major forces now at work in teacher education. They are mostly negative forces, I regret to say. I gather them together here merely for the reader who would like a summary view of matters. They are discussed in detail at appropriate places in the book. I do not discuss here my recommendations or suggestions for reform, which of course grow out of these findings, since they are the business of the final chapter.

These findings are not of equal weight, though all are important in making the field what it is. Nor are they, obviously, discrete conditions independent of one another; all are closely interrelated, so that changes in any one of them immediately affect the others. Still, the prevailing conditions in teacher education are best clarified if we consider them separately.

(1) There is, to begin happily, a greater ferment throughout teacher education now than has been evident for a very long time. There is more internal criticism than ever before, more pressure for reform, more support for raising standards, more actual change (though small), and more active interest on the part of academic faculty members, their scholarly associations, and government agencies. All this is a promise of better things to come. There has been some genuine effort in recent years on the part of educationists to gain support from scholars and scientists for their teacher education programs and to make the rest of the college community active in these programs. These efforts have met with some success, though the majority of academicians are not much more involved as yet than they have been in the past. Nevertheless, limited progress on so

important a problem is to be appreciated. There is also an increasing recognition by educationists of some of the more flagrant abuses that have characterized teacher education for many years and at least a willingness to talk about remedies. There are a number of experimental programs that are significant, especially the so-called fifth-year and Master of Arts in Teaching programs, going forward with support from the Fund for the Advancement of Education or other foundations. How applicable to teacher education generally will be such programs, which demand first-rate students, five years of preparation, and unusual amounts of money, remains a large question; but the experiments are important in themselves. More important, at least potentially, than any of these developments is the fact that a few of the younger men one finds coming into the field of Education here and there are much abler and better educated than their older associates. While their number is still very small in relation to the number of new doctors turned out each year in Education, they could exert a large influence in the future. They will need time and stamina to overcome the basic inertia of the field, and they will need a lot of help from the academic faculty, but they are probably the best single sign now on the professional horizon.

So there are good things happening in teacher education that deserve praise and support, and if the best minds in the field can eventually have a controlling effect, there will be many more improvements. It might even be said, if one is willing to settle for a kind of mild meliorism in the education of teachers, that one can look to the future with a certain amount of optimism. But if one feels, as I do, that meliorism is not good enough in view of the conditions of modern life, then one sees the field more darkly and the need for reform more urgently.

(2) Professional education suffers very greatly from a lack of congruence between the actual performance of its graduates and the training programs through which they are put. There is what can only be called an appalling lack of evidence

to support the wisdom of this or that kind of professional training for teachers. This does not mean that professional training has no value. It means that, until a reliable method is developed for connecting the training programs with the on-the-job performance of teachers, there should be much less rigidity in these programs and much more modest claims made for them. It also means that there should be many routes, not just one, to the teaching license.

(3) Education as an academic discipline has poor credentials. Relying on other fields, especially psychology, for its principal substance, it has not yet developed a corpus of knowledge and technique of sufficient scope and power to warrant the field's being given full academic status. That it has been given this status in most of our colleges — or, more accurately, that it has achieved this status through the abdication of responsibility by the academic departments — does not make Education a genuine discipline; it only makes possible the building of more academic empires on sandy foundations.

(4) As is true of many other fields, one of the greatest obstacles to reform in Education is administrative inertia. Having grown into an immense academic industry with a top-heavy bureaucracy, and thus with a giant complex of jobs, power, and vested interests to protect, Education has been stuck on dead center a long time. Educational administrators look with the same misgiving as those in other areas on the innovator, or on any radical departure from the *status quo;* in Education, in contrast to other fields, there are as yet insufficient forces to oppose the policy of stagnation.

(5) It is an indecorous thing to say and obviously offensive to most educationists, but it is the truth and it should be said: the inferior intellectual quality of the Education faculty is *the* fundamental limitation of the field, and will remain so, in my judgment, for some time to come. Although a number of able men are to be found, as I have said, in Education, particularly among the younger people, their number is minute in relation

to the whole. Moreover, there is still a strong strain of anti-intellectualism that runs through the typical Education staff, despite their increasingly frequent apostrophes to academic quality. Until the question of the preparation and the intellectual qualifications of faculty members is faced head-on in Education, the prospects for basic reform are not bright.

(6) Likewise, the academic caliber of students in Education remains a problem, as it always has. Fortunately, there is some progress here, more so, ironically enough, than with the faculty. Many schools in the last few years have succeeded in raising the level of admission requirements to the teacher-training programs, which has been possible chiefly because the requirements were so low to begin with. Other institutions that still take pretty much anyone who appears at the door are beginning to practice "selective retention" with some seriousness. As a general thing, Education students still show up poorly on standardized tests and still impress members of the academic faculty as being among their less able students. In short, although something has been done, much remains to be done.

(7) Course work in Education deserves its ill-repute. It is most often puerile, repetitious, dull, and ambiguous — incontestably. Two factors make it this way: the limitations of the instructor, and the limitations of subject-matter that has been remorselessly fragmented, sub-divided, and inflated, and that in many cases was not adequate in its uninflated state. That some teachers and courses in Education can be found to equal the best in any of the academic areas is a happy fact; but it does not change the basic fact that the intellectual impoverishment of the course work remains a major characteristic of the field. And not a great deal is being done about it.

(8) The quantity of Education courses in the typical teacher-training program also deserves the harsh things that have always been said about it. According to my survey of transcripts of credit, secondary teachers of academic subjects take an average of 27 semester hours in Education. This is

close to a year's work in most colleges and is clearly excessive. Elementary teachers take an average of 49 semester hours in Education. This is about 40 per cent of their undergraduate careers and is, I submit, wholly indefensible. These averages go even higher among teachers colleges and many university schools of Education; they are brought down nationally by the liberal arts colleges. The figures speak for themselves: a severe curtailment in the quantity of these courses is needed.

(9) The graduate programs in Education offered for administrators and special school personnel usually suffer from all the deficiencies of the teacher-training programs, only in aggravated form. Admission standards are low and sometimes non-existent; course work is continuously atomized with little restraint; dissertations, when they are done at all, are frequently triumphs of trivia. Graduate programs, even those that extend over many years, frequently include *no work in any liberal arts field,* while they pile up a record of courses in the specialties and sub-specialties of educational administration, guidance, and curriculum construction. At the doctorate level, the Ed.D. degree has long since outdistanced in popularity the Ph.D. in Education, itself a weak degree, for the obvious reason that it is an easier degree to take.

(10) The centripetal nature of authority in Education, which prevented many improvements in teacher training in the past, is still much in evidence. For every move toward greater institutional autonomy, there is often an opposing one toward ever greater centralization of power; for every move toward the involvement of academicians in teacher education, there is often an opposing one toward the old exclusionist policies. The movement toward national accrediting of teacher-training programs, as embodied in the National Council for Accreditation of Teacher Education, is an excellent example of how the concentration of power in a relatively few professional hands can threaten any real progress. The ultimate effect of NCATE, unless the organization undergoes a major transformation, will

be to impose a rigid pattern of training on the entire field of teacher education and perhaps to hamstring it worse than it has ever been.

(11) The academic component of a teacher's education, which remains, after all, the primary one, is also badly in need of attention. Course work in academic areas is sometimes not much stronger than in Education, a fact that academicians ought to face with candor. The freshman and sophomore survey courses are too often in the hands of graduate students and inexperienced instructors who, despite the administrative rationalizations, do not make up in youth and vitality what they lack in depth. Even the advanced courses are poorly done much too often. Although academic teachers have certain advantages over their Education colleagues in training and in the natural viability of their material, and although they are certainly more effective in their students' eyes than are Education professors, all indications are that course work in the liberal arts areas could be immeasurably better than it is. Academic competence and teaching skill are not easily secured in public school teachers without the demonstration of similar virtues on the part of their college teachers. Also, the sequence of courses approved by academic departments for teachers who are majoring in academic subjects usually ignores the special needs of secondary teachers, and fails much too often to constitute a genuine *sequence* that turns out teachers who really know and love their subject. If high school teachers are often incompetent, a large share of the responsibility must be accepted by the academic departments.

(12) And finally, I must cite a phenomenon that is everywhere encountered in Education and that plays a much larger role than educationists imagine in depressing the field. This is the abandonment of the English language and the creation in its place of a pernicious patois that can most charitably be called Educanto. Although educationists have been joined by many other people in this rape of the language, they have been

by far the most grievous offenders. Their unremitting assault upon the mother tongue often makes impossible any communication between educationists and academicians, except by sign language. Educationists even find it difficult to communicate anything important to one another, for it is not easy to express ideas in Educanto. Despite its ludicrous excesses, Educanto is a deadly serious phenomenon: it masks a lack of thought, supports a specious scientism, thrives on slogans and incantations, and repels any educated mind that happens upon it. Until Education can carry on its business in decent English, most other reforms are handicapped, for they cannot even be discussed intelligibly. Educanto, being a rather special problem which I treat in a special way, is perhaps best discussed apart from the main body of the report; I therefore reserve it for a kind of *l'envoi* that follows the last chapter.

CHAPTER II

Professional Education as an Academic Enterprise

All other reforms are conditioned upon reform in the quality and character of those who engage in the teaching profession.

— John Dewey

Development and Scope of the Field

THE FIELD of Education is very much larger than is implied by the term most often used to identify it: "Teacher Education." While the training of teachers is indeed the business of Education, the field also encompasses extensive training programs for a wide variety of other jobs in the educational world. There are master's and doctor's degree programs in dozens of specialties and sub-specialties of educational administration and of college teaching in Education. There are also "field service" branches of schools of Education that conduct school surveys and do other kinds of evaluative work; there are well developed and very lucrative consulting practices, with school systems as the usual clients, on the part of both individual educationists and institutional agencies; there are many research projects carried out by the Education divisions of colleges and universities under the sponsorship of foundations and government agencies. And there are numerous organizations of great size and influence outside the institutions themselves that are an integral part of the world of Education.

Professional Education constitutes a considerable industry. It is the largest single field in higher education. It awarded 143,000 bachelor's degrees in 1962, about a third of all those awarded by U.S. institutions. It produces nearly half of all the master's degrees awarded each year. And it produces more doctorates by far, 1,500-2,000 a year, than any other single field. By the latest count, 1,148 schools, over 80 per cent of all accredited colleges and universities, have teacher-training programs or are otherwise involved in professional Education. The Education field employs over 20,000 full-time faculty members, more than any other discipline in higher education, with the possible exception of English. Moreover, the training programs are buttressed by an extensive professional structure outside the institutions themselves. There are state and national professional associations of great wealth and influence, most notably the National Education Association and its several dozen departments, committees, and commissions, and its state affiliates; there are governmental agencies, such as the United States Office of Education and the state departments of Education; there are accrediting agencies at the state, regional, and national levels; and there are innumerable lesser organizations and associations.

Professional Education, in short, is very big business. And that is, as discussed in Chapter VII, an important part of the problems it presents in the education of teachers. When any social enterprise, certainly any academic enterprise, approaches the size and scope of Education, the forces within it working for rigidity and increasing bureaucratization, for the maintenance of jobs and established programs, are inevitably large. In Education they are more than large; they are overwhelming. In one sense Education, which is usually cited for its failures, has had too much success: it has grown too large too fast on too slippery a foundation. It now has an established market of such size and diversity that it spends 95 per cent of its energies and resources supplying that market, instead of shoring the foundations of the field, producing important research to verify its own assumptions and to improve its programs, and raising its standards all around. Thus it remains the most diffuse and formless field in higher education at the same time that it is the biggest and busiest.

No one is quite sure, or has ever been, just what the proper business of Education is. It still lacks, after three-quarters of a century of grappling with the problem, a usable definition of what it is supposed to do or be. The men who brought teacher training and the professional study of Education into American colleges and universities during the last quarter of the nineteenth century had only general notions about the functions of this new field and the research methods, if any, it might follow in its own development. In seeking to establish Education as an academic discipline, they were responding to powerful pedagogical ideas from Europe and to the rocketing school enrollments at home. They felt that training teachers was properly the business of institutions of higher learning, and that a bona fide discipline could be evolved; but they had few specific ideas about the purposes or procedures to be followed.

Justifiably, the early educationists felt that the one and two-year teacher-training programs of the normal schools could not cope with the developing problems of American public education. The normal schools[1] began in the 1820's as private schools but were quickly followed by public institutions. Together they gave almost the only formalized instruction in pedagogy that was available in the United States until the 1870's and 80's when institutions like Johns Hopkins, Teachers College (Columbia University), the State University of Iowa, and the University of Michigan began to institute course work in Education. For nearly a century the normal school was not really a part of higher education, but was a technical school, a sort of orphaned starveling in a limbo between the public schools

---

[1] Interestingly enough, I find that the word "normal" has lost its meaning for most educationists, who no longer recall the derivation of the word. It came into English, according to the *Oxford English Dictionary*, from Latin through French, from words that meant "rule" or "model" or "pattern" — signifying that the job of the normal school was to give rules or models for teaching.

and the colleges. It often took students who had little or no high school work themselves and trained them, under a staff of former school teachers, chiefly for the elementary schools. In the twentieth century many of the normal schools, able to get high school graduates as students, became four-year institutions; that is, teachers colleges, and began to train large numbers of high school teachers. Today, the evolutionary process still goes on as the teachers colleges become, in name if not always in function, general purpose colleges and drop "Teachers" from their titles. Some indeed have become large universities. But they were in no position at the turn of the century to contribute much to the development of a discipline of Education, and so attention turned to the universities instead.

The early educationists were by no means oblivious to the need for building a sound theoretical and empirical foundation under the new field. But, while they talked often about the problem, they had few ideas about how such a foundation might be formulated. They knew that training teachers was important and that there should be a discipline of Education to do it, but they found it difficult to go beyond inspirational hopes in seeking a solid bedrock upon which to build. "None of us," as James Earl Russell, dean of Teachers College from 1898 to 1927, said, reflecting upon the early years of the College, "had any settled philosophy of education." [2] Forty years after the beginnings of Education in the universities, Boyd Bode, one of the most critical of the progressives, spoke for all of Education in recognizing that it was no nearer a defined purpose than it had been in the beginning. "Unless we know where we are going," he said, "there is not much comfort in being assured that we are on the way and traveling fast." [3] And in 1962, after forty more years of being on the road and

[2] *Founding Teachers College*, Bureau of Publications of Teachers College, 1937, p. 49.
[3] *Fundamentals of Education*, Macmillan, 1921, p. 241.

traveling fast, Education still suffers from the imprecision with which it began. Today educationists are still trying, as one of their spokesmen recently put it, "to identify, clarify, and delineate the knowledge, skills, and attitudes that are essential to teaching and to other educational services" [4] — still trying, that is, to find out what their job is and how to do it. So after three quarters of a century of attention to the problem, Education still lacks a significant corpus of knowledge and practice that its graduates can use with confidence and that can form the base for the research and intellectual advancement of the field. This lack accounts for many of the continuing problems and controversies of teacher education.

Part of the difficulty is merely a reaction to a similar difficulty in public education. Progressivism was never strong on educational priorities or on the delineation of purpose in education, and thus created what I. L. Kandel aptly calls a "cult of uncertainty" that affects the programs of teacher training as much as it does the programs of the public schools themselves:

> The chief failure in the cult of uncertainty has been the refusal to accept any responsibility for a clear definition of values, for a clear statement of the purpose of education, for which the thousands of objectives and aims, the results of factfinding analyses, have been no substitute. [5]

But essentially the difficulty lies in the premature birth of Education as a major academic enterprise. Most disciplines, certainly the basic ones, are built upon the sustained efforts of many generations of scholars working at the task of intellectual discovery and development, and at the task of perfecting the methodology of investigation that best fits a particular subject. These disciplines are the *culmination* of countless individual and group efforts over prolonged periods of time and become

[4] Don Davies, Executive Secretary of the NEA's National Commission on Teacher Education and Professional Standards, in the Keynote Address given to the 1962 Regional Conferences of the Commission.

[5] *The Cult of Uncertainty*, Macmillan, 1943, p. 30.

recognized only when they have developed a substantial body of specialized knowledge of proven worth and techniques for continued investigation and advancement of the subject. But Education, like business administration, social work, and perhaps other fields, reversed the procedure and came into being, not because educationists had already developed a body of knowledge and research technique, but simply because enough people thought that Education ought to be a separate field.

Lacking a consensus, even among themselves, about the proper functions of Education, the logical result of the lack of an established body of knowledge, educationists are free to explore the question as they individually choose and to assign to Education whatever concerns they happen to think appropriate. Some therefore say that the principal concern of Education should be with the learning process, how to understand and improve it (which would seem to be the province of psychology). Some say it is with the history and development of schools as arms of society (which would seem to be the province of history). Some say it is with the exploration and codification of educational goals, values, and purposes (which would seem to be the province of philosophy or perhaps of society itself). Some say it is with all of these things and many more.

Typical of the more thoughtful attempts of educationists to explore the question of Education's role is that of Laurence D. Haskew, dean of the College of Education at the University of Texas. He begins with a three-part assumption to support a claim that Education is a legitimate academic discipline: "The academic field of Education," he says, "derives whatever significance it may have from three sources — (1) the importance of its central concern, (2) what it (Education) is attempting to do, and (3) the potency of its impact." [6] He claims, that is,

[6] *The Discipline of Education and America's Future,* the Horace Mann Lecture for 1959 at the University of Pittsburgh, published by the University of Pittsburgh Press, 1959, p. 7.

as the first ground upon which Education is to be justified as an academic discipline, the fact that it is the only component of higher education whose *central* concern is with schooling; and that, because schooling is by common consent so important to the individual and the nation, the dedication of an academic field to it alone is in turn important. The second ground is the importance of what Education "is trying to do," which is "to develop a discipline — a field of organized human knowledge" as well as to act as the co-ordinator of programs to train teachers and conduct needed research, and to serve "as a social institution" which strives to effect changes in people through education. The third ground upon which Education should be considered a qualified academic field, says the author, is the "potency of its impact" on American society — that is, the practical effects it has been able to produce so far, particularly in responding to the current needs of society and in preserving certain values when the tide of popular opinion seems to be running the other way.

It is evident that the principal qualification *not* cited by the author in his defense of Education as a discipline is the principal *raison d'être* of most other disciplines: a body of knowledge of demonstrable power and a research methodology to support and expand it. He says only that Education is "attempting to develop a discipline — a field of organized human knowledge" about what people should learn in schools, how they should learn it, and how schools should be conducted. While recognizing that Education has not yet done any of these things and is not yet a real discipline, he asserts that it should be regarded as one anyhow because it is becoming one and because what it does is important — which is about the position taken by the founders of Teachers College in 1889.

The absence of the means and methods of genuine scholarship is one of the chief reasons for the low esteem in which Education is still held by members of the academic faculty. It was one of the chief reasons for the dissolution in 1958 of the

Department of Education at Yale — an extraordinary step, in view of the fact that departments and schools of Education, once established on the campus are almost never curtailed, not to say abolished. The obituary of the Yale Department, written by six members of its faculty, makes it clear that they considered the action unjust and peremptory, even though they recognized the gulf between their discipline and the others that made up the institution. Yet they felt, not surprisingly, as does Haskew and no doubt educationists generally, that the Education field should enjoy full academic status because of what it may become rather than what it now is:

> According to Professor Brubacher [one of the six authors], never in the history of education has there been so intensive a development of pedagogy as in the last seventy-five years; yet at the end of that period the teacher of pedagogy still falls short of achieving professional respectability in nearly everyone's eyes but his own. What is basically weak in this situation, he believes, is *a failure to develop a proper regard for the theoretical study of education.* There are two aspects of this failure: (1) teacher training has been painfully slow to base itself on theory; and (2) many eminent American educators sincerely feel that teacher training is inherently incapable of developing a theoretical dimension.[7]

The efforts of educationists to develop a bona fide discipline lured them for many years into the trap of scientism. Convinced that a "science of Education" was waiting to be developed, they set about, with a rather unscientific show of faith, trying to quantify the field, searching for the "laws" and irrefrangible principles they supposed governed the ways in which learning took place. All that was necessary for solving educational problems, as Charles H. Judd, one of the best known of the early psychometricians, made clear in a book devoted to the subject, was the systematic application of the

[7] John S. Brubacher, *et al., The Department of Education at Yale University,* privately printed, 1960, pp. 44-45.

scientific method.[8] The field of psychology, very little older than Education, lent great support to the idea that such a study of the learning process could yield a body of firm, scientific knowledge upon which to base teacher training. Psychology itself, evolving somewhat haphazardly out of philosophy and physiology, faced the same problems of definition and procedure as did Education. Thus they developed together in an effort to put a scientific base under instruction. While this pursuit of a science of Education did yield some useful results, it has fallen far short of the promise educationists saw. The "laws of learning" have, as one of the most perceptive professors at Teachers College, who began his own career with faith in a science of Education, observed, "an irritating habit of collapsing as evidence accumulates."[9] Or, as another of the "Essentialists" at Teachers College later put it: "The search for incontrovertible laws on which education and instruction could be based has not been and probably will never be successful and the hope of developing a science of 'human engineering' is fortunately unrealizable."[10]

Although there is less talk now among educationists about a science of Education, the old-time religion is still very much alive. Educational psychology continues to turn out 6,000–7,000 studies a year, almost all of which are trying to solve problems through quantitative means. There continues to be a pretentious display of mathematical-statistical lingo throughout writings in Education, and an unseasoned attempt to adapt to Education the research techniques of the behavioral sciences. Questionnaires are everywhere — pretested, tested, prepared by a committee so as to represent some kind of consensus, evaluated by another committee using esoteric formulae. Machine-scored tests are everywhere — standardized,

[8] *Introduction to the Scientific Study of Education*, Ginn, 1918.
[9] William Chandler Bagley, *Education and Emergent Man*, Thomas Nelson, 1934, p. 192.
[10] I. L. Kandel, *American Education in the Twentieth Century*, Harvard University Press, 1957, p. 95.

validated, and tested themselves for reliability. Sociologists make learned, scientific excursions into the "behavior" of students, parents, or school superintendents. Committees of educational psychologists devote whole books to "taxonomies" of education, than which no more revealing term could be chosen! Everywhere in the writing and research of the field, more so now than ever, is the drift toward quantification, toward classifying all things educational, measuring them, counting them, listing them, finding their modes, means, and medians, and coefficients of correlation. Only partly is this preoccupation a reflection of the educationist's belief in the ubiquitous usefulness of the scientific method; partly it is the old problem of concern for status and professionalism; and partly it is a refuge from the necessarily imprecise, intuitional, frustrating means that must be used in any effort to solve the really important problems of education. Not only does scientism in Education produce little of value in relation to the numbers of people, time, and resources devoted to it, but it also has a great many harmful effects in the education of teachers. It diverts them from some of the most important professional problems that they might otherwise deal with, and encourages the pernicious belief that their teaching can be based on some kind of exact or scientific foundation. It tends to produce teachers who "are afraid of offending the golden calf of 'empiricism,' " as one eminent educationist puts it, and adds:

A large part of the responsibility for this situation falls on the spirit that reigns in our institutions for the training of teachers. There, during the past decades, a timid relativism has often been advocated, an admiration for statistical procedure irrespective of whether the subject lent itself to the quantitative approach, an imitation of science instead of an independent investigation into the methods of research most appropriate to the enormously complicated field of education. Naturally, where this mentality dominates, the humanist, historical, and philosophical studies have been neglected. The sense of tradition declines. The suggestion that the education of nations has something to do with their metaphysical and religious beliefs, and consequently cannot be understood without some insight into their origin, is buried in a slightly embarrassed silence.[11]

What then is the condition of Education today as an academic enterprise? It continues to be one of the intellectually weakest, most nebulous, and generally unsatisfactory fields in higher education, although it is the biggest. A foreign educationist visiting American colleges records that:

> The relative absence of reference to the intellect is one of the most immediate impressions received by a Canadian professor [of Education] visiting schools of education in the American west for the first time.
>
> For example, it was the consensus of informed opinion — and I saw little that would enable me to controvert this — that schools of education provide an intellectual training less adequate than that of any other university department.[12]

Education continues to want for a viable definition of its own purposes and for a theoretical foundation to give form to its multifarious programs and activities. It is no closer now than it was 25 or 50 years ago to basing itself on scientifically derived principles, though it continues to pursue the scientific will-o'-the-wisp as ardently as ever; meanwhile, it gives short shrift to the non-quantitative and unscientific parts of professional Education that are, in all probability, the most important for the training of teachers. Educational research continues to be afflicted with inconsequential subjects, inadequate methods, and unused results. Jacques Barzun's characterization of it as "the science of nonthought" [13] is apt enough. Or, to let an educationist specializing in research characterize it himself:

[11] Robert Ulich, *Professional Education as a Humane Study*, Macmillan, 1956, pp. 59, 60.
[12] Charles C. Anderson, "A Canadian Critic on Teacher Education in Western U.S.A.," *School and Society*, April 23, 1960, p. 204.
[13] *The House of Intellect*, Harper, 1959, p. 137.

There is another reason why I cannot get excited about the failure to disseminate research findings in education: many of the so-called findings are not worth disseminating. Indeed, the general quality of research in education is so inferior that I feel we had better attack the question of research standards before we worry too much about disseminating findings that possess only dubious dependability.[14]

Educational and professional journals, another index of the condition of the Education field, are especially depressing. With a very few exceptions, such as the *Harvard Educational Review* or *Teachers College Record,* they are ill-conceived, ill-written, and ill-edited. The periodical of greatest circulation is the *NEA Journal,* which goes automatically to all NEA members, thus giving it an enormous circulation but probably a small readership. It is done up handsomely in the coated-stock, multi-colored format that is the NEA's expensive custom, and is a monument to effusive sentimentality and sophomoric inspiration. It is the Norman Vincent Peale of Education. Two of the most elaborate journals in the field, *Overview* and *The Nation's Schools,* are for educational administrators, and are the equal of any commercial periodical in layout, quality of paper, color illustrations, and the other accouterments of expensive magazine-making. But they are devoted, not to the intellectual stimulation of the administrator, but to pedestrian discussions of the mechanics of school operation. They particularly favor articles on running the school lunch program, on the transportation or janitorial system, on audio-visual aids, and on similar matters. Their extensive advertisements almost never concern books or things of the mind, but are reserved for the hawking of such wares as school office equipment, stoves for the home economics program, floor wax, folding tables, padlocks, and tape recorders. One can only hope that these journals are not symptomatic of the intellectual life of

---

[14] Andrew W. Halpin, "Problems in the Use of Communication Media in the Dissemination and Implementation of Educational Research," in *Educational Research,* the Third Annual Phi Delta Kappa Symposium, published by Phi Delta Kappa, 1962, p. 176.

school administrators. If one were to judge the field of Education by the quality of its professional periodicals, the verdict would be harsh indeed.

All this is not to say that Education as an academic enterprise is illegitimate, or any more out of place in universities than schools of business administration or social work. No standards exist that determine the degree of legitimacy of an academic discipline. But it is to say that until Education develops the minimum qualifications that are found in most fields — a theoretical dimension on which to base training programs, a practical application which produces some kind of demonstrable results, and verified methods of investigating the phenomena of the field — until it has this equipment, it ought to be more modest in its claims, far more restrained in its demands on student time, and more humble in its general expectations. Educationists ought to abandon the manifestly absurd claim that people can become competent teachers only when they have been through orthodox training programs, and its corollary that all teachers, before the advent of professional Education, must have been blithering idiots who knew nothing about their job. Educationists need to recognize that the ideas and claims upon which professional work in Education is now based are extremely tenuous; they should recognize that, despite the fact that almost all teachers now in the public schools have been through the standard preparatory programs, the level of public school teaching lends no particular support to the efficacy of these programs. In short, Education, recognizing that its record has been more one of promise than performance, ought to reconstruct itself as an academic enterprise, bringing its claims to power and authority into reasonable relation to its demonstrated virtues and improving its standards at every point in the system.

The Faculty and Students of Education

If it is true that almost all improvements in public schooling must start with the teachers themselves, or no improvements will be made, it is equally true of the teacher-training programs in the colleges. In Education, perhaps even more than in other departments, the quality of the faculty is controlling. Unfortunately, the quality is low. And so one quickly reaches the limits of what can be done to improve other areas of the teacher-training programs. All other reforms, as Dewey remarked, are conditioned upon reform in the quality of personnel in Education.

Little is known in any formal way about what attracts people to the academic life in any field. Some psychologists think they know but avoid saying so in public. The explanations hazarded by academics themselves suggest that intellectual factors are not always dominant. Personal freedom, vacations, prestige, and sheer accident play a part. Also, the commonly held assumption that college teaching offers a kind of withdrawal from life, a shelter for those who fear, are not able, or do not choose, to compete, is not without its truth. The student who once asked his professor, "If you weren't teaching, what would you be doing in *real* life?" was probably getting at the most important of the non-intellectual reasons that people become professors. Non-intellectual reasons certainly play a sizable role in the determination of members of the Education faculty; the conditions under which one does graduate work in Education and goes on to join an Education faculty often suggest that intellectual drive is not the motive power of the field. A desire to get out of public school teaching or administering, an inability to do graduate work in other fields, an attraction to the amenities of academic life, the need to put a capstone on the accretion of Education courses taken at a considerable investment of time and money over the years — all these and no doubt many other similar motives are behind many an advanced degree in Education.

In any case, the fact remains that educationists as a group are near the bottom of the academic ladder. A number of comparative studies of the subject have been made over the last twenty years, some confined to the faculty of one institution, some constituting broad manpower studies, some using scores on such standardized tests as the Graduate Record Examination and the Miller Analogies Test, and some comparing other factors. One of the most recent studies compares people in all academic fields who took the doctorate degree in 1958, on a three-criteria scale: intelligence (as adapted to the Army Standard Scale), math-science aptitude, and rank in class. Holders of the doctorate in Education were on the bottom rank in each computation. "The trailing position," said the report, "of doctorates in education is apparent on all three measures. This group includes both Ph.D.'s in Education and Ed.D.'s; the differences in findings for holders of these two degrees were very minor." [15]

Such findings are merely the formalized statement of what has been known informally in higher education for many years. When members of the Education faculty are compared in non-statistical ways to members of other faculties on the same campus, the results are the same. Whether one compares faculty members in educational background, in the quality of their teaching, in the quality and performance of their graduates, or in the quality of research and of publications in their fields, Education invariably is found on or close to the bottom. To these measures I would add a further one, though one that would hardly be acceptable to most educationists. That is the judgment one reaches after having talked, often at some length, with hundreds of faculty members across the country in Education and in academic areas. The cumulative effect of these conversations, however impressionistic, is surely worthy of note. The interview or the informal discussion is still rightly relied upon as a serviceable measure of ability in most areas of life, including the training programs in Education for teachers and administrators. One's principal impression of educationists

[15] The study was made by Lindsay Harmon, Director of Research of the Office of Scientific Personnel of the National Academy of Sciences–National Research Council. It is reported in the journal, *Science*, for March 10, 1961, pp. 679-88.

at the end of such a safari as mine is that of a sincere, humanitarian, well-intentioned, hard-working, poorly informed, badly educated, and ineffectual group of men and women. Naturally, many exceptions to this judgment must be made, but the general judgment is, I have no doubt, thoroughly just. In all of those timeless and imponderable ways in which comparisons and judgments are made in person-to-person situations — involving clarity of discourse, subtlety, force, depth of knowledge, intellectual penetration, and many related virtues — in all of these, the Education professor comes off poorly in relation to the academic professor on the same campus. That such virtues are simply not the forte of the Education faculty would be clear to anyone who had the opportunity of lengthy discussions with many professors on many campuses.

The circumstances under which teacher education is carried out frequently have much to do with the caliber of the Education professor. Teaching loads, especially in teachers colleges are often 15 semester hours or more, which is excessive if either good teaching or good research is to be expected of the faculty. The instructor sometimes finds himself, not only with three or four different preparations to make for his classes, but with supervision of student teachers as well. Thus the faculty of Education is often identified, perhaps in self-defense, as a "teaching faculty," suggesting that research in Education should be done somewhere else where time and money are available. The deleterious effects on whatever talent an instructor has of teaching too many poor students in too many courses over too many years and in too intellectually thin an atmosphere are quite devastating. But of course the faculty itself makes many of the conditions of its own work. Many Education professors are retired or retreaded school administrators; others have spent their careers mostly in schools of Education, having taken their advanced degrees and perhaps their undergraduate degrees in Education. In either case, the chances are not good that the individual will be himself an educated person capable of constructing and carrying out strong programs for the education of teachers. Graduate degrees in Education simply do not very often equip people intellectually for this job.

In the early days of Education, before it became an academic field with codified graduate degrees to supply its faculty, it was able to attract a number of outstanding men. Nicholas Murray Butler, a competent philosopher in his own right, not only served for several years as president of the New York College for the Training of Teachers (which later became Teachers College) but continued for many years afterwards an active interest in professional Education. He remarks in his memoirs,

> It is difficult to convey my sense of the real distinction of the men who in so great numbers adorned our educational system at that time [the 1890's, when Butler was most active in teacher training]. They were certainly a most extraordinary group. They were not all philosophers by any means, but they were almost without exception scholars. They were admirable administrators and, what is more important, they were powerful personalities.[16]

Today, one gets few nominations when one asks educationists themselves to name the "scholars," the "powerful personalities," or the men of "real distinction," now leading the field of Education. Instead, one sometimes gets a candid comment like that of one well-known educationist in a Midwestern university: "I think we should kick everybody in Education out as incompetents and then reorganize the field with *able* people."

Able people there are, as I have said; the problem is that their number is so small in relation to the whole. Fortunately, what few there are tend to be found among the younger members of the faculty, who have a long future in the field. Education treats them well, on the whole, and rewards their ability with high salaries and fast promotions — advantages for which some of them, by their own admission, entered the field to get,

---

[16] *Across the Busy Years*, Scribner, 1935, volume I, p. 200.

realizing that they probably could not enjoy the same benefits so quickly if they were competing in academic departments of the same institutions. However that may be, the fact is that Education is able to attract and hold some excellent people, through whom others may also be attracted. With luck this can make a difference over time in the caliber of Education faculties in general. But the direction of the future is not at all clear at present. Each year more institutions add the doctoral degrees in Education to their offerings, a tendency that, in view of the nature of these programs, is probably the exact opposite of what should be happening. And other fields are bidding with increased attractions in the marketplace of graduate talent. One thing is certain: Education, like any other field, will continue to be just as good as its faculty; and until it has the will to face this fact and do something about it — which means, among other things, doing something about the doctoral candidates and programs — most other reforms in teacher education will be seriously hamstrung.

Weak students gravitate to weak faculties, thus compounding the problem of inferior personnel in Education. By about any academic standard that can be applied, students in teacher-training programs are among the least able on the campus, along with students in agriculture and business administration. All major studies that have been made of the subject have arrived at the same conclusion. One of the first such studies, and still a classic of its kind, was done under the sponsorship of the Carnegie Foundation for the Advancement of Teaching in 1928-32 in Pennsylvania. Using scores made on standardized tests by various kinds of students within the state, the investigators reported:

The results concern two large groups of prospective teachers about to graduate from college — 1,422 out of a total of 4,412 students tested in 1928, and 1,410 out of a total of 2,830 tested in 1932. In both tests the teachers' average was below the average total score for the entire group and was below all other group averages except those of the business, art, agriculture, and secretarial candidates. In the second part, the artists scored above the teachers.

The authors went on to compare the teachers' scores with those of *high school graduates* — students, that is, four years below them in education:

> It is unnecessary to enlarge on such findings. So far as this study goes, the fact seems to be that high-school teaching attracts college students who differ widely in the fundamental quality of their abilities and who fall below a knowledge minimum in a large proportion of cases. While a theoretical minimum may be difficult to fix, a practical minimum becomes extremely easy when we find pupils at a level where these teachers will work surpassing them on their own territory. A superior fund of matured general knowledge, though perceptible in the average, is evidently not an indispensable qualification for the individual teacher as prepared in these Pennsylvania institutions, nor is it necessary that he command even the verbal tools of education to an extent equal to that of many whom he will seek to instruct.

There was no reason, the authors pointed out, to consider the findings restricted to Pennsylvania. "One tends to conclude," they said, when putting all the findings together, "that they [teachers] have inferior minds." [17]

Subsequent studies have been more comprehensive but have

[17] William S. Learned and Ben D. Wood, *The Student and His Knowledge; a Report to the Carnegie Foundation on the Results of the High School and College Examinations of 1928, 1930, and 1932*, The Carnegie Foundation for the Advancement of Teaching, 1938, pp. 39, 43, 64, 351. This well-made study was preceded by another, more restricted one, sponsored by the same Foundation, and very much worth the attention of anyone interested in teacher education at the time of the transition from normal schools to teachers colleges: William S. Learned and William C. Bagley, *et al.*, *The Professional Preparation of Teachers for American Public Schools, a Study Based Upon an Examination of Tax-Supported Normal Schools in the State of Missouri*, The Foundation, Bulletin No. 14, 1920.

come to the same result. In 1951-53, for example, the Selective Service College Qualification Test was given to nearly half a million college men to help to determine their draft status. The SSCQT is an intelligence test divided between "verbal" and "quantitative" items. Data from the three years were collected and interpreted by the Educational Testing Service. Scores were compared by fields of study, among other ways. Table I, on the next page, lists some of the results.

Of the men examined in all fields, 62 per cent scored 70 or higher, which was considered the critical score because it equaled the per cent of male college students who scored 120 or higher on the Army General Classification Test. The pattern of scores was consistent throughout the tests for most fields; it was thoroughly consistent for those who gave Education as their college major: they scored lowest in every grade in every year the test was given. These findings have some limitations, however: they are scores for men only; they probably do not include large numbers of men who were preparing for secondary teaching, and who therefore gave an academic field, not Education, as their major. Thus those who gave Education would be prospective elementary teachers, an unknown number of secondary teachers, and majors in various kinds of administrative specialties in Education. The report lists 20 "Central" and "Related" specialties, such as "School Administration," "Secondary Education," and "Guidance," that were subsumed under "Education" in the tabulation of the data.[18] This is some of the most comprehensive information available. Putting the best possible light on the matter, one must obviously conclude that Education attracts very large numbers of men (a total of 35,890 men out of 482,403 examined gave Education as their major) who consistently exhibit the lowest academic ability of any major group in higher education, far below that of students in the basic academic areas.

[18] *Statistical Studies of Selective Service Testing, 1951-1953,* a report of the Educational Testing Service (SR-55-30, November, 1955), p. 108.

TABLE I

Selective Service College Qualification Test, 1951-1953
Scores by Major Field of Study

Major field of study	Per cent exceeding critical score of 70% Freshmen	Per cent exceeding critical score of 75% Seniors
Engineering	68	67
Physical Science and Math	66	68
Biological Science	60	46
Social Science	56	51
Humanities	52	47
Agriculture	40	29
Business and Commerce	38	43
Miscellaneous	32	32
Education	*28*	*20*

Source: Data derived from *Statistical Studies of Selective Service Testing, 1951-1953*, a report from the Educational Testing Service (SR-55-30, November, 1955), p. 89.

Another major study was reported in 1954 which surveyed the distribution of talent in all fields of higher education. The study tabulated scores on standardized intelligence tests for a sample of 10,000 college graduates from 41 institutions, and 4,500 graduate students from between 40 and 50 liberal arts colleges and universities (no teachers colleges included). All scores were converted to appropriate ratings on the Army General Classification Test. The average score for all college graduates on this test is 121. Figure I indicates the results. Special efforts were made to put graduates in the most appropriate category, thus insuring that secondary teachers would be listed under Education and not lost in the various academic fields.[19] Even so, the lowest two categories in Figure I, Home

[19] Dael Wolfle, *America's Resources of Specialized Talent*, a report of the Commission on Human Resources and Advanced Training, Harper, 1954, pp. 286-96.

Economics and Physical Education, contain a large but undetermined number of Education students, since majors in these fields commonly take the usual sequence of Education courses and are considered in many schools to be bona fide Education students. The Education score here indicated, in other words,

FIGURE I

Intelligence test scores, expressed in AGCT ratings, for a sample of 10,000 students with bachelor's degrees

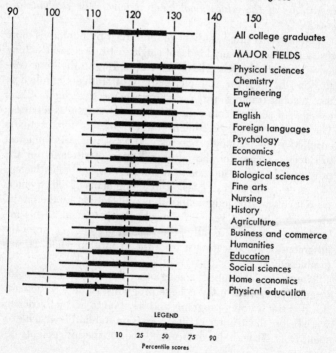

Source: *America's Resources of Specialized Talent*, a report of the Commission on Human Resources and Advanced Training, prepared by Dael Wolfle, Harper, 1954, p. 199. Reprinted by permission.

is probably higher than it would be if all Education students had been included at the bachelor's level. The Education student, regardless of the point in his career at which he is examined, consistently scores close to the bottom. A similar consistency, which the study considered an important finding in itself, was evident in most of the other fields: "This consistency means that some fields attract, or admit, students of a higher intelligence level than are attracted to other fields, and that *the differences among the fields are about the same regardless of the educational level at which the students are studied.*" [20]

The previous three studies are reinforced by numerous more restricted ones of many kinds, of single institutions, of teaching fields, and of other classifications, all pointing to the same conclusion. In 1959 for example, a study of students enrolled in the teacher-training programs for prospective high school teachers of 16 New York colleges and universities was reported. The study involved 580 students out of a total of 1,300 actually enrolled in the training programs.[21] It was principally an effort to develop means for the better selection of students for the programs, based on judgments about the teaching effectiveness of a large group of graduates. Three judgments of effectiveness were involved: the judgment of the pupils taught by the graduate during his first year on the job; the judgment of his immediate superior, usually the school principal; and the judgment of an educationist from the institution where he was graduated.

The study determined, among other things, that of the 1,300 originally enrolled in the college programs, those who actually finished the training programs and went on to become teachers were below the average of all students on standardized achievement tests. It was also determined that of the instruments de-

---

[20] *Ibid.*, p. 197, italics in original.
[21] John E. Bicknell, "The Prediction of Effectiveness in Secondary School Teaching; a Summary Report," The New York State Education Department, June, 1959.

veloped to predict the teaching success of graduates, "The college recommendation scores, which represented the best estimate of a student teacher's probable effectiveness on the job, were of no value in a prediction of effectiveness." The report concluded:

> If the findings of this study have applicability beyond the groups of students and colleges here studied, teaching is a profession in which a premium is placed on mediocrity. The findings that the average high school academic performances of the teacher group exceeded only those of the group who dropped out of college with failing marks, and that the average academic aptitude of the teacher groups, as measured by the ACE test, exceeded only that of the group who failed in college, together with the finding that academic performance and ability were not predictive of teacher effectiveness, tend to support this possibility.[22]

The pattern seems to be consistent, whether we look at well-supported state institutions in New York or at prestige private universities. At Harvard, for example, a survey of the student body (including Radcliffe students) in 1957 indicated that very few students were attracted to teaching at all and that those who were attracted came from the lower academic ranks:

> There are, and probably will continue to be, a small number of students who are drawn to secondary teaching. The 3 per cent of the class of 1957 who have indicated their intention of embarking on such careers stand off markedly from the rest of the student body. They have a lower academic rating than the students who intend to go into college teaching. They are less demanding with regard to status; this is the only group in the class that expresses contentment with its salary expectations, although those expectations are lower than average.[23]

[22] *Ibid.*, p. 25.
[23] Oscar Handlin, *et al.*, "Report of the Harvard University Committee on Teaching," May 15, 1957, pp. 22-23. A pamphlet printed by the Harvard University Printing Office.

Again, all this is merely the statistical statement of what has been known in higher education for a long time. To some extent, teaching has probably been a low-status job attracting low-talented persons in many nations for many centuries. Western literature is full of unhappy profiles of teachers, sometimes satirical as in Dickens, and sometimes despairing as in Rousseau. Montaigne refers to the schools and schoolmasters of his time as

> mere jails, where youths are corrupted by being punished before they have done any wrong. Go into one of these institutions during lesson hours, and you hear nothing but the outcries of boys being punished and the thunderings of pedagogues drunk with fury. A pretty way it is to tempt these tender and timorous souls to love their books — a furious countenance, rod in hand! O wicked and pernicious manner of teaching!

In Carlyle's astringent frolic, *Sartor Resartus,* Teufelsdröckh characterizes his childhood teacher as "My schoolmaster, a downbent, brokenhearted, underfoot martyr, as others of that guild are, did little for me, except discover that he could do little . . ." Rarely, outside classical literature and often not there, are school teachers described in our literary heritage as intellectual persons, certainly not in America. Here the teaching profession, as one caustic comment went some years ago, "consists largely of timid and unimaginative persons to whom moderate comfort, a moderate competence, and moderate security are the reward for a moderate amount of moderately conscientious drudgery."

Today teaching continues to attract the poorer students for a combination of social, economic, emotional, and educational reasons. And the bland acceptance of this condition by the field of Education serves, of course, to perpetuate the condition. Sometimes the educationist simply refuses to recognize the problem, holding that Education students are probably about as good as any others — as if *that* were reason for satisfaction, even if true. Sometimes he takes the position that intellectual ability is only one of the qualifications needed in teachers, not necessarily the most important one. And sometimes he defends low standards on the grounds of expediency ("We have to get *somebody* into those classrooms"). One of the newer texts on educational psychology, in reviewing the research on "teacher effectiveness," notes, as though it were a startling discovery: "At no point, however, has research shown that being intelligent, achieving high [sic] while in college, or getting a good general education is a handicap to teaching." [24] Despite this comforting reassurance, a good many educationists honestly continue to believe that intellectual ability is sometimes irrelevant to teaching, sometimes downright dangerous, and in any case is merely one of many abilities the teacher needs. But sometimes the modern educationist takes a more candid look at the problem of low admission standards, though even when he does he is apt to blame forces outside Education for the situation. Here is a typical assessment:

I should like to comment about the admission standards [to teacher education]. I think in this we stand perhaps convicted as in scarcely anything else. Our standards have not been as high as we would want them to be. I think this is because we have felt a commitment to get teachers for the children in school, even if the teachers were only the so-called "warm bodies." We have had to accept the average and sometimes below average. None of us want to do that, but until we have made some fundamental changes in American values it is going to keep on being that way. [25]

Rarely does the modern educationist face the problem head-on, in the way I. L. Kandel did in the thirties:

[24] Herbert J. Klausmeier, *Learning and Human Abilities*, Harper, 1961, p. 95.
[25] Felix Robb, president of the George Peabody College for Teachers, in "Preparation of Secondary School Teachers; Report of a Regional Conference Sponsored by the Council on Cooperation in Teacher Education," American Council on Education, 1959, p. 32.

In the vast accumulation of literature on secondary education
everything from the management of cafeterias to the promotion
of health and worthy home ownership through Latin has been
discussed. The only solid foundation of an educational system,
the qualifications of teachers, has virtually been ignored. . . .
To erect fine buildings and to seek to meet the needs and abilities of all individuals who desire to avail themselves of the opportunity so generously offered without providing teachers with
qualifications commensurate with the ideal is a sham.[26]

Some progress is being made. A great many teacher-training
programs that used to admit virtually anyone have raised admission standards in recent years. A grade average of "C" or
a shade better is becoming a common requirement in these
programs. This is helpful, though it may not in itself mean
much; grade averages are most significant when one knows
what the quality of the instruction is, what the grading practices are, and what groups a given student is competing
against. A "C" average is not an impressive requirement, nor
is it comparable to the averages required for admission to other
professional schools or programs. Also, it should be remembered that as soon as a certain grade average is established as
a prerequisite for anything in education, the tendency is for
professors to begin awarding that grade as standard practice.
Even so the grade requirement is on the rise in Education and
in time should make some difference in the quality of teachers
coming out of the programs. Eventually, the field may even
conclude that prospective teachers ought to demonstrate ability that is considerably *above* average. In those few programs
that do require outstanding ability of their students, the principle seems to have been well established that high entrance
standards attract rather than deter greater numbers of able
people.

No headway is being made, so far as I am able to see, on
admissions standards at the all-important graduate level. With

the exception of those persons enrolled in the Master of Arts in Teaching programs (described in Chapter VI), who are usually good students, candidates for the various master's and doctor's degrees in Education are rarely screened as they are in other fields. Wolfle's study, cited earlier, found graduate students in Education fifth from the bottom in a listing of intelligence scores for 19 separate fields. Below them were Dentistry, Business and Commerce, Home Economics, and Physical Education.[27] Ironically, it is often easier to be admitted to graduate study in Education than to undergraduate programs in the same institution. A bachelor's degree that might be twenty years old or more from a third-rate institution is often adequate for admission, especially to those degree programs that are wholly under the control of the Education division. Teachers College, for example, until quite recently, has always accepted virtually anybody who presented an undergraduate degree, as have other graduate schools of Education, including those attached to the prestige universities. Whatever reasons there may have been historically for taking low-caliber people in the programs for classroom teachers, there has never been and assuredly is not now any reason for taking them in the graduate programs. The ramifying influence of low admission standards in graduate Education is plain: The masters and doctors turned out become administrators who hire teachers, construct curricula, and set standards in public schools; they also staff professional associations and accrediting agencies and become professors of Education. It is they, in short, who make Education as an academic enterprise what it is now and what it will be in the future.

[27] *America's Resources of Specialized Talent*, a report of the Commission on Human Resources and Advanced Training, Harper, 1954, p. 200.

CHAPTER III

The Conduct of Education Courses

The general principles of any study you may learn by books at home; but the detail, the colour, the tone, the air, the life which makes it live in us, you must catch all these from those in whom it already lives.

— John Henry Newman

The General Rationale

IF EDUCATION as an academic field has so far failed to develop a significant body of knowledge and technique, it follows that the course sequences in particular programs will suffer from a like deficiency. The professional courses required of elementary and secondary teachers — courses that still constitute the main business of Education — are not constructed around programs of proven worth. Rather, they represent a half-century's haphazard accretions for which no very specific rationale, either theoretical or empirical, exists.

What rationale there is seems to be made up of certain broad assumptions, the grounds for which are indeterminate. The training programs assume, for example, that prospective teachers, who as students have spent somewhere between 14 and 18 years in educational institutions, have observed nothing useful about the teaching-learning process in that time; and that the training must therefore begin at the beginning, as though the student's mind, in matters pedagogical, were a *tabula rasa*. It is further assumed that the best pedagogical preparation for such people lies in a series of specialized courses in subjects that, it is again assumed, teachers are most in need of, such as educational psychology, the history and "philosophy" of education, and the methods of teaching various subjects. Finally, it is assumed that people who have been exposed to such a series of courses become better teachers than people who have not; indeed, that people who have not had this orthodox training are incompetent to teach. The trouble is that so little evidence is available to support any of these assumptions. Considerable evidence exists to refute them.

Public school teaching is the only major field in which the "professional" training does not constitute the bulwark of "practice" by people on the job. The professional training of doctors *is* the body of knowledge with which the graduate begins his career and which constitutes his field, just as it is with lawyers, architects, chemists, or veterinarians. They do not "practice" their general or liberal education, whatever it might be, but their professional education only. What they learn in their professional school is the bulk of what they begin their careers with. Thus there is a direct relationship between the professional preparation and the actualities of the job, and there is an almost total reliance upon the training by the graduate. There is also a more or less immediate "proving out" of the training: the practitioner learns very early and under very specific conditions how well or how badly his training prepared him. The architect's building falls down, the doctor's patients consistently die, the engineer can't design a circuit, or the pharmacist dispenses poison in place of aspirin; or in a thousand less spectacular ways the practitioner learns very early whether his training was adequate. In teaching, however, the practitioner does not practice his professional training. He is not a specialist in pedagogy or Education. He is not an expert in it. He "practices" his teaching field or fields, where, if he is fortunate, he is an expert of sorts. His truly professional training has not been in Education, but it has been, in contrast to all other fields, in the liberal arts. No way has yet been discovered of measuring the connection, if any, between Education courses and the actual performance of teachers in classrooms.

The research specialty in Education known as "Teacher Effectiveness," in which many educationists have worked for prolonged periods of time, is mostly significant for explaining how much we don't know about what makes a good teacher and for its persistent failure to prove the broad hypotheses upon which Education courses rest. A. S. Barr, of the University of Wisconsin's School of Education, has devoted a lifetime to trying to find out what makes good teachers good and how to predict which students will be most effective as teachers. In 1948 he reviewed and summarized all of the studies of any consequence, 138 of them, that had been done during the previous 50 years on "teacher effectiveness." What his discussion reveals is the chaotic nature of the whole effort. It lists an infinite variety of criteria used to identify the desirable characteristics of teachers and an equal variety of criteria by which observers were to measure these characteristics in the classroom. It indicates in a hundred different ways the hopelessly vague and subjective instruments relied upon by the investigators. Despite the fact that little in the way of usable results came out of these 138 studies, Barr felt cautiously optimistic about further research in the subject: "By and large, the overall picture and future for the measurement and prediction of teaching efficiency and its prerequisites seem promising." [1] But thirteen years later, in another summary of his own work and of many other studies done under his direction, he says,

In looking back over the investigations herein summarized, one might ask what progress has been made? In brief, progress would appear to have been made in clarifying the problem [of teacher effectiveness], in indicating some alternative way of structuring teaching ability, in indicating some of the components of teaching ability, and in indicating some matters that

[1] "The Measurement and Prediction of Teaching Effectiveness: A Summary of Investigations," *Journal of Experimental Education*, Vol. 16, 1948, pp. 203-283.

need to be kept in mind in developing designs for future research.[2]

In other words, Education is still exploring ways of finding out how to measure "teacher effectiveness" and its relationship to training programs. Recently, three psychologists, after exploring the lack of apparent relationship between training programs for teachers and the jobs teachers actually do, entitled their book: *The Preparation of Teachers: an Unstudied Problem in Education,* thereby indicating their central theme that very little is yet known about how best to prepare public school teachers.[3]

Another major investigator, in organizing the most extensive research project yet done on what characteristics good teachers have in common, observed that,

> in spite of universal recognition of the importance of the teacher, relatively little progress has been made in defining "good teaching" or in specifying the distinguishing characteristics of competent teachers. Personnel decisions are constantly being made by teacher education institutions in admitting students and by school boards and administrators in selecting and promoting teachers, but there is little agreement about the relative importance of qualifications such as intelligence, formal education, pedagogical training, interests, and various personal and social characteristics.[4]

With this as the starting point, the study, running over a period of ten years, sponsored no fewer than 98 separate research projects involving a total staff of 75 persons and some 6,000

[2] *Wisconsin Studies of the Measurement and Prediction of Teacher Effectiveness: a Summary of Investigations,* Dembar Publications (Madison, Wisc.), 1961, p. 113. Barr also reduces to 15 the traits that most investigators found good teachers to possess: he mentions virtues like "buoyancy," "cooperativeness," "forcefulness," and "judgment." As the fifteenth, he lists "scholarliness" — p. 136.

[3] John Wiley, 1962.

[4] David G. Ryans, *Characteristics of Teachers,* American Council on Education, 1960, p. 370.

teachers in 1,700 schools that volunteered to participate. Extensive use was made of personal interviews, questionnaires, classroom visits, "projective" personality tests, and similar devices, all directed at discovering the "components, patterns, variations, and relationships" of "teaching behavior." The aim, that is, was not so much to determine what particular value a characteristic may have for teaching effectiveness as to determine what characteristics, if any, could be consistently associated with what kinds of teachers.

Once again the approach is self-consciously scientific and statistical, and once again the findings indicate the sharp limitations of this approach in any attempt to "objectify" human characteristics. It would not be unfair to say that the conclusions of this massive piece of research into the personal qualities of good or bad teachers are pretty much those that anyone would arrive at by addressing himself for a few minutes to the question: "What do you think are the characteristics of good teachers?" The reader might try this experiment: Think about the above question for a few minutes and jot down ten or a dozen characteristics that occur to you. Then compare your "findings" with those in the following paragraphs in which the study's findings are summarized:

A growing body of evidence is accumulating that indicates certain characteristics which may contribute to the model of the teacher. Certain generalizations are suggested, based not only on the results of investigations conducted by the Teacher Characteristics Study, but also on data growing out of various other researches, employing quite different approaches and criteria.

Superior intellectual abilities, above-average school achievement, good emotional adjustment, attitudes favorable to pupils, enjoyment of pupil relationships, generosity in the appraisal of the behavior and motives of other persons, strong interests in reading and literary matters, interest in music and painting, participation in social and community affairs, early experiences in caring for children and teaching (such as reading to children and taking a class for the teacher), history of teaching in the family, family support of teaching as a vocation, strong social service interests, and descriptions similar to those noted in this chapter [more of the same] appear to apply very generally to teachers judged by various kinds and sets of criteria to be outstanding.[5]

Good teachers, that is, usually are nice, intelligent persons who have traits that everyone would expect good teachers to have. One thinks of Horace's well-known line, "The lab'ring mountain scarce brings forth a mouse." Educationists, at the end of fifty years of mountainous labors on the problem of what makes a good teacher, bring forth the commonplace conclusions that teachers ought to be bright, well-balanced, well-educated people who like youngsters and who are interested in intellectual and cultural matters. How far does this take us? Certainly, the investigators discovered nothing to suggest that the effectiveness of a teacher had much to do with his or her pedagogical training.

Still another educationist, in reviewing the entire state of research in teacher effectiveness, says,

> More than a half-century of research effort has not yielded meaningful, measurable criteria around which the majority of the nation's educators can rally. . . . Perhaps most of all we need a comprehensive theory of teacher behavior and learning to channel the research effort that undoubtedly will be undertaken. A comparison of contemporary teacher competence research with that engaged in forty years ago suggests that little progress has been made toward theory formulation.[6]

Yet, even in the face of this persistent lack of support for the efficacy of their training programs, educationists hold fast to their faith in the orthodox sequence of Education courses. The hard truth about these courses is that, whatever they may claim

---

[5] *Ibid.*, p. 366.
[6] Harold E. Mitzel, "Teacher Effectiveness," in *The Encyclopedia of Educational Research*, Third Edition, Macmillan, 1960, pp. 1481, 1485.

to do and be, they deserve the ill-repute that has always been accorded them by members of the academic faculty, by teachers themselves, and by the general public. Most Education courses are vague, insipid, time-wasting adumbrations of the obvious, and probably irrelevant to academic teaching. Ideally, the goal of special training for teachers is no doubt what Horace Mann had in mind:

> The statement has been sometimes made that it is the object of Normal Schools to subject all teachers to one, inflexible, immutable course of instruction. Nothing could be more erroneous, for one of the great objects is, to give them a knowledge of mode, as various as the diversity of cases that may arise, — that like a skilful pilot, they may not only see the haven for which they are to steer, but know every bend in the channel that leads to it.[7]

But these laudable ideals are not realized in practice, where the "one, inflexible, immutable course of instruction" prevails far more often than Mann's worthier object. It is precisely because Education courses so often fail to give teachers "a knowledge of mode" or sensitize them to "the diversity of cases that may arise" that they seem so unrelated to actual teaching. Perhaps these are virtues best learned on the job, or perhaps they come naturally to teachers with good minds and good educations. Or perhaps they *can* be inculcated through the medium of courses, but not in the passive and intellectually thin air of the average Education course. As one prominent educationist candidly put it:

> In principle, no educationist denies that knowledge of the fields in which a teacher works is essential. But lip-service to the principle does not negate the fact that this knowledge as provided by the average school of education is often cursory indeed. Most impartial observers would admit, moreover, that typical teacher-training programs are littered with time-wasting, repetitious, and obvious courses in "know-how," many of which could

[7] *Fourth Annual Report*, 1839.

be eliminated without loss except to the entrenched instructors of these courses.[8]

In the summer of 1960 the Fund for the Advancement of Education sponsored a lengthy conference at the Center for Advanced Studies in the Behavioral Sciences that produced a report of some significance to our discussion of course work in Education.[9] The conference brought together over a period of two months thirteen educationists of leading reputation, plus a number of occasional participants. The conference addressed itself specifically to four questions, listed in the report as follows:

1. Is there anything of essential importance to a teacher in the way of teaching beyond knowledge of the subject he teaches?
2. If so, what are these essentials?
3. How best can these essentials be imparted or acquired?
4. How can you tell when a teacher possesses these essentials?

To my knowledge, this is the first time that a representative group of educationists has sat down for a prolonged period to consider these basic questions, though the need for such an examination has been clear, as we have seen, for many years. The results of their efforts are therefore important and worthy of attention from anyone interested in the education of American teachers. The first thing that strikes one about their report, apart from the fact that the conference took place at all, is its forthright recognition of the evils and abuses that have characterized course work in Education for a long time. The eight authors whose papers constitute the report exhibit little of the cant, sentimentalism, or dogmatism with which edu-

[8] Theodore Brameld, *Cultural Foundations of Education,* Harper, 1957, p. 256.

[9] The report, called *Teacher Education: A Reappraisal,* was published by Harper & Row in the fall of 1962. My consideration of it is based on galley proof and is therefore without page references. I should like to express my thanks to Alvin Eurich of the Fund for the Advancement of Education, for making an early typescript of the report available to me, and to Elmer R. Smith of Brown University, who edited the report, for checking the accuracy of my quotations against the final proof.

cationists so often defend the professional curriculum. Instead, they examine the fundamental justification of professional work by asking after the practical effects professional and liberal education have on teacher performance in the classroom; in so doing they find much to quarrel with in present programs. Among other conclusions of the report are listed 14 "charges" that are worth quoting in full:

1. The charge that many competent teaching candidates are being forced to take formal professional courses which they don't need.

2. The charge that education courses in some colleges are being proliferated beyond the warrants of valid information, concepts, ideas, and, in some instances, beyond the abilities of their instructors.

3. The charge that the study of education in too many institutions is predominantly missionary, sentimental, and tender-minded in nature, and that research has not validated methods being widely promoted.

4. The charge that some teachers are misusing concepts, generalizations, and methods of inquiry in the behavioral sciences which are valid only in terms of the constructs arranged by behavioral scientists in unique experimental situations.

5. The charge that some teachers lack specialized knowledge of the subjects they are teaching, and that they are offering their students thin and truncated copies of the courses they have taken themselves, without reference to the needs and problems of their students.

6. The charge that prospective teachers through practice can learn to analyze, criticize, and control their own teaching behavior, but that many teacher preparatory programs fail to make systematic provision for the development of this important ability.

7. The charge that school systems are playing a laggard role in the development of functional, continuing training programs for the beginning and specialist teachers, and that wide opportunity exists for much greater collaboration between school systems and universities in increasing teacher competence.

8. The charge that the schools are lacking in adequate numbers of trained supervisors capable of guiding the practice teaching of beginning teachers. The analysis of teaching behavior requires highly specialized skill, knowledge, and training which many supervisors lack. As a result, much practice teaching for beginners amounts to little more than uncritical immersion in tasks of the school.

9. The charge that many teacher education programs are deficient in the extent to which they aid beginning teachers to carry on inquiry into the educational process — the act of teaching — and in the decision-making which must both precede and follow the teaching act.

10. The charge that professional educators have not yet developed an adequate unifying theory and that until such schema are available the design of alternate programs of teacher education must go begging.

11. The charge that no respectable basis for professional education is likely to exist until studies in depth are undertaken by responsible scholars to validate content.

12. The charge that teacher education programs are not based on a clear and consistent theory of teacher education that rests on clear-cut assumptions about secondary school teaching as distinct from both elementary and college teaching.

13. The charge that the main efforts of teachers to upgrade their profession have thus far been devoted chiefly to improving the conditions under which they perform their traditional functions, but rarely have they tried to improve the profession through changes in the intrinsic structure or content of the teaching job itself.

14. The charge that teaching, unlike other professions, has been slow not only in employing ingenuity and inventiveness in extending the effectiveness of its practitioners, but also in rewarding those who possess unusual skills and competence in teaching.

All this, especially in view of its source, comes to a considerable indictment of the professional program and is certainly consistent with my own analysis of teacher education. However, from these negative findings the report goes on to make a strong case for the customary *pattern* of teacher education — that is, a program made up of three components: general and liberal education, specialization in one or more academic fields, and the usual course work in Education, to which the report gives principal attention. In the collective view of the authors, the Education program should include courses in the history and philosophy of education (or in the "Role of the School," as an alternate rubric), in methods of teaching, in practice teaching, and in applications from the behavioral sciences, especially psychology. In other words, the authors propose a major job of renovating the existing structure of professional Education courses but see no need to alter the structure itself.

In arriving at their conclusions, the authors show a refreshing lack of reverence for what usually passes as research in Education; and most of them are free of educational jargon. But it is significant that they find they must base their conclusions and recommendations on something less than concrete and palpable information. Elmer R. Smith, for example, who edited the report, says,

> If it can be proved, perhaps on the basis of accumulated testimony, if not on the basis of tight research, that a thorough liberal education is sufficient to equip an elementary or secondary school teacher to carry on high level teaching that secures high standard student performance, it will be unnecessary to ask for further preparation. If, however, evidence appears to indicate that a liberal education must be joined only by specialization in the subject or field to be taught, this would seem to set the limits on his preparation, especially if the teacher is able on the basis of these alone to insure desirable student performance. . . .
>
> If both liberal education and some specialization fail to equip the teacher to meet with competence the obligations imposed upon him in the modern classroom, adequate justification for a program of professional education which provides this assistance would appear to exist.

The contributors find the last of these speculations to be true, chiefly on the basis of "accumulated testimony": the general experience of those who run teacher-training programs, the exploration of plausible hypotheses about the teaching job, and a certain amount of exhortation. All of the authors consider the question of what kind of evidence exists to justify the professional courses, and two of them do a persuasive analysis of this kind;[10] but ultimately both must rest their case, not on the demonstrable or measurable, but on the possible or the probable as they see it.

The conferees agreed on the need for a "more flexible system to supplant the present rigid method of state certification with its mandated courses"; they also agreed that a fifth year of preparation is probably essential for teachers, and that whatever form the professional work takes, it needs to be far more rigorous and scholarly than it now is.

They further agreed, and this is important, that "preparation for teaching may well take various forms not restricted to formal courses and to traditional practice teaching. A plea was made for exploration of the many interesting ways in which intellectual inquiry via seminars, independent study, examinations, and internships may be made to substitute for the formal courses which appear to make up the bulk of the average teacher's preparation." Unfortunately, the report does not follow up on this crucial recommendation, which would fall on highly sympathetic ears among academicians and other folk who have long felt that, in view of the lack of evidence for the effectiveness of traditional training programs, there should be many paths, not one, to the teaching certificate. The bulk of the report, that is, concerns itself with the traditional Education courses and the traditional ways of training prospective teachers. The candor with which the report

[10] John Walton (Johns Hopkins University), who explores a pragmatic rationale for some kind of special training for teachers, and Judson Shaplin (Harvard University), who does the same for practice teaching.

assesses these programs is commendable, but it would have been an even stronger analysis had it explored alternate ways of training teachers, such as internship programs with no courses whatever.

The problem of establishing a clear and defensible purpose in teacher education is the main theme of one essay called "The Need for a Unifying Theory of Teacher Education," by Paul Woodring, Consultant to the Fund for the Advancement of Education. He points out that present training programs are not founded on any discernible "unifying theory" — that is, a stated rationale that takes into account the actual functions teachers are expected to perform as well as the question of educational purpose in public schools, and synthesizes from these a coherent training program for teachers. He says:

> Unfortunately, the teacher education programs found in these colleges [general state colleges that formerly were teachers colleges] today are not based upon a clear and consistent theory. When the normal school became a teachers college and began preparing secondary teachers, it did so without first asking whether the theories underlying its programs for elementary teachers were equally appropriate for the education of secondary teachers. The faculty members who were holdovers from normal school days often seemed to assume that what was good for an elementary teacher was equally good for a teacher of adolescents, and that the high school teacher, too, should take courses in child growth and development, methods of teaching, and the conventional period of practice teaching.

He then moves on to an analysis of the various "roles" that teachers are called upon to fill. They must act, for example, as dispensers of knowledge, taskmasters, disciplinarians, surrogate parents, therapists, and evangelists. He then deals with the implications of these roles for the training program. It is an interesting and useful analysis that points up the central flaw in teacher education today. However, any unifying theory must make judgments and establish priorities in teacher education. The analysis of roles that a teacher fills in a classroom, important as that is, should not lead automatically to programs that prepare teachers for these roles. The designer of any teacher-training program must first make some judgments about (1) which of these roles a teacher *should* be filling, (2) which are sufficiently important and difficult to deserve time in a training program, (3) which cover matters that Education, or some other field, has solid and verified knowledge about, and (4) which can best be learned in some way other than formal course work.

The report also contains a basic inconsistency often encountered among educationists. One of its recurring themes is the lack of a verified body of knowledge on which to build the professional curriculum, the lack of supporting research, and the need for scholarly validation of the content of courses in Education. Until such validation is at hand, the report rightly concludes, "it is not likely that any worthy base for professional education can be brought about." Yet the report also calls for continued recognition of the "valid content" of professional Education, and presents as one of its principal conclusions the idea that teachers-to-be do need an organized program of professional work in addition to their academic work. The conferees seem to be saying, on the one hand, that people cannot teach effectively without specialized work in pedagogy, and, on the other, that the field does not yet know what such work ought to be. At other times the report seems to be saying that the field does know in general what such work ought to be, but that we have no way of knowing whether in fact it will make people better teachers than they might otherwise have been — which would seem to take the conferees back where they started in asking whether professional work has yet any "valid content."

This report is valuable and illuminating both for what it does and what it does not do. It does constitute an honest and searching critique of many abuses and weaknesses of course work in Education; it does present both solid recommendations for meeting the problems and useful defenses of certain components of the traditional training programs. It does not offer an adequate theory of professional Education (nor, presumably, was it meant to), and does not go beyond plausible ratiocination and suasive discourse in its claims for the efficacy of professional work. That it does not do these things is no fault of its own; it merely reinforces the point with which we began this chapter: that enough is not yet known about teaching and learning to give professional Education a developed corpus of knowledge of proven usefulness, and that course work in Education, lacking such a foundation, is among the most formless and ill-defined in higher education and is perhaps the most susceptible to waste and vacuity.

One of the very few studies of the relationship between Education courses taken by a teacher and his subsequent performance on the job was done in 1960 under the direction of John R. Beery, dean of the School of Education at the University of Miami.[11] Like the Stanford report, the report of this study, although mostly for professional consumption, throws a good deal of light on the theme of this chapter. The report alleges to prove that teachers who have had the usual sequence of Education courses do a better job than those who haven't. If it had proved this, the study would be important indeed. The fact is that it proves nothing of the sort. If the report proves anything, it is, I believe, the precise opposite: that the professional sequence is mightily ineffective.

Briefly described, the study sought to compare the classroom teaching of 152 new teachers of academic subjects in southeastern Florida during the 1959-1960 school year. Half the teachers were fully certified and had completed the customary sequence of Education courses; they were matched as closely

[11] "Professional Preparation and Effectiveness of Beginning Teachers," Graphic Arts Press (University of Miami), 1960.

as possible in age, background, academic education, and other factors, with 76 emergency teachers who had not completed such a sequence. Each teacher was visited five times during the year, either by one of eleven educationists or by one of six laymen, or both; the quality of teaching was rated by the observer on each visit according to a prescribed rating scale. When all the returns were in and arranged in rather tortuous statistical tables, the fully certified teachers were adjudged better.

What is significant, however, is that, despite the badly stacked deck with which this Florida game was played, the fully certified teachers came off no better than they did. Their performance was rated consistently better than that of the emergency teachers, but by such a small margin as to suggest that, when their unfair advantages are factored out of the study, their opposite numbers, the emergency teachers, may have been a shade better! The directors of this study no doubt earnestly believe they have proved what they say they have proved. But consider some of the bias built into the study:

1. It was wholly designed by and under the direction of educationists. No representative of any academic field was involved at any point in the study, despite the fact that it was the teaching of academic subjects that was being judged. The assessment of Education courses, which was the basic aim of the study, would not seem to be done best by those who have the highest stake in the courses.

2. Three of the six lay observers were social workers, whose field has an obvious affinity for professional Education; the fourth observer was an osteopath, the fifth a lawyer, and the sixth an engineer. How they were chosen we are not told. Complementing them in visiting classrooms and judging the quality of teaching were eleven educationists whose principal experience was in educational administration, plus one "Senior Observer" who visited all teachers and whose qualifications

were three years of experience as a teacher and thirty-six as an educational administrator.

3. The study assumed, as is unfortunately customary, that the way to judge good teaching is not by the progress students make under a given teacher but by the teacher's display of personality characteristics the observer thinks good teachers should display. The rating scale used by the observers asked them to make judgments about whether the teacher on any particular day seemed to be "bored" or "constructively busy"; "autocratic" or "democratic"; "restricted" or "understanding"; "excitable" or "poised"; "pessimistic" or "optimistic"; "erratic" or "steady"; "evading" or "responsible"; "disorganized" or "systematic"; "immature" or "integrated"; "stereotyped" or "original"; *et cetera*. How anyone — educationists, laymen, or anyone else — can make useful judgments about such qualities on the basis of a hit-or-miss visit to a classroom is a question the investigators apparently did not consider. Yet this kind of rating scale is one that is often used by educationists in their experiments to determine "teacher effectiveness." Also, the question of what discernible effect these characteristics, even if accurately judged, have on students in the class is not considered. You might try measuring Socrates, for example, against the above "criteria."

4. We are not told where southeastern Florida obtains its emergency teachers, who were being compared to the regular ones. We are told, however, that they were older than the regular teachers, out of college longer, and that *none of them had had any practice teaching experience*. Practice teaching is the one Education course, not really a course, universally recognized as useful. It consistently gets a vote of confidence from professors and students alike as being by far the most valuable part of the professional training. Thus it seems highly probable that the slight edge finally given by the judges to the fully certified teachers was due to the fact that these teachers had had, not the full sequence of Education courses, but some

experience in actual teaching which their opposite numbers lacked.

5. Teachers knew a day ahead of time when a "visitation" was to be made by one of the observers. The fully certified teachers would naturally set about preparing a lesson they thought the observer (12 out of 18 of whom were education-ists) would like to see. Presumably, the other teachers, not having the benefit of professional training, would prepare a lesson *they* thought best.

6. The differences between ratings by the educationists and the laymen turned out to be substantial. The "reliability co-efficients," as educationists are wont to call such things, were not very high between the ratings of the two groups. This simply means that the groups were not in much agreement about what constitutes good teaching, or how to judge it. How much the totally subjective nature of the rating scale had to do with these differences is not clear from the report.

7. The school principals under whom the 152 teachers were employed also rated the teachers, once near the end of the fall semester and once again near the end of the spring semester. When the teachers were thus rated by their super-visors, who worked with them throughout the year and pre-sumably knew their abilities far better than the occasional observer, the difference between ratings for the emergency teachers and those who were fully certified "was small and statistically insignificant."

8. This was a study of first-year teachers only, a year in which any person with no introduction whatever to teaching and no practice teaching would clearly have problems not faced by fully certified teachers. More important might be a study of their comparative performances two or three years after they started teaching.

9. From the particular counties involved in the study, the researchers took *all* the emergency first-year teachers, thus including all those persons who were hired for jobs that

administrators could find nobody else to fill. Against this group, who in the nature of things would seem to be something less than top-rank, the investigators selected a "matching" group from the fully certified first-year teachers in the same counties. The sample, that is, is 100 per cent of the group that, on *a priori* grounds, would be assumed to be less competent, while the sample chosen to match it represents only a fraction of the possible choices.

In short, despite the pervasive evidence of bias in favor of the fully certified teachers in this study, these teachers still came off better by such a small margin as to point to exactly the opposite conclusions from those reached by the investigators. Even giving the professional point of view the benefit of every doubt, this study lends but poor support to the professional training program. What it does do, like the other studies already discussed, is call sharply into question the idea upon which professional courses for teachers is based; namely that educationists know in some organized and validated way not only what professional abilities and qualities make for good teaching but also how to measure these virtues and equip their graduates with them. Their own research, however, either ignores the question altogether or indicates quite clearly that such knowledge does not yet exist.

The Quality of Textbooks

The conduct of Education courses is conditioned more than educationists like to admit by the textbooks used. Far more reliance is placed upon them, and far less on the professor's teaching skill, than is consistent with the educationist's own pedagogical principles. Thus the quality of textbooks becomes a problem of some consequence in Education. Early in my survey of teacher training, I made an attempt to determine what textbooks were used most often in the professional courses. I did this simply by using the required textbook lists from a representative sample of 160 institutions across the country, about 15 per cent of the total. In most cases I got the lists directly from the campus bookstore. It turned out that these schools required a total of 348 separate works for use in Education courses. About 60 per cent of these books were not used often enough to be considered significant, many of them appearing only once or twice in the booklists; another 20 per cent were used somewhat more often but probably not enough to be called typical; and the final 20 per cent appeared with considerable frequency, covering all the usual subjects of the professional sequence. It is this final 20 per cent to which I have given most of my attention and which I consider quite representative of textbooks in the Education field. Some generalizations are in order, which I offer with the qualification that they *are* generalizations that apply to the overwhelming majority of the 70 or so textbooks that are used most often in Education courses:

1. The first thing that strikes one in studying these texts is the scarcity of recognized authors. Like the textbooks used in public schools, the authors are generally educationists of no particular reputation, and of no scholarly standing whatever. Rarely is a book on educational philosophy, for example, written by a philosopher or scholar in philosophy, or one in the history of education by an historian, or one in educational psychology by a psychologist. This happens partly because established scholars are not interested in writing such textbooks and are never encouraged to write them by educationists. But also it happens because a kind of Gresham's law is always at work in Education, in which good teachers, good students, good courses, and good textbooks are driven out, or never allowed to enter, by bad ones. As one distinguished university scholar and teacher in the field of chemistry put it, when asked why he did not complement his criticism of science textbooks in public schools by writing better ones: "Who would adopt

them?" Until the authorship of educational textbooks is improved, not much else can be done about them.

2. Physically, Education textbooks are often handsome examples of bookmaking. Good type, clear and elaborate illustrations (and often ludicrously irrelevant), sturdy coated stock, and well-designed covers. They tend to be lengthy, heavy, and very expensive, although no one has yet explained why. Since they are sold in substantial numbers, they might well be turned out in paperback editions, or other available paperbacks might be used; but, like the public schools, which still break students' backs with four-pound textbooks to take home and wrestle through classes with, schools of Education have yet to make friends with the paperback and discover its many uses.

3. A third striking characteristic of most of these textbooks is their low intellectual level. Compared to textbooks in other professional fields, those in Education reflect a low estimate indeed of the comprehension of the students who are to read them. Often they seem to be written *for* rather than *about* the elementary or secondary school student. They invariably carry an elaborate editorial apparatus, including a teacher's guide that contains everything the non-teacher needs: questions to ask and answers to them, topics for discussion and student papers, examinations, and sundry other helps for any teacher who does not or cannot do such things for himself. The books themselves have extensive summaries of simple material, sometimes at both the beginning and the end of chapters or subjects; they have lengthy lists of questions for "thought and discussion"; they sometimes have even a perfunctory gloss in the margin; and they always have a full covey of typographical gimmicks, lessons from the audio-visual aids specialists, for "greater readability." Presumably, the ultimate sin for these authors is to assume that people who mean to be teachers should be able to make their way through demanding material set forth in a normal, straightforward format devoid of meaningless illustrations and clutter. Stylistically, the books, *all*

that I have seen, are under the dead hand of Educanto. When one thus brings together a weak author discussing thin material by means of a bizarre format and an unknown tongue, the ensuing textbook is not likely to be a triumph of intellectual stimulation.

4. Duplication of material both within the books and among them is probably higher than in any other field. One reason Education students feel they are on a treadmill in their professional courses is the continued repetition of ideas in classes and in textbooks. Take, for example, the subject of how to use the "resources" of the community for school purposes — its public and private institutions, its outstanding citizens, its recreational facilities, etc. The Education student covers this material the first time in his textbook in educational psychology, again in his textbook on school and society or modern educational problems, again in his textbook on methods of teaching, again in his textbook on audio-visual aids, again in his textbook on curriculum development, again in his textbook on secondary, or elementary, education. And this material appears in sundry other places along the way. The same is true of countless other subjects, such as classroom discipline, the importance of "individual differences," motivating students, evaluating "learnings," democratic living, constructing "meaningful experiences," and the theories of how learning takes place. By the time the student has been through two or three such books, all he hears is echoes.

5. A strong strain of anti-intellectualism often shows itself. It is particularly evident in the psychology and methods books, where the prospective teacher is repeatedly warned of the intellectual limitations of students and the need to "adapt" instructional material to the "non-intellectual needs" of students. Despite a great deal of pious genuflection in the direction of the academic subjects, the bias of the authors of these books is plainly in the other direction, toward permissive education, toward the idea that all school subjects are created

equal, toward the ever-broadening curriculum, and toward the idea that intellectual excellence is just one of many virtues, not necessarily the most important one, that schools are to foster.

In addition to the foregoing deficiencies, which apply to Education textbooks in general, the major divisions of the professional curriculum — psychology, history and philosophy of education, and methods — have textbook problems of their own. To wit:

6. Textbooks in the vast sub-specialty of educational psychology (there are about 25 textbooks in print called *Educational Psychology*, plus an uncounted number of others that deal with the same material) are something of an anomaly in themselves. Most research psychologists agree that there is no such thing as "educational" psychology or "educational" psychologists. There are only psychology and psychologists. And neither has much information that teachers can put to immediate classroom use. William James, in his tough-minded *Talks to Teachers*, was at pains to disabuse his listeners of a fallacy that has now become practically universal in Education courses:

> To know psychology, therefore, is absolutely no guarantee that we shall be good teachers. To advance to that result, we must have an additional endowment altogether, a happy tact and ingenuity to tell us what definite things to say and do when the pupil is before us. That ingenuity in meeting and pursuing the pupil, that tact for the concrete situation, though they are the alpha and omega of the teacher's art, are things to which psychology cannot help us in the least.

What psychology had to offer the teacher, in James's view, was fundamental information about mental processes and the opportunity to sensitize oneself to the variety of possible approaches to the teaching job. But he felt that this was a relatively simple and uncomplicated matter:

Fortunately for you teachers, the elements of the mental machine can be clearly apprehended, and their workings easily grasped. And, as the most general elements and workings are just those parts of psychology which the teacher finds most directly useful, it follows that the amount of this science which is necessary to all teachers need not be very great. Those who find themselves loving the subject may go as far as they please, and become possibly none the worse teachers for the fact, even though in some of them one might apprehend a little loss of balance from the tendency observable in all of us to overemphasize certain special parts of a subject when we are studying it intensely and abstractly. But for the great majority of you a general view, one may say, might almost be written on the palm of one's hand.

And James proceeded to outline what he thought the most valuable material that teachers might take from psychology. It is instructive to compare the lecture titles of James's *Talks to Teachers* with the chapter titles of a modern textbook on educational psychology; I will choose for the purpose one of the most recent and well-received textbooks:[12]

JAMES	KLAUSMEIER
Psychology and the Teaching Art	Human Abilities and Teaching — Learning Processes
The Stream of Consciousness	Educational Objectives and Learning Efficiency
The Child as a Behaving Organism	Pupil Characteristics and Efficiency of Learning
Education and Behavior	Teacher Characteristics and Efficient Pupil Learning
The Necessity of Reactions	Classroom Interactions and Efficient Learning
Native Reactions and Acquired Reactions	Cognitive Learning Outcomes I: Facts and Concepts
What the Native Reactions Are	Cognitive Learning Outcomes II: Problem-Solving and Creativity
The Laws of Habit	Psychomotor Abilities and Skills

[12] Herbert J. Klausmeier, *Learning and Human Abilities; Educational Psychology*, Harper, 1961. Reprinted by permission.

James covers his ground in about 70,000 words, Klausmeier in something over 300,000. Of course, psychological knowledge potentially useful to teachers has grown since James, but modern textbooks, of which Klausmeier's is better than most, are not written by genuine researchers like James, but by persons who summarize, synthesize, and very possibly misconstrue and glamorize the research of others. Thus their books all contain the same information, draw upon the same set of experiments, quote one another for support, and depart from one another only in the degree of specificity they are willing to advocate. All the books I have seen violate James's principle about the distinct limitations of psychology to classroom practice. They all tend to be prescriptive to a degree that would horrify James, and they all tend to extol the illimitable reaches of educational psychology instead of making clear that practically everything they say is tentative and speculative. They illustrate perhaps better than any other texts the capacity of Educanto to inflate perfectly ordinary ideas and extend a discussion of them to the limits of the space available. If economics is, as it has been accused of being, the art of stating the obvious in terms of the incomprehensible, it must have gone to school to educational psychology.

The basic information most helpful to teachers remains, as James showed, general and not educational psychology. Here, for instance, are the chapter headings from one of the better books of general psychology such as are used in regular undergraduate liberal arts courses:[13]

Psychology as a Behavioral Science
The Human Organism
Infancy and Childhood
Adolescence and Adulthood
Physiological Motives
Social Motives
Emotion
Conflict and Adjustment
Mental Health and Readjustment Techniques
The Nature of Learning
The Management of Learning
Remembering and Forgetting
Thinking, Language, and Problem-Solving
The Sensory Basis of Perceiving
The Perception of Objects
Statistics and Psychological Measurement
Individual Differences and Their Testing
Intelligence Testing
The Nature-Nurture Issue
Personality
Group Dynamics
Attitudes and Opinions
Vocational and Professional Applications of Psychology

By the time most prospective teachers are ready for their Education course work, starting usually in the junior year, they

[13] Ernest R. Hilgard, *Introduction to Psychology*, second edition, Harcourt, Brace, 1957. Reprinted by permission.

have had a course of this kind in general psychology, in which the principles relating to their work as teachers have been covered. Yet the educationist says they must have another year of something specifically named educational psychology, a derivative of the general field; and beyond that they must often take a course in "human growth and development," perhaps one in child or adolescent psychology, plus another one in guidance and counseling.

7. Textbooks in the history and philosophy of education, the second major division of the professional curriculum, come in all sizes and shapes, but mostly large and lengthy. A few of them are very decent, workmanlike jobs. Cubberley's history of Western education is a standard work and very useful (though it now seems to be undergoing a critical reappraisal by historians), as is I. L. Kandel's for the twentieth century in the United States.[14] Others, unfortunately those that are most highly regarded by educationists and used most often, are quite pedestrian and derivative compilations,[15] thoroughly dull, deserving of the low esteem in which Education students commonly hold them. Educational history is badly neglected by historians as an uninteresting and inferior specialty in which to work. In able hands, however, it need not be, as Lawrence A. Cremin amply demonstrates in his excellent history of the progressive movement in American education.[16] Although things are looking up a bit in the history of education field, there is still much room for improvement in the textbooks most often used in Education courses.

Books in educational philosophy are a sadder story still. If historians are scarce in Education, philosophers are scarcer. The typical textbook in the field does not concern itself with

[14] Ellwood P. Cubberley, *The History of Education*, Houghton Mifflin, 1920, 1948; I. L. Kandel, *American Education in the Twentieth Century*, Harvard University Press, 1957.
[15] For example, R. Freeman Butts, *A Cultural History of Western Education*, McGraw-Hill, 1947, 1955; or Luella Cole, *A History of Education*, Rinehart, 1950, 1957.
[16] *The Transformation of the School*, Knopf, 1961.

much that would be recognized as philosophy, but rather with various theories and pseudo-theories about the purposes of schools in a democracy and the implications therefrom for the curriculum and the organization of the school. One such text, for example, devotes its chapters to everything from "The Structure and Dynamics of Personality," to "Organization of an Educational System," to "The Economic, Health, and Educational Values."[17] Another widely used text is given over to a summary and discussion of current "philosophies" of education, which turn out to be the various notions of some twentieth-century educationists about educational purpose; the author's bibliography for the most philosophic of his chapters, "The Theory of Knowledge," lists 21 works, only two of which could reasonably be considered to have much to do with philosophy.[18] Still others represent attempts to fuse perennial philosophical questions with contemporary educational theories, but without great success.[19] What strikes a trained philosopher probing into the specialty called "philosophy of education" and its textbooks is best described by Sterling M. McMurrin, a philosopher who served for 17 months in 1961-62 as United States Commissioner of Education:

Or consider the body of large problems suggested by the term "philosophy of education." Much that passes as the philosophy of education in the schools today is confused and superficial jargon that fails to come to grips with real issues and does little more than produce an appearance of profundity and learning where none exists. More than that, if taken seriously at the point of the common assumption that from a particular theory of reality a correlative theory of education can be deduced, this discipline would tend to produce, as apparently it does,

[17] Harry S. Broudy, *Building a Philosophy of Education*, Prentice-Hall, 1954-1959.

[18] John S. Brubacher, *Modern Philosophies of Education*, McGraw-Hill, 1959.

[19] For example, Philip H. Phenix, *Philosophy of Education*, Henry Holt, 1958; or Van Cleve Morris, *Philosophy and the American School*, Houghton Mifflin, 1961.

dangerous orthodoxies and party lines in educational policies and procedures. There is great need for careful work in this field by scholars of the highest philosophical competence, classroom and seminar work that would be exciting and rewarding to the best student brains on any campus.[20]

What the student in his educational philosophy courses is likely to wind up with is a potpourri of unconnected ideas from sociology, anthropology, psychology, philosophy, plus a lot of material about the ordinary day-to-day problems of running schools. As in psychology, perhaps there is no such thing as "educational" philosophy. Perhaps there is only philosophy. The subject is not a clearly delimited one now, with the result that it shades off into other kinds of courses that are simply discussions of one sort or another about modern education. Sometimes the course is only a review, under the guise of educational philosophy, of current criticisms of education and how to meet them,[21] sometimes it is simply an extended "orientation to teaching" course that dabbles under the name of philosophy in almost anything having to do with schools and society and teachers. The variety of books subsumed under the category of history and philosophy of education, or school and society, or introduction to education, or educational foundations, and similar names merely emphasizes once again the abandon with which superfluous courses can be created in the professional curriculum.

8. Textbooks in the area of methods of teaching offer the least substance of all. Why they should be as poor as they are is something of a mystery. Method is obviously important in teaching, and certainly it is a matter of great concern to

[20] "The Teacher and His Education for a Free Society," a speech delivered at the 1962 annual convention of the American Association of Colleges for Teacher Education, and reprinted in the 62nd Yearbook of the Association, p. 34.
[21] Using, for example, a book like C. Winfield Scott, and Clyde M. Hill, *Public Education under Criticism*, Prentice-Hall, 1954 — a badly loaded collection of critical writings about education and "answers" to them.

the future teacher, who is likely to worry above all about *how* to proceed when confronted with a class; there ought to be limitless amounts of good material on the subject of teaching method. Yet there are not. "I have been teaching for twenty years myself," says Gilbert Highet in the introduction to what *is* a fine book on teaching method, "[and] I have several times tried to find a book which would help me learn more about what I was doing. Having failed to find any, I have decided to write this one . . ." [22] The usual textbook on methods is a dreary and unimaginative collection of vague recommendations, anecdotes, and lists of skills and objectives. The case history, which is potentially a device of great usefulness in methods instruction, is rarely used effectively. Most attention is given, not to actual case histories, but to hypothesized and idealized classroom problems that teachers find have little relevance to what their work turns out to be. There is also a strong tendency, despite contrary statements in the texts, to give ready-made answers to instructional problems instead of exploring with the future teacher a dozen different illustrative approaches to common problems.

Most of all, there is a depressing emphasis on pseudo-educational activities in public schools instead of on organized intellectual training. Here is how a widely used book in the teaching of social studies presents a case history in the use of "laboratory practices":

A general term used to designate various kinds of student participation in civic action is laboratory practices. This term is in keeping with the view whereby not only the classroom but the entire community is looked upon as a laboratory for social studies instruction. One example of a laboratory practice actually carried out by a social studies class involved the improvement of an automobile traffic bottle-neck in the community. Although much previous talk had taken place about the bottleneck, no action was taken by city officials to eliminate it. The students

[22] *The Art of Teaching*, Knopf, 1950.

conducted an opinion survey among local merchants, pedestrians, and car owners; tabulated accidents; interviewed a traffic officer and members of the city council; took pictures of hazards; and presented a petition based on this evidence to the city council. The council acted on their petition and the bottleneck is now an efficient one-way street.[23]

By no means an atypical fable. There seems to be universal preoccupation in methods books with the "flexible" curriculum, with adjusting students to their community and their society, with democratic living, with meeting student "needs," with constructing "core curricula" around "centers of interest" such as Home Life, the Natural World, Healthful Living, Social Experiences, Transportation and Communication, and with courses of study that meet the "real life needs of youth." Conversely, there is a pronounced bias against what is regarded as the "fixed" curriculum, or the "classical-cultural" approach to schooling, or to the cultivation of the intellect as the principal goal of public schools, or to the primacy of basic education. The degree of anti-intellectualism that characterizes most textbooks on the methods of teaching can only be appreciated through an extensive exposure to these books.

Moreover, they suffer from a pervasive banality, whatever the immediate topic under discussion. Whether the subject be field trips in social studies, the functions of schools in a democratic society, the relationship of administration to the core curriculum, or "incidental language experiences" for bright students in the 12th grade English class, the *ideas* developed by the author are thoroughly commonplace and, one would think, superfluous in professional college courses. Some substance there is, to be sure, and useful to new teachers, but it is usually so inflated as to lose for them a sense of proportion and emphasis. I would hazard the guess that the typical textbook in methods of teaching, or in curriculum develop-

---

[23] Edgar B. Wesley, and Stanley P. Wronski, *Teaching Social Studies in High Schools*, fourth edition, D. C. Heath, 1958, p. 484.

ment, or in school administration could be reduced by 75 per cent without the loss of anything important.[24]

The principal responsibility for the quality of textbooks in teacher education must rest squarely on educationists themselves. They have consistently produced, and adopted for use in courses, patently inferior stuff, and have done very little to encourage the preparation of anything better. They have shown themselves content with the second– and third-rate while they could have the first-rate at any time they chose. Publishers of textbooks, for their part, must bear some secondary responsibility for the inferiority of the product. Educational publishers are not a venturesome lot. They like a sure thing and are wont to stick with a known market for a poor book rather than open up a new market with a high-quality book that departs from the orthodox. They rarely seek out or encourage the unconventional textbook writer. Although they may have what they regard as sound financial reasons for this attitude, the effect is to entrench inferior authors and textbooks in Education. It must be said in the publishers' behalf that they would just as eagerly fill a high-quality market as a low-quality one, and no doubt would rather, but they prefer to wait until the market itself has been created by the field. And so far the Education field, despite all the talk about "upgrading" teacher training, has shown few signs of including textbooks in the movement.

The Quality of Instruction

Few things illuminate the true nature of an educational field so well as actual visits to a wide variety of classes and talks

[24] Impartial readers, I believe, would agree that textbooks like the following, which are no different from most, are about three-quarters water: George A. Beauchamp, *Basic Dimensions of Elementary Education*, Allyn and Bacon, 1959; B. Othanel Smith, *et al.*, *Fundamentals of Curriculum Development*, World Book Company, revised edition, 1957; and Edgar L. Morphet, *et al.*, *Educational Administration: Concepts, Practices, and Issues*, Prentice-Hall, 1959.

with many different students. From the beginning of my survey of teacher education, I made a special effort to visit classes at all levels and to discuss them with Education students. I managed to visit about 200 classes, chiefly in Education but also in the academic subjects that most often are a part of teachers' programs. Let me say at once that I do not see how any observer, having made such visits to a large number of institutions, could fail to conclude that Education courses fully deserve their ill repute. Like the textbooks, they suffer from a high degree of dullness and superfluity. In the lifeless, gray miasma of the typical Education class, where the student never seems to exercise his right to expect stimulation, the cogent remarks of Alfred North Whitehead apropos of the main reasons for having courses in colleges become grimly laughable:

> The universities are schools of education, and schools of research. But the primary reason for their existence is not to be found either in the mere knowledge conveyed to the students or in the mere opportunities for research afforded to the members of the faculty.
>
> Both these functions could be performed at a cheaper rate, apart from these very expensive institutions. Books are cheap, and the system of apprenticeship is well understood. So far as the mere imparting of information is concerned, no university has had any justification for existence since the popularization of printing in the fifteenth century. Yet the chief impetus to the foundation of universities came after that date, and in more recent times has even increased.
>
> The justification for a university is that it preserves the connection between knowledge and the zest for life, by uniting the young and the old in the imaginative consideration of learning. The university imparts information, but it imparts it imaginatively. At least, this is the function which it should perform for society. A university which fails in this respect has no reason for existence. This atmosphere of excitement, arising from imaginative consideration, transforms knowledge.[25]

[25] *The Aims of Education*, Macmillan, 1929, pp. 138-39.

In *none* of the Education classes I attended was the "atmosphere of excitement" or the "imaginative consideration of learning" noticeable. Instead, what was evident most often was the poverty of the instructor's scholarship, the thinness of the material, and the conspicuous consumption of student time. I am, of course, aware of the sweeping nature of these judgments, which I make advisedly; for they are, however unrestrained they may appear, fully justified. Here are thumbnail sketches of a dozen representative classes, all mandatory in the teacher-training programs. I draw the material from notes I made at the time of the visits:

1. A class in "The Principles of Secondary Education" taught in the school of Education of a private Midwestern university by a former superintendent of schools. The class begins with the instructor's writing eight "study questions" on the board, four concerning the advantages and disadvantages of using textbooks in public schools and four on the uses of libraries in public schools. Then he directs the students to copy the questions into their notebooks; he takes the roll while they do so. About 20 minutes go by. He then says that these questions are all answered in the textbook and gives the page numbers as an assignment. He notes that the class will discuss these questions the next time. Then he proceeds to the day's subject, which is the place of mathematics and science in the high school curriculum. "What do you think," he asks of the class, "is the place of mathematics in high school?" No one responds. He calls on a student. "You mean, why should it be taught?" asks the student, "Well, it's important in lots of fields." "Yes," says the instructor, "it certainly is, isn't it." He calls on another student with the same question. The student says, "Because it is required to get into college." The instructor agrees and moves on to another student, then to another and another. No one volunteers anything. When twenty or so opinions are in, the instructor says, "Now, you see why it is difficult for people to agree on what the schools ought to teach." Then he moves over the class with this question, "What do you think is the

place of science in the high school?" with the same results. Then he reads from a typed sheet about the new developments in mathematics and science — the Physical Science Study Committee at M.I.T. and the various mathematics groups that have been at work in recent years. Most of the students are neither math nor science majors and will not teach these subjects. They gaze around the room, squirm in their seats, doze, and watch the clock. Before the instructor can finish reading, the bell rings and he says smilingly, "You have your study questions for next time."

2. A class in "The Principles of Teaching" taught in an Eastern teachers college by an Ed.D. specializing in "group dynamics." At class time the instructor is absent, but five students are to carry things forward. They turn out to compose one of several groups into which the class was divided early in the semester. In accordance with the principles of group dynamics, each group has been deciding all semester what it will do during the course and how it will do it. The group of five on hand this particular day is discussing its future plans; after considerable talk, it decides to spend the next few "class" periods visiting public schools and uses the rest of the time deciding where and when to meet to accomplish this goal. The instructor makes a brief appearance at this point but, seeing that all is going well, departs. Another group that belongs to the course meets each class period by itself in the basement of the library to discuss whatever it has mapped out for itself to discuss. During the second half of this hour, I seek out the library group, made up of eight students discussing integration. Having chosen "current events" as their semester's work in "The Principles of Teaching," they are devoting this week to exploring "the Negro problem."

3. A class in "The History and Philosophy of Education" taught in the school of Education of a large Eastern state university by an Ed.D. in educational psychology. The subject of the day is Comenius. The instructor lectures from note cards.

He has an extremely poor carrying voice and focuses his eyes on the far corner of the room at the ceiling, staring there throughout the class. "Comenius," he says, "was a sense realist. You know what that is." No response from the class. "A sense realist," he says, reading from a card, "is one who believes in the evidence of his senses only. But Comenius was also very religious." He drones along for the remainder of the period, during which no student says anything, reading data about Comenius's life and what he takes to be Comenius's "philosophy." He succeeds in making the generous Moravian a thoroughly dry and unattractive character; he overlooks all the attributes of Comenius's great humanity; and he obviously has not the slightest understanding of Comenius's ideas or of how applicable *The Great Didactic* is to contemporary education. Perhaps it doesn't matter: the class is singularly uninterested in the proceedings; some students talk with one another while the instructor reads from his cards; some read magazines; some are preoccupied with their attire, their lipstick, or their tennis shoes; and some few, bent closely over their desks, furiously scribble in their notebooks, apparently trying to record the lecture verbatim.

4. A class in the methods of teaching social studies in high school taught in the school of Education of an upper Midwestern university. The instructor is a former high school principal and has a doctoral student as his assistant. Today's class is about the "public relations problems" of the social studies teacher and is begun by the assistant, who has never taught social studies in a high school. He gives a 40-minute talk about the political dangers confronting the social studies teacher. A teacher must, he says, "get the community orientation," must understand the politics of the community, and if they conflict with his own, the teacher must yield. He then reviews the case of a social studies teacher who, not sensitive enough to the need for good public relations, was dismissed by his school board through pressure from the John Birch Society.

"You must sell the school," says the assistant, "enhance it to the community." He then reviews the famous Pasadena case of 1950 as a classic dramatization of what can happen when stalwart, able educators, heedless of their public relations, are beset by "a small vociferous minority like the John Birch Society." At this point, a thing happens that I had never seen take place before in an Education class: a student challenges his instructor, though mildly. He says, "Is there some sort of data to back up all these things you have been saying about public relations and the dangers of the job, or are they just your own ideas?" The assistant colors a bit and allows that the ideas are his and not based on any "systematic information." The hour is nearly finished and the professor now stands up and takes over the class from his assistant. He says, "Now, of course, most of you are not going to get fired or in any trouble. Mr. ———— was simply trying to give you an idea of what can happen. You will find it easy to get along. Go to the card parties, go to the PTA's, sponsor the Boy Scouts, make yourself popular — get some news coverage, and you'll have plenty of academic freedom."

5. A class in advanced grammar taught at a Northeastern state teachers college, one of the relatively few institutions that require advanced grammar for secondary teachers. The instructor has a master of arts degree. The entire class period is given over to a discussion of the active and passive voice, the chapter of the text that happens to be up for discussion. The instructor opens the text to the chapter and directs the students to follow. He reads the better part of the chapter to the class, including the examples, and adds a comment here and there of his own. At the end of the chapter, he takes up the exercises. Four members of the class volunteer in turn to recite the 20 exercises. They just finish when the period ends, and the instructor says, "Next time we will take the next chapter."

6. A class in the methods of teaching elementary school

science taught at the school of Education of a private university by an M.A. in general science. The course is listed in the institutional catalogues as one of several in "General Science" and is mandatory for all elementary teachers, though the school is at pains to say that it is not a methods but a content course in science. The room is arranged with a number of large tables seating eight or ten students each; on the tables are placed numerous kinds of rocks labeled with their identifying names. Business matters take about 15 minutes, involving the clarification of assignments, test dates, examination questions, and similar items. The instructor then directs the class to spend a little time looking over the rocks on the tables. When that is done, she holds up a few specimens asking the class to identify them. When they do so, she asks, "Is that a big learning?" All agree that it is not. She then asks questions about the strata in which the specimens are found, and the class, by referring to a wall chart, gives the information. "Is that a big learning?" she repeats. They are not sure. "Well, it could be," she says, "depending on why you are using it in school."

She then moves on to a different subject, the photosynthesis of plants. She holds up a sprig from a maple tree. "A sugar maple," she says, "has opposite leaves." After a pause, she asks, "Is that a big learning?" "No," says the class. She then says, "Green plants make their own food. Is that a big learning?" "No!" "Then let's make it profound," says the teacher. "Let's ask: What difference does that make?" Before this can be answered, the bell rings for the end of the hour.

7. A class in the methods of teaching "Language Arts" in the high school taught in a Western college by an M.S. in Education. The instructor opens the class by referring to the "visitations" the students have been making over the past two weeks to English classes in local high schools. He asks them to report on their "experiences." No response. He asks, "What did you see that was good, and what did you see that was bad?" No response. He calls on a student. "Well, the class was

reading an O. Henry story. They read it the first half of the period and discussed it the second half." The instructor asks, "What impressed you about it?" The student squirms and finally says, "It was very well done." The instructor moves on to another student, with the same kind of result. He then asks, "Didn't any of you see anything that you would like to talk about? Anything that seemed particularly good or bad?" The students, in a general embarrassment, search their minds for something to say. They find some small items of procedure to discuss and then finally get involved in a discussion for the remainder of the hour on the question of whether grammar should be taught in high schools.

8. A course in educational psychology taught at a West Coast state college by a retired president of a junior college with a master's degree in administration. The subject of the day's work is "arranging learning situations." The instructor opens the textbook and summarizes the appropriate contents for the class. Then he says, "Before establishing the learning situation, you must analyze the desired learning. Is it primarily psychomotor, for example, or is it perhaps cognitive? Or is it a combination of the two? What is the difference between them?" After a long silence, one student puts up his hand and says, "Psychomotor has to do with physical skills, and the other with intellectual. There is a third one too, called affective learning, and it has to do with the emotions." "Quite right," says the instructor. "Yes, I had forgotten that one for a moment." He goes on to explain the importance of the teacher's analyzing everything he does according to these three criteria; only then will he know what "units" to teach by, what "outcomes" to teach for, and what "methods" to use. He then goes around the class asking each person to comment on his recent classroom "visitations" and to analyze according to the three terms what kind of learning was taking place.

9. A class in elementary education taught at the school of Education of a large Southern university by an Ed.D. in ele-

mentary education. The class is discussing the controversy about reading, part of a "unit" on the subject of current issues in education. (At this institution, elementary teachers are also required to take a course in orientation to teaching, one in methods of teaching reading, as well as the usual psychology and other professional courses, in all of which, as one student observed, the same ground about the reading controversy was covered.) "Reading is not a subject, you will remember," says the instructor, "but a skill. It is a means to an end. And the end is [she writes on the board in giant letters]: PUPILS WHO *CAN* READ, WHO *DO* READ, AND WHO *LIKE* TO READ. You remember that from your book." She goes on to explain that reading is more than pronouncing words, that phonics is, of course, important in teaching reading but is not a major part of the job. The most important method is the word-recognition method, the "configuration" or "context" or "sight" method. She does not call it the "look-and-say" method. "Reading," she says, "is gaining experiences, and so the words must *mean* something to the child. It does no good for him to be able merely to *pronounce* the words; he must know them, which he can only do through contextual reading skills." She explains that all the furor over reading is taking the subject back to the nineteenth century, when children were often made to read before they had developed a proper readiness. "Many six-year-olds are not ready to read, and great damage is done by making them. You must wait until the child himself feels a need to learn." The students say nothing but carefully record all that is said in their notebooks, since an exam is due the next week on the subject.

10. A class in the psychology of learning taught at a Midwestern state college by a Ph.D. in educational psychology. The subject of the day is examinations. The instructor spends the first half of the period reading, in slow motion so that students can copy it all into notebooks, the advantages and disadvantages of certain kinds of tests — the essay type, true-

false, multiple-choice. He gives several pros and cons for each one, but leaves it clear that any kind of machine-scored test is to be preferred to the essay type, which research proves is "outmoded in practically all fields." He uses no examples of any sort, no sample questions to illustrate his points, no demonstrations of the shortcomings and virtues of the several examination systems. When he is finished, he says, "Now let's see how you would use these examinations in actual teaching. How would you use an essay exam in mathematics?" No response. "You see what I mean," he says, "about the limitations of essay exams. You wouldn't use one in math, you would use a machine-scored test. Now how would you use an essay test in social studies — does anyone think they could do better with it in social studies than a machine-scored?" No response. Finally a student says, "It depends on what you are trying to test, doesn't it?" The instructor says, "Does it? Research proves that *any* subject can be tested better by machine-scored methods than by essay." The rest of the hour is taken up with the ensuing discussion among the instructor and three students, while the remaining four-score students gaze out the window, massage their eyes, tie their shoes, and otherwise occupy themselves.

11. A class in "School and Society" taught at a Southern university by a Ph.D. in Education. One of the textbooks for the course is an anthology of readings about current educational issues. Today's business is to discuss what the readings say and what the students think about the "philosophical aims of education." The first 20 minutes are used to discuss what the final exam will be like; then the instructor, an advocate of the discussion method, turns to the topic at hand. "What do you think the present educational controversy is about?" he asks of a dozen students in turn and writes their answers, after an extended refining process, on the board as a series of equations: traditional vs. progressive, liberal vs. vocational, general vs. specific, classical vs. pragmatic, old vs. new. "Now," he says,

"what are some of the arguments for these two positions?"
He sets up the answers in reciprocating form: "Old says there
is a basic morality; New says there is only a changing morality.
Old says that thinking is a process and that academic subjects
give training in it; New says there is no evidence that academic
subjects 'train' the mind. Old says that human nature is un-
changing; New says it changes all the time." The instructor,
making it clear that the New is the only acceptable position
for the students to have, recognizes no gray areas. All is black
or white in his philosophy.

12. A course in educational psychology taught in a Midwestern college by a Ph.D. in educational psychology. The
class is two hours long and meets twice a week. For the first
hour, the instructor plays back a speech on tape that was recorded the previous year when a Teachers College professor
visited the campus and was discussing the educational controversy in general. Both the instructor and students sit
quietly for about 50 minutes while the tape runs. Then, after
a break, the class begins its second hour, which is given over
to a discussion of the speech. The instructor says, "What did
you think of Professor ———— speech?" No response. "He
is a very effective man. Did you like it?" No response. He
looks at a sheet of paper on which he has written a number of
questions. "What did Professor ———— say about the purpose of schools in a democracy?" He calls on a student. The
hour is consumed with similar questions directed at the
students in an effort to evoke "discussion." The students volunteer little, and the relationship of the day's work to educational
psychology, the presumptive subject of the course, is never
clarified.

And so it went through the great majority of classes I visited.
Some were naturally better than others, but none were what
could be called outstanding, and few could be called reasonably good. If my dozen examples seem one-sided, it is because
the experience was one-sided. Of course, the students them-

selves, as do students in any field, affect the quality of instruction. In Education, they contribute much to the general sterility of the courses. They almost never question sharply anything they are told in class, and on the whole are resoundingly uninterested in much of what takes place. An intellectually timorous attitude seems endemic among them. That some classes in Education can be found to equal the best in the liberal arts areas is a happy fact. A course in the history of American education taught by, say, Lawrence Cremin of Teachers College, or one in the psychological theories of how learning takes place, taught by Ernest Hilgard of Stanford, or one in the methods of teaching high school English, taught by Edward Gordon of Yale — such courses could be as stimulating and valuable as any on the campus; but the mere effort to identify such courses and such men testifies to their scarcity in Education.

The irony of the situation is that the teaching of the Education division of our colleges and universities ought to be a model for the entire institution. Educationists should consistently exhibit the finest teaching on the campus. Men who profess to be experts in pedagogy, in the understanding of "the learner and the learning process," in stimulating student interest and in "creating effective learning environments," ought to demonstrate these virtues, one would suppose, in their own classes. One might fairly ask of experts in teaching methodology just what methodology they use in their own classes, when the results are as poor as they normally are. Some Education professors have done no public school teaching themselves, and almost all do none whatever after joining an Education faculty. The closest that most of them get to actual teaching in a public school is in the process of observing and supervising student teachers from the college or in carrying out well-paid consulting jobs. Rarely do they "practice" their profession in the way that, say, members of a medical faculty do; and almost never are they required to *demonstrate* in an actual public school classroom the teaching methodology they discuss *in vacuo* with their students. Prospective teachers must be somewhat uneasy about the professional prescriptions of Education professors who are known to be among the worst teachers on the campus.

In addition to the inabilities of the Education faculty, other factors play a part in making Education courses what they are. One is the simple fact that too much time is available, indeed mandated, for the professional work. This means that the Education professor often has a heavy teaching load and becomes known as part of a "teaching faculty," the implication being that important research is not expected of him. A 15-semester-hour load, for example, often drives the Education professor to rely on classroom busywork to consume the time — field trips, panel discussions, student projects and reports, and the ubiquitous "general" class discussion signifying, as it most often does in public schools, an undirected, generalized bull session. Heavy teaching loads also contribute to the regular employment of such time-killing classroom procedures by the instructor as writing out, or slowly reading aloud, material that is readily available in other forms or that most professors would mimeograph if they thought it sufficiently valuable, or taking the roll, or discussing at length at the start of classes housekeeping matters like tests and reading assignments and current events in education. The answer here is not to hire more professors to take the excess classes, but to eliminate the classes.

Important, too, as a factor in the redundancy of Education courses is the lack of a clear definition of purpose and scope of particular courses. A course, for example, in "Introduction to Teaching" or "Orientation to Teaching" almost never has a clear mandate. Just what is such a course supposed to cover that is essential for future teachers? It covers whatever any given instructor thinks he would like to cover. So the chances are he spends lots of time discussing (1) the organization of American education, (2) who runs schools and how and to what purpose, (3) the "professional" field of Education, meaning the NEA and its affiliated state teachers' associations, and why the teacher should support it all, and (4) current controversies in education. When the student gets to his course in the history and philosophy of education, he will cover the same ground again. His course(s) in methods will go over these matters once more. And he will likely find the same perennial subjects coming up yet again in his courses in educational psychology as well as in his elective courses in Education.

The recurrence of these ritualistic themes carries a good deal of indoctrination for the student, through sheer repetition if nothing else. He absorbs the orthodox position on many controversial issues — everything from the flexible curriculum to reading readiness and how to refute criticism. In specific subjects there *is* an orthodoxy that is perpetuated in this fashion, despite the denials of many educationists. Of course, professors in any field manage to convey their convictions to their students, but in Education the opposing view rarely gets anything like an equal hearing.

Not surprisingly, the only part of the professional course work that gets a general vote of confidence from the students themselves, and from practically everybody else, is practice teaching — the time students spend, usually in their senior year, actually teaching under supervision in a public or a demonstration school. What is surprising is that the implications of this fact escape the educationist. The students' vote for practice teaching is merely a common-sense vote in favor of coming to grips with the practical, everyday problems of the job, and against the drudgery of dealing with ambiguous and poorly supported theory in Education courses. It suggests, among other things, the possibilities of extended apprenticeships or internships for teachers with very little or no formal work in pedagogy.

Not that practice teaching is always well done; indeed it is wretchedly done very often. School systems have far too little interest in training student teachers, usually have no organized program for doing so, and devote little time or energy and no funds to the matter. Systems that cooperate with colleges in taking student teachers for a few weeks of practice do so by means of assigning the cadets to specific teachers, who are paid a paltry stipend, or nothing, by the college to oversee the cadets' work and introduce them to the intricacies of actual teaching. If the cadet is lucky enough to draw an accomplished teacher, an interested principal, and a capable college supervisor, the practice teaching will probably be a great success. If he draws a mediocre teacher who visits him and his class two or three times during the whole practice period, an uninterested principal, and an incompetent college supervisor — the experience may still be the best part of his training, but the entire burden for making it so will be on him. The fact is that there are simply not enough outstanding teachers available to act as supervisors for cadets; even the best training programs of the most respected colleges have never beaten the chronic problem of staffing the practice teaching programs with first-class supervising teachers. For that matter, they haven't beaten the problem of supplying first-class college supervisors to their cadets. A good deal of the time, the college supervisor has done very little public school teaching himself, sometimes not any, and sometimes not any for the last twenty years or so. Moreover, he may very well have cadets who are teaching in several different fields and find himself "supervising" some students who are teaching English, some social studies, and perhaps some even in science or in one or two other subjects. Yet he is supposed to visit all of them and advise them about their teaching skill. Educationists used to be accused, somewhat facetiously, of believing that if you knew how to teach, you could teach anything; but the accusation does not seem so fantastic when one sees a college supervisor presuming to counsel cadet teachers in a number of different academic subjects.

A final problem of practice teaching is its failure to weed out the incompetent cadets. It is supposed to be a proving ground for neophyte teachers, but it rarely fulfills this obligation. By the time students get to the final stage of the program, few schools or educationists have the fortitude to wash out the incompetents, even if practice teaching effectively identifies them.

On the whole, then, the quality of instruction in Education courses is perhaps lower than that of any other department. Only the extraordinary docility or uninterestedness of the Education student permits the low level of instruction from being called more often to public, as well as campus, attention. When students do have an opportunity to evaluate their professional work, the verdict is rather clear, as is demonstrated in the next chapter.

CHAPTER IV

Consumers' Reports

Most of us believe that all American boys and girls should have experiences, at least in the elementary and secondary schools, that are maximally meaningful to them at the time, and that their judgments are necessary if we are to know what is meaningful.

— Stephen M. Corey, former dean of
Teachers College, Columbia University

The Assessment of Student Opinion

AWARENESS of the opinions of one's students and of their reaction to what is being taught is, says the modern educationist, one of the first duties of the teacher. Only then will the teacher be able to plan his classroom work around what Dean Corey calls "maximally meaningful experiences." No other field in higher education has made so much for so long of the importance of this interaction between teacher and student, the importance of adjusting instruction to the "needs" of students and of regularly determining student response to instruction. Yet Education has done almost nothing by way of applying these precepts to its own courses. Despite the fact that Education courses have drawn the continuous critical fire of both students and academicians for many years, the educationist seldom solicits the views of his own students about the Education program.

Student opinion must itself be critically weighed; no one suggests that it be accepted at face value. Students are not always in a position to see the potential value of their courses, nor able to appraise them dispassionately. Also, the testimony of students who are usually among the less able on the campus, as is true of Education students, needs to be assessed with particular care. Nevertheless, students in any subject are presumably qualified to judge with some accuracy the conduct of the courses they must take and the effectiveness of their instructors' presentation. Perhaps it is significant in itself that even low-ability students react as negatively as they do to Education courses; considering the opinion that recent Education graduates commonly share of their professional preparation, one can only guess at what the opinion of large numbers of bright students might be to the same work. The few attempts of any importance that have been made to measure student opinion in Education do indicate a reasoned and honest response on the students' part, though a clearly negative one. When the temper of student opinion is as consistently one-sided as it appears to be in Education, one would suppose this phenomenon to be of some significance to the faculty members involved. One would suppose that they would set about re-examining the content and conduct of their courses and perhaps effecting some adjustments in response to the criticism. Rarely does this occur in Education.

One of the few efforts made in recent years to solicit student opinion and to adjust courses in response was made by the School of Education at the University of Wisconsin; students enrolled in Education courses were sent a questionnaire about the quality of instruction. The results in part were:[1]

	Satisfied	Satisfaction about 50-50	Dis-satisfaction
Degree of over-all satisfaction with Education courses	50%	25%	25%
Reaction to [Education] courses in comparison to non-education courses	28%	30%	42%

The student paper at Wisconsin, *The Daily Cardinal*, published an editorial on the survey which points up nicely the

[1] Lindley J. Stiles, "Student Attitudes Toward Education Courses at the University of Wisconsin," Education Document 89, mimeographed, dated October 13, 1958, p. 3.

whole question of soliciting student opinion in higher education, and which I therefore reprint in full:[2]

ED SCHOOL SURVEY . . . Fine Project

We doff our fedoras to the Education school, for its recent poll of students and graduates for their opinions on the school's courses.

This sort of continual testing and re-evaluating of course material is one which many other departments should attempt.

WE FEEL THAT any department is apt to lapse into stagnancy unless it allows its students to evaluate the course material. All departments continually re-evaluate their courses; however, in these departments, the judging of a course's merits is done by the faculty.

But who knows better the value of a course than the students?

We feel there is but one flaw. As Dean Lindley J. Stiles, of the Ed school, told the Cardinal, "We felt there would be students taking a pop at the Educational school just because we asked for it."

Perhaps such a bias exists, and could distort the statistics. (As it turned out, 50% of the students expressed overall satisfaction with Ed school courses, and different phases of the department's courses met with more favorable comment. The idea of practice teaching met with almost complete approval.)

THE PRACTICE of course evaluation by students is relatively young at the university, and is a program in which the university lags behind several others.

Last year, the Wisconsin Student Association (WSA) requested that department heads and individual professors pass out sheets to their students, so that the students could criticize the course they were just finishing.

Some professors liked the plan, and have since commented that it turned out satisfactorily. Some, perhaps afraid of frigid frankness by their students, turned down the WSA plan.

The English department instructed all of its teachers not to accept the WSA offer.

It is our opinion that course evaluation shouldn't have to be a function of student government.

[2] From the October 18, 1958, number. Reprinted by permission.

WE FEEL THAT it is very difficult for any professor to know whether his course is being accepted properly by his students. Because of the vicissitudes of class attendance, the quiz instructor system, the student-lecturer distance, it is particularly hard for a lecturer in the larger classes to sense his audience's reaction to his deliveries.

Thus, the student must have the right to express his opinion, and the department involved must not be over-incredulous in evaluating it, or read too much bias into the results.

AND THERE was another thing we liked about the Ed school survey.

There appeared to be no covert activity associated with the study. The findings were released to the press — and it was a story which could have easily been sensationalized and made to reflect unfavorably on the school.

The School of Education deserves our plaudits.

And we hope that other departments and schools will be deserving the same praise in the near future — by doing the same thing the Ed school has done.

Wisconsin's School of Education is regarded by educationists as one of the best in the field, and its self-survey probably represents about the most favorable results that Education could expect anywhere. Even so, half the students were less than "satisfied" with the courses and nearly three-quarters did not compare the courses favorably with those in liberal arts departments. (Even more interesting would be the results of a similar questionnaire that Wisconsin sent out to *graduates* of its Education programs who had been teaching for a number of years; but these data are not yet available.)

A state-wide survey was made in California in 1960 of the opinions of high school and junior college teachers on a variety of issues. The first question asked in a 42-item questionnaire was:

There has been considerable debate in recent years about the value of many of the education courses required of teachers. How important do you believe the education courses you took to obtain your credential were in making you an effective teacher?

Of the 1,391 high school teachers who answered the question, 6 per cent said that their Education courses had been "most important," 44.7 per cent said they had been of "some importance," 42.2 per cent said "little importance," and 7.1 per cent said "no importance."[3] One can only speculate about what would happen if a similar verdict were obtained against professional courses from, say, a large group of practicing doctors in California or people in other professional fields. If only half of them could say that their professional preparation was of some or great importance, it seems probable that the matter would get a bit of attention from the public and the profession. To my knowledge, there has never been a national survey in which a large and carefully gathered sample of graduates of Education programs from many institutions could render a series of opinions about their preparation. It would be a valuable undertaking, especially if the sample could include teachers who had been teaching for varying lengths of time. The closest approach to it is in a national study of beginning teachers done over the last few years by the United States Office of Education.[4] It sent a questionnaire to a well-drawn sample of 7,150 new teachers, asking them many questions about their background, teaching situation, and plans. Unfortunately, it included only two items out of 59 on the subject of the teachers' opinions of their professional preparation, and these turned out to be rather loaded questions which I reprint here (from page 196 of the report):

57. Helpfulness of Education Courses: In general, do you feel that the education courses you had in college have been helpful in your present position?

    1 ☐ Very helpful
    2 ☐ Fairly helpful

[3] Gustav Albrecht, "A Survey of Teacher Opinion in California," *Phi Delta Kappan,* December, 1960, p. 104.

[4] Ward S. Mason, *The Beginning Teacher,* being the "Final Report on the Survey of New Teachers in the Public Schools, 1956-57," OE-23009, Circular No. 664.

   3 ☐ Not very helpful
   4 ☐ Not helpful at all
   5 ☐ I haven't had any courses in education

58. Helpfulness of Practice Teaching: In general, do you feel that the student or practice teaching you did in college has been helpful in your present position?

   1 ☐ Very helpful
   2 ☐ Fairly helpful
   3 ☐ Not very helpful
   4 ☐ Not helpful at all
   5 ☐ I did not have any practice teaching

The results were reported for the whole sample in several different ways. Here they are broken down by the size of the school district (from pages 45 and 145 of the report):

Type of school district	Per cent replying that education courses were —					
	Number in sample	Very helpful	Fairly helpful	Not very helpful	Not helpful at all	Not applicable
All beginning teachers	7,150	20	41	29	7	2
Large urban	1,689	17	41	31	8	2
Medium urban	2,122	19	44	29	7	2
Small urban	1,773	20	37	31	9	3
Rural	1,566	26	41	24	5	4

Type of school district	Per cent replying that student or practice teaching was —					
	Number in sample	Very helpful	Fairly helpful	Not very helpful	Not helpful at all	Not applicable
All beginning teachers	7,150	53	24	8	2	14
Large urban	1,689	57	25	7	2	9
Medium urban	2,122	59	23	7	1	10
Small urban	1,773	49	26	8	2	15
Rural	1,566	45	22	9	2	22

Combining the two tables, the results are (from page 45 of the report):

Type of school district	Per cent replying that practice teaching was very helpful or fairly helpful, by teaching level and sex (based on the number reporting having had practice teaching).				Per cent replying that education courses were very helpful or fairly helpful, by teaching level and sex (based on the number reporting having had education courses).			
	Elementary		Secondary		Elementary		Secondary	
	Men	Women	Men	Women	Men	Women	Men	Women
Large urban	86	92	86	89	63	65	56	34
Medium urban	95	91	89	90	67	70	59	48
Small urban	91	88	88	84	61	68	54	50
Rural	82	87	86	87	73	77	63	59

Put in the appropriate context, these results constitute, I believe, a pretty severe verdict against professional Education by its own graduates. In reading the above tables, one should consider that:

1. The data are for first-year teachers only, the time when the professional preparation is supposed to be the most valuable. Many educationists say that their greatest objective in the ordinary training program is to get the teacher past his first year. New teachers should feel the most sanguine about their Education courses during their first year of teaching.

2. Of the elementary teachers, fully 24 per cent did not have the bachelor's degree, meaning that they would be relying even more than usual upon their professional work to see them through the first year.

3. We do not know what the ratings might have been by specific teaching fields, but we do know, as the report states: "With reference to the type of secondary subjects taught, teachers of nonacademic subjects [home economics, industrial

arts, physical education, etc.] were most likely to feel that education courses had been helpful, and teachers of academic subjects least likely." (Page 43.) Exactly half the teachers of academic subjects checked Education courses "very" or "fairly" helpful, but we are not told the specific percentages for the two categories; most of the other data indicate that the "fairly" column gets two or three times the votes that the "very" column gets. This would mean that perhaps 15 to 20 per cent of the teachers of academic subjects found their Education courses "very helpful."

4. The wording of the questions made a favorable answer the easiest to mark. Even the strongest opponent of professional Education would suppose Education courses to be "helpful" to beginning teachers. Hundreds, perhaps thousands, of things a college might do for prospective teachers would prove "helpful" — anything from instruction in the phonetic alphabet to how to pour coffee at the PTA meeting; the important question is, What are the best things the college can do for future teachers in the time available? But the respondents to the questionnaire had no opportunity to comment on whether they felt the time spent in Education courses was the best possible use of that time; nor did they have a chance to make any comparative ratings of their Education courses with their academic courses.

In other words the questions themselves and the circumstances of the questionnaire put the best possible light on the effectiveness of professional Education. Even under these circumstances, only half the teachers of academic subjects could say that Education courses were helpful, and even that figure is skewed to the high side by the votes of teachers in rural and small urban areas. In the large cities fully 46 per cent of the men teachers and 66 per cent of the women teachers said that Education courses were not helpful in *any* degree. One would suppose this to be about as poor a showing as any "professional" field would care to make.

In almost all the classes I visited, I made a point of talking to the students afterward. Often I would simply question them as to whether the class had been a reasonably typical one in that course and ask how they felt about the course and about their preparatory program in general, both in Education and in the liberal arts areas. I also made particular efforts on each campus to talk informally with as many Education students as possible, sometimes in small groups in the campus cafeteria and other such places, sometimes singly in any place that was convenient. How many students I talked with I have no way of calculating, but the number was not small. I feel that in the aggregate these students, considering the variety of campuses I visited, can be considered representative of the whole field. For what it is worth, I should like to record that the overwhelming weight of student opinion thus measured of Education courses is negative. Sometimes mildly, often bitterly so. When students have a chance, not to check a box on a questionnaire or fill in a blank, but to *discuss* their opinions about Education, the picture they draw is rarely a happy one. Even in the preparatory programs, including the fifth-year plans, of our more exalted institutions, the students find far more to criticize than to praise. In general, their grievances are the familiar ones: Education courses are dull and directionless; the instructor is nice but uninformed and uninteresting; the time and tuition are being wasted; practice teaching is the best part of the program; more academic work is needed. Occasionally, there is a vote of confidence in a particular Education course or professor. Often there are hard words for the academic courses as well, chiefly on grounds that the instructor remains too aloof or that his lectures are too specialized.

But it is not alone the negative verdict rendered so often against Education that is significant. Equally revealing is the almost total absence of any kind of enthusiastic *support* for Education by its own students. Even among those students who are most sympathetic in assessing their own programs one seldom finds any really active, positive support for Education. What is conspicuously absent is the kind of excitement and enthusiasm that one often finds among students in other professional fields and the active defense of the training programs. When only 20 per cent of a sample of over 7,000 new teachers can call their professional preparation "very helpful," something is seriously wrong either with the students or the preparation or both.

Opinions from One Hundred Graduates

In addition to the informal expression of opinion discussed above, I tried to gather some opinions on a more formal basis from recent graduates of Education programs. I therefore gathered a sample of 827 names of persons who had graduated recently from the teacher education programs of a variety of institutions. This sample was by no means a systematically drawn one, nor is it one that I would offer as statistically representative of the whole field. I believe indeed that the results are reasonably representative, but offer them only as a rather disorderly array of reactions from one large group of recent graduates.

To these 827 teachers I sent a neutral questionnaire (reproduced in Appendix B) that asked them to evaluate both their Education and academic courses. In contrast to the usual type, the questionnaire had ample room for respondents to write in their opinions, as well as to answer specific questions. One hundred thirteen of the questionnaires were returned address unknown, leaving 714 graduates who presumably had the opportunity of responding, assuming that mail to old addresses, parents' homes, etc. was forwarded and received by the intended persons. Three hundred seventy-six or 52.8 per cent responded. This is not an overly impressive response, though perhaps not too bad under the circumstances. Following up on a number of non-respondents with personal interviews, I found that their most frequent reason for not responding was fear of administrative reprisal. They simply did not trust the assurances of the questionnaire that their anonymity would be protected, and they were suspicious about how their names were "chosen" in the first place. That these and other fears did play a part with the non-respondents is further supported by a number of notes or letters from those who received the questionnaires asking how their name happened to be included and what use was to be made of the information. This kind of fear is present in all such questionnaires, particularly those done by single institutions or professors of their own students, and it no doubt tends to elicit somewhat restrained opinions.

In any case, almost all of the 376 who replied took advantage of the opportunity to write comments about their college work. Many did not bother with the specific questions at all, and others did so erratically, so that their free comments are perhaps the most reliable gauge of their feelings. Two hundred eighteen wrote both a general comment on the Education and academic program and comments about specific courses. These free comments, taken together, seem to me to illumine most of the problems and criticisms of professional Education. They offer little reassurance to the educationist regarding the attractiveness of the training programs. In some ways they also offer little reassurance to the academic departments.

These responding teachers, while they have opinions enough about the proper training for a teacher, are not strong on English composition; they often ignore the fundamentals of grammar, punctuation, and usage in their comments, as well as the correct spelling of words. Here, for example, are some of the misspellings that turned up:

persuits	choosen
valuble	overlaped
immensly	wasteing

conglameration
preperation
parr (for par)
repeatetious
repitious
professer
proffesion
forsee
idle (for idol)
two (for too and to)
studing (for studying)
then (for than)
chalenge
condenced

scholasticly
suppliment
uterly
repetoire
agressive
relevent
opiniated
prefered
equiped
excellant
their (for there, and vice versa)
mimeographers (for Education graduates who imitate learned men)

Obviously, the academic departments, especially English, that turned out these teachers might also look to the effectiveness of their work.

Of the 218 who commented at some length on their questionnaires, three were strongly favorable in evaluating their professional Education, and 62 were somewhat favorable; 152 (or 70 per cent) were unfavorable, either somewhat or strongly. Almost all of the 218 evaluated their academic work favorably, regardless of their attitude toward their Education work. From the 218 replies, I have chosen to reprint 100 that seem to me to represent all of the positions taken and to reflect the appropriate ratio of favorable to unfavorable comment. Ninety-three of these 100 practicing teachers came from 39 different institutions in 16 states; seven declined to identify themselves, so that there was no way to determine their college or state. I reprint 20 of the comments here verbatim, each from a different institution, and the remaining 80 in Appendix B:

1. [Secondary teacher of social studies] In the school of education I attended it was necessary to cross-register in the

college of liberal arts for any credits needed in that area. This leads to much guessing. It is common knowledge that two professors teaching the same subject may be teaching two different courses. By this I mean, one may be so involved in his subject that he can see nothing else. He speaks its jargon. He expects his students two; He takes for granted a thorough background in his subject. The type that may only be built up by an abundance of outside reading (perhaps unassigned). He is the sort of man that should be the idle of some one who is a major in his subject. He'll make them work and this is good. The other type of professor may have as much knowledge as the first but have different personality traits. He makes an effort to find out who is in his class, there backgrounds and he takes due consideration when teaching.

It is my feeling that a person studing education in a four year program can't afford to spend time being academic about Liberal Arts subjects; the place for this is in the Liberal Arts College and for its students.

2. [Elementary teacher] Every education major wishes she had chosen something else. The courses are one dull, repetitious thing after another. I had 3 courses [she had 45 semester hours of Education, total] in a row which were straight repeats, Statistics, Teaching and Guidance (last two under the same professor, a psychological testing bug). Every course starts out with 6 weeks of "developmental psychology" — which means such labored truisms as "The whole child comes to school," "Children develop at different rates," "You have to start where the child is," etc.

Not one thing about how you go about teaching — you are left to find out the practical, down-to-earth dealings with children completely on your own. Generalities are all right for a base, but do you little good when a supervisor is looking over your shoulder. Such things as "How to plan," "How to establish routines," "How to teach in 24 hours a day," "How to conduct parent conferences," "How to deal with the compulsive talker, busybody, slow-learner, back-talker in the classroom"; none of these is touched upon. How to juggle social studies books of 3 series, science likewise, make up "independent learning activities" at midnight, steer a course between what can be done and what the administration would like to see you do (they won't tell you till you've done it wrong) — why can't these so-called educators communicate some real information?

My prescription would be: good, heavy content courses for most of three years — history, science, literature, geography, some of the newer math, English composition. Perhaps a basic "Psychology of Learning" and "Backgrounds of Modern Education" in the third year. Then I would like to see methods courses coordinated with student teaching in a laboratory school situation, where the student observed a master teacher, planned a similar or follow-up lesson and taught it, then evaluated it with the teacher-professor. Professors should have to demonstrate with real children.

3. [Secondary teacher of history] I found on the whole that all my education courses were a complete waste of time. I learned more about teaching in my 8 weeks of practice teaching than I did from all the other education courses put together. As for my major and minor subject training, both were excellent.

4. [Secondary teacher of English] Most courses very good quality; interested me to some extent in most areas. Prepared me for a lifetime of enjoyment in literature, history and psychology and the knowledge of what to look for and where to find it. Liberal arts, of course, unlike engineering, does not usually prepare one for a definite career, but provokes interest and the desire to go on in a certain area. Many times liberal arts background prepares you insufficiently for a vocation, but I would have gone no other route.

I think education courses are a waste of time (bear in mind I had four general ones) as a preparation for teaching. Provide good cultural and historical knowledge, but almost nothing which can be beneficial in the classroom. I discussed this answer with several teachers and these ideas of mine were reinforced:

1. You learn more *psychology* in a class in a week than you do in a semester course.

2. Your *methods* come naturally with the type class you have.

3. *Practice teaching* valuable in that it gives you six weeks, two months head start on procedures.

4. *Philosophy* good as philosophy without the "education" follow up.

5. *History* more interesting than others, but how beneficial is this?

I also, and it follows, think little of the "teachers colleges" which take in average and *below* average high school students, water down the courses and produce quantity but not quality. Too much time is spent on education courses and not enough on major studies. I had 48 hours in my major which, I think, qualifies me as being better prepared than a teacher who had 24 hours of English and 24 of education.

Get some school committees who are willing to let a few moths out of their wallets and education will benefit by getting good students from good colleges into teaching. (I *would* like to afford a master's degree from a good school — started at _____ State College and almost lost my lunch.)

5. [Secondary teacher of English] In general, I have found that the education courses I had to take (with the exception of six weeks of student teaching) have been altogether useless and totally irrelevant to the practice of teaching, which evidently cannot be learned from a textbook or a lecture. Even the few education courses which were interesting and had good professors have been very little help.

The liberal arts courses have been much more useful. I found, however, when I began teaching, that my knowledge of my major field, English, was extremely weak, and this weakness has been a real handicap to me. The English courses I did were good, in general, but I didn't have enough of them.

Judging from my own experiences, I would suggest that the number of education courses required be greatly reduced, except for practice teaching, which should begin as early and last as long as possible. I would require students to take about half the total amount of work in their major fields. Such a program would perhaps help prospective teachers from being in my position — having wasted time with education courses useless in helping me to teach and being placed in a classroom in order to teach English, about which I don't know enough to teach well.

6. [Elementary teacher] I thought that a liberal education with a minor in elementary education prepared me very well for teaching. I think, however, that more science would have been beneficial. At my college we could not major in education. I think this is an excellent idea because it gives you time to spend on subjects you might never have another chance to explore and cuts down on unnecessary education courses. I felt the most valuable course, and the one that prepared me best was the Observation and Practice Teaching.

7. [Secondary teacher of botany and zoology] In general, my biggest disappointment in the education department is the method in which the courses are taught. Most education courses stress the importance of new types of teaching, practical experience, good tests, motivation, and so many fancy sounding things. The trouble is that most of the instructors preaching this wouldn't have the faintest idea of how to teach this way.

Most people in the education department preach the need of more education courses. I have some startling news for you. Some of my best instruction in college has come from professors who have never seen the inside of an education class room, let alone taken any education courses.

Methods — Both of my methods courses were way below expectations. The general methods course in education was a complete waste of time. Most of the discussion was not on the subject, and most of the course did not give any help on methods of teaching. My methods course in my major field was somewhat better, but in general poor in quality.

Guidance — My only guidance course has been "Introduction to Guidance," and if I thought all would be as poorly taught, I would never take another. In general the instructor comes in, opens his notebook, and lectures straight from notes for 2 hours. Once in a while we have an exam which consists of memorizing dates, names, etc., which we will never use again. It seems a shame to expose graduate students to this type of instruction [respondent was half way through a master's program in Education], especially when this is an introductory course. At the very least it should stimulate, if it does nothing else.

8. [Elementary teacher] I found the education courses which I took (and the one I am currently taking) almost entirely worthless. The most worthwhile courses I studied were liberal arts courses. I feel the "so called" methods courses I had failed completely in giving me a realistic or practical understanding of education.

9. [Elementary teacher almost through the master's in Education] I feel that a complete overhaul of my school's education program is essential. I feel that there were entirely too many education courses and as a result they overlapped into each others field. You can only hear something a certain amount of times before you stop listening because you know what the answer will be. Many of the methods courses could be combined into a general program and the rest of the time could be devoted to more liberal arts courses to develop the teacher as a more complete and educated person and not someone who just knows how to teach.

10. [Secondary teacher of social studies] I believe the course of studies I had was very good. It prepared me with a well rounded education for the profession of teaching. Much has been said about the values of education courses but I find most of mine were very helpful. They bring to life many of the problems faced in the classroom. Also they inform prospective teachers with information on where to get and how to use outside sources. This I found especially helpful and the older teachers I gave this information to found it equally helpful.

11. [Secondary teacher of English, also with a master's in curriculum development] My graduate courses in education I can not rate as particularly fascinating. I do not think that the professors were necessarily lower in potential [than academic professors] — they were rather interesting people — but more interesting outside than in. The reason for this was the philoso-

phy of the department that lecture courses were to be avoided, and as much as possible done by committees, panels, and student reports. The purpose is, I suppose worthy, but it seems to be ill-timed. . . . As a graduate student whose time was even more valuable to me than the tuition involved, I resented sitting in a class which was far too large for effective discussion while ill-prepared classmates exchanged ignorances or my classmates and I squirmed through a boring presentation of something we could have learned more about through reading a good textbook. . . . I would try to raise standards of teaching in the Schools of Education. Too many graduate courses are simply a rehash of the undergraduate course under a new title. I would decrease the number of courses offered — and concentrate on making them "meaty." And I would require the teachers to spend as much time on preparation as they would if they were teaching in the public schools.

12. [Elementary teacher] I feel that I received an excellent education for preparing me to become a teacher. I also feel though that further studies are necessary to really tie together all that you have learned as an undergraduate. I am now studying for my Master of Education Degree and am finding it much more meaningful since I have now had actual teaching experience.

13. [Secondary teacher of English] In _____, the quality of teacher preparation is in such a state that it will take an amazing amount of correction to pull it up to satisfactory standards. Since 1960, the teachers college at _____ has made many desperately needed requirements [improvements, presumably]. *Before* 1960, it took pure will power for the students (those who were in the least bit intelligent) to stay there. 90% of the students were those who *could not* enter any other college because they were not intellectually competent enough to be accepted. Thus the academic atmosphere was practically non-existant.

The motto of the faculty (average age 55) was to lecture material that was required by the Board of Education [of the state], and to demand that the students learn by rote. Any questioning or even natural discussion about the curriculum was NEVER encouraged and, in fact, was squelched as quickly as possible with the age-old reprimand that "tradition dictates that . . ."

(Do I sound bitter? I am. It was a daily chore to force myself to attend class. Why did I stay on? Lack of funds to transfer and a strong desire to get through for a degree and to learn as much as possible under the circumstances.)

14. [Secondary teacher of history and political science] I feel that my undergraduate courses in liberal arts were, for the most part, excellent. While I have only been teaching half a year, I think that if I had to repeat my undergraduate training, I would take the same courses at the same college. I find them valuable not only in teaching, but in my general life.

On the whole, I was disappointed with my education courses. I felt that I could have learned more if my credits and time had been used in liberal arts rather than in education. History methods and practice teaching were the only useful courses and I feel that these two alone prepared me for teaching; the other courses contributed little and could have been dispensed with. The thing wrong with my education courses was that they were taught by college professors who hadn't been in high school classrooms in 30 years, if ever. To make education courses more meaningful, I think they should be taught by those who are currently high school teachers or administrators or by college professors who have had recent experience in the schools.

15. [Elementary teacher] I sincerely believe that in order to attract the needed intelligent people into the field of elementary and high school education, the entire curriculum and program must be drastically revised. There are far too many poor instructors and a definite vagueness about the subject matter which should be taught. To be frank, most of my education courses were big unchallenging, unstimulating bores. Anyone with a minimum of common sense could have done well in them. The textbooks were poor, on the whole, also.

I think we should throw away most of the methods courses, retaining only one which would include method theory and curriculum. Then, the rest of the college education could consist of courses in all fields of liberal arts including a lot of physical and biological sciences. We must have teachers who are as well informed and well educated as humanly possible. Education, instead of appealing to mediocre students should be revised so it will appeal to the superior student. An intelligent person with a fine education and a great fund of knowledge will be a better teacher with no "education courses" than an average person with all the method in the world.

16. [Secondary teacher of English] Education for teachers at state colleges has been much criticized. On the secondary level, it is not as bad as reputation has it. I feel the liberal arts colleges do a far poorer job of preparing teachers in that they do not prepare students to communicate with the young pupils. It is true that the state college gives less depth of knowledge and this is lamentable, but it is preferable to a high level of knowledge and no awareness of how to best transmit that knowledge. At least teacher training institutes prepare future teachers to organize their curriculums and daily work; a liberal arts graduate too often has no idea of how to proceed. Thus, he gets involved in discipline problems which arise from his own incompetence. If some way could be found to eliminate superfluous courses and make room for a few more intensive courses in the major field of study, the teacher-training institute would produce a more satisfactory product.

One factor relating to the poor reputation of the teacher-training institute is the fact that it accepts students with too low an academic record. If it would raise its admission standards, its reputation would rise accordingly. The main fault with the product of teacher-training institutes lies within themselves, rather than with their training, but the poor teaching done by these individuals casts unjustified criticism upon the institute from which they were graduated.

17. [Elementary teacher] I firmly believe education courses are *a complete waste of time* at any college and most of my friends agree with me. The only worth-while and truly helpful course is student teaching — the length of student teaching program should definitely be extended while the other "superficial" courses cut out or at least clipped to the bare essentials.

18. [Secondary teacher of history] Had some good courses in Education especially at M.A. level. . . . However, I believe the best training a teacher can get is through the study of his (her) subject matter field. This is the prime requirement as I see it. Education courses could be cut in half or practically eliminated in some cases as far as their usefulness is concerned until one has had some teaching experience.

Must explain contradiction in the preceding statement. Enjoyed Education course at undergraduate level probably because of having interesting teacher and because he dealt with many interesting and novel ideas. Their practical usefulness, however, is very questionable without having had any previous teaching experience.

19. [Secondary teacher of English] I consider my training in my major field, English, excellent. My other courses in the liberal arts field, especially history and biology, were also good. My education courses, however, except for methods, were generally repetitive and composed of idealistic theory that doesn't work. My student teaching was also helpful.

I believe that I would lower the amount of education courses required, leaving the student more time for study in his subject matter. I would also try to make the education courses that were required a bit more practical.

20. [Secondary teacher of mathematics and physics] I feel the M.A.T. program is an excellent concept for teacher training provided that there are faculty members who have had experience in American public schools. Two things are essential for secondary teachers: 1) Competence in subject field; 2) desire to work with young people. The rest can follow from these two.

CHAPTER V

How Much Is Enough?

The tremendous waste of time in the American educational system must result from the fact that there is so much time to waste.

— Robert Maynard Hutchins

State Requirements vs. Institutional Practices

As I SURVEYED the literature relating to that most enduring of controversies between scholars and schoolmen — the question of how many courses future teachers take in Education and in the liberal arts — it was soon apparent that nobody had the answer. Everybody had an opinion but nobody had any real data. For some curious reason no educationist had ever attempted to settle this important question by gathering data from the one incontestable source of information on the subject: the transcripts of credit for graduates of the several degree programs in Education. I therefore undertook to gather a national sample of such transcripts and to make numerous tabulations from them. The results indicate that graduates of teacher training programs take far more work in professional Education than demanded by state certification requirements and considerably more than claimed by educationists who have looked into the matter.

The historic rationale for licensing teachers at the state level is the same as it is for medicine, law, or other fields: to protect the public from charlatans and incompetents. In contrast to other fields, however, the teaching license presumes to assure minimum quality both in the subject field involved and in the individual's ability to teach. This has meant that state certification laws have specified semester hour minimums in general education, in the subject or subjects to be taught, and in professional Education. The licensing function has been carried out by the state departments of Education, manned chiefly by educationists. Certification laws have been enacted by state legislatures with the advice and consent of these departments and reflect the educationist's convictions about how teachers ought to be prepared.

In the past state requirements have been justly accused of being excessive in professional Education and disastrously weak in academic education. They frequently gave rise to bizarre incidents and became the object of many jokes. The stony and self-defeating inflexibility with which they have characteristically been administered has kept large numbers of able people out of teaching and continues to do so today, though some changes are in prospect. Only in very recent years have state departments of Education and legislatures responded to the traditional criticisms of certification requirements. A few states are beginning to increase their requirements in academic areas, though they show no sign of a proportionate decrease in Education requirements. Nationally, requirements are still too high on the professional side and much too low on the academic.

Table II illustrates just how far we have come in the last few years, during which there has been a great deal of talk about overhauling the requirements. As is evident, the semester hours' requirement in Education has remained practically static for both elementary and secondary teachers, while the requirements for teaching majors at the secondary level have shown a very small rise. Note that the requirements for teaching academic subjects are still well below what any self-respecting college would consider a decent major. Note also that the state departments of Education still feel that one is competent to teach, say, physics or chemistry in American high schools with exactly half the work in these subjects that the

TABLE II

Comparison of State Requirements in Education and in Certain Subjects, Nationally in Semester Hours, for Certificate to Teach in 1959 and 1961.

Subject	Basic requirement		Minimum requirement	
	1959	1961	1959	1961
Biology	18	20	15	15
Chemistry	18	20	15	16
English	24	25	19	20
General Science	22	22	17	18
Mathematics	20	21	16	17
Modern Languages	22	23	17	18
Physics	18	20	15	15
Agriculture	37	40	30	32
Commerce	30	31	25	27
Home Economics	34	34	26	28
Industrial Arts	30	32	24	25
Physical Education	30	30	25	26

	1959		1961	
	Elementary	Secondary	Elementary	Secondary
Education	*23*	*18.8*	*23.4*	*18.7*

Source: Data derived from W. Earl Armstrong, and T. M. Stinnett, *A Manual on Certification Requirements*, 1961 edition, National Education Association, 1962, pp. 61, 62, 24; and 1959 edition, pp. 37, 19. The "Basic Requirement" is the minimum for full-time teaching in the subject; the "Minimum Requirement" is for teaching the subject part-time, or for a minor fraction of a day, or teaching it full-time in the lowest classification of schools.

state requires of teachers of agriculture to have in agriculture! In fact the states continue to require substantially more semester hours in the major field for non-academic teachers, in all subjects, than they do for academic. Apparently, the state departments of Education still feel that it is more important to keep standards high for teachers of home economics, commerce, or industrial arts than for teachers of mathematics, foreign languages, or English.

Still, improvements are under way in states like New York, California, and Texas that are not yet reflected in the national statistics. Usually these improvements are toward the mandating of a fifth year of college work for a permanent teaching license, but not toward any decrease in pedagogical requirements. While these developments can hardly be considered a "revolution" or a "vast overhaul," as one prominent educationist recently characterized them,[1] they are another sign of the melioristic nature of teacher education today. Obviously, great changes are still needed in state certification requirements and procedures.

Important though the laws governing state licensure are, even more important are the actual practices followed by the preparing institutions. How many semester hours do colleges and universities in fact devote to professional and to academic training for their future teachers? It has long been evident that the colleges, while controlled to some degree by state requirements, have generally followed programs that go far beyond these laws. To the academician who has always inveighed against what he regarded as an excessive number of Education courses in teacher training, the usual response of the educationist has been to say that the number is really quite reasonable and that the academic did not know whereof he spoke. Often the educationist would speciously point out that state requirements were not at all excessive but would fail to say that the institutions require much more. Of course, the important question in teacher education is the intellectual quality of the training programs, not the quantity of this or that component. If the quality were high, the question of quantity would not even arise. But because the quality is low, and be-

[1] T. M. Stinnett, "A Vast Overhaul of Teacher Certification," *The Saturday Review*, March 17, 1962, pp. 87-88.

cause it reflects the ways in which the time available is used in the programs, the question of quantity becomes quite important.

As I have said, there seemed to me very little reliable information on the quantitative problem. Some contradiction existed among the studies that had been done, most of which relied on risky sources of information such as college catalogues and reports from institutions. Although most studies are not far apart on their estimate of time devoted to professional Education in the secondary training programs, they are not in much agreement on the elementary programs — and their estimates are all low on both programs. One author, for example, made tabulations for certain programs described in 114 college catalogues ("haphazardly" selected, as he indicates). He arrives thereby at a national figure of 19 per cent as the amount of time given over to professional Education in the typical undergraduate program for secondary teachers.[2] Another investigation, using more detailed information from the institutional reports of nearly 300 schools, arrives at these figures: an average of 34.8 semester hours devoted to professional Education nationally in programs for elementary teachers; and an average of 23.6 semester hours in secondary programs — that is, about 28 and 19 per cent respectively of the undergraduate programs.[3] Still another study, the most recent and probably best known, was based on tabulations made from the catalogues of 35 colleges and universities — the sample having been drawn to represent an appropriate variety of institutions around the country. Results indicated that in the elementary training programs an average of 36 per cent of the four undergraduate years was given over to professional Edu-

[2] Morris L. Cogan, "Professional Requirements in Collegiate Programs for the Preparation of High School Teachers," in *The Education of Teachers: New Perspectives,* National Education Association, 1958, pp. 317-21.

[3] "Analysis of Quantitative Requirements in Teacher-Education Programs of 294 Colleges and Universities," in *The Education of Teachers: Curriculum Programs,* National Education Association, 1959, pp. 173-92.

cation; and in the secondary programs an average of 17 per cent.[4]

Additionally, there have been a number of small studies, often institutional self-studies,[5] that are naturally of limited application. In all of these investigations, too much use is made of what might be called "secondary" sources, and in none of them are we given sufficient information to draw reliable conclusions about the amount of time actually devoted to Education and to liberal arts or about the various patterns of preparation for elementary and secondary teachers. What has been needed for a long time is a review of transcripts of credit, not of college catalogues, from a sufficient sample of institutions to yield representative national results.

What the Transcripts of Credit Show

In an effort to draw an accurate academic profile of typical graduates of teacher-training programs, I collected in the course of my survey of teacher education a sampling of transcripts of credit from 32 institutions. My sample included graduates at all degree levels in Education in very recent years. The sample was drawn from the commencement rosters of the institutions and varied inversely with the number of prospective teachers turned out by the schools, so that in the case of a very small number of teacher-graduates, the sample might be 100 per cent for adequate representation of the school involved,

[4] Earl J. McGrath, and Charles H. Russell, "Are School Teachers Illiberally Educated?" Published for the Institute of Higher Education by the Bureau of Publications, Teachers College, 1961, pp. 2-3. This report does not list the institutions used in the sample; the Institute has kindly furnished me with the list, however, and I reproduce it in Appendix A.

[5] A typical example is a survey done at the University of Oregon in which the transcripts of 108 graduates from the secondary training programs were used for data. Results indicated that the average time spent in professional Education by high school teachers of academic subjects was 14% at the University of Oregon. Marshall D. Wattles and Henry Osibov, "The Content of Teacher Education," *The Journal of Teacher Education*, Vol. XI, No. 4, 1960, pp. 464-69.

whereas in the case of a large number, the sample would be appropriately reduced, the smallest being 10 per cent. In all but a few cases the transcripts were gathered in this fashion.

A total of 3,459 transcripts was collected, and 1,684 (48%) were actually used in my tabulations. Those not used were thrown out for many reasons: some were clearly special cases in which an individual had done one or two years of work many years before and had returned to complete his degree, or was part of a "retread" program; a great many more were non-academic cases — that is, teachers of non-academic subjects such as home economics, industrial arts, commercial subjects, nursing, physical education, art, and music; and in a few cases early in the study, 100 per cent samples from large institutions were made, before it became clear that this method of "depth" sampling was superfluous because of the lack of variety among the transcripts, necessitating a random reduction of them later on.

In addition to taking samples from the 32 institutions involved, I also included other samplings as a check against the main findings. I took, for example, a sample of transcripts from recent applicants to Brown University's National Science Foundation's institutes in mathematics and science as a check against the main group of math and science people; and I took a large sample of elementary and secondary transcripts for recently certified teachers in the state of Connecticut as a check against my findings for the 32 institutions that made up the main sample.

All told, 503 transcripts for elementary teachers were tabulated (435 in the main sample), 514 for secondary teachers of *academic* subjects (446 in the main sample), 481 transcripts for holders of the master's degree in Education, 172 for holders of the Doctor of Education degree, and 46 for holders of the Doctor of Philosophy in Education degree. (The graduate records are discussed in Chapter VI.)

Here are the 32 institutions, together with the designation

given them in the only standardized classification system now widely recognized, that of the United States Office of Education. Type II schools are those giving only the bachelor's or first professional degree and include many of the better liberal arts colleges; type III schools give the master's or second professional degree; and type IV the doctorate or equivalent. The lower case letters refer to types of programs offered (see Table VI, Appendix A, for a breakdown of this classification system).

1. Ball State Teachers College (Ind.)   III e
2. Boston College   IV k
3. Carleton College (Minn.)   II e
4. Cedar Crest College (Pa.)   II e
5. Concord College (W. Va.)   II e
6. Danbury State College (Conn.)   III d
7. Drake University (Iowa)   III k
8. Eastern Illinois University   III e
9. George Peabody College for Teachers (Tenn.) IV f
10. George Washington University (D.C.)   IV k
11. Grinnell College (Iowa)   II e
12. Indiana University   IV k
13. Keene Teachers College (N.H.)   III d
14. Montclair State College (N.J.)   III d
15. Oberlin College (Ohio)   III j
16. Occidental College (Calif.)   III e
17. Pennsylvania State University   IV k
18. St. Louis University   IV k
19. San Fernando Valley State College (Calif.) III e
20. Southern Connecticut State College   III e
21. State College of Iowa   III d
22. State Teachers College at Towson (Md.)   III e
23. State University of Iowa   IV k
24. Teachers College, Columbia University (N.Y.) IV g
25. Troy State College (Ala.)   III d
26. Washington University (Mo.)   IV k

27. Western Washington State College	III e
28. University of California at Santa Barbara	IV k
29. University of Southern California	IV k
30. University of Washington	IV k
31. University of Wichita	IV k
32. University of Wisconsin	IV k

From these 32 schools, 435 transcripts of credit for the graduates of programs for elementary teachers were tabulated, practically all of them graduates in 1960 or 1961. For secondary teachers of academic subjects, 446 transcripts were tabulated, practically all for 1960 and 1961. The tabulation procedure involved the classifying and recording of every item of information from every transcript — the school and the individual (each given a code number), the degree awarded, the year it was awarded, every course taken, the credit hours, the grade, and other items.[6] Courses were recorded in three major categories: "Academic," "Non-academic," and "Professional." In the "Academic" category courses were recorded in those subjects generally identified with that name, or with the name "liberal arts" or "arts and sciences" — embracing the humanistic fields, the sciences, mathematics, psychology, and general education courses. In the "Non-academic" category were recorded mostly courses in physical education and ROTC, and an occasional course in home economics, industrial arts, business, and similar subjects. In the "Professional" category were recorded those courses customarily considered pedagogical — educational psychology, methods of teaching, history and philosophy of education, guidance, audio-visual aids, etc. Under methods of teaching were included courses, especially for elementary teachers, in what is sometimes called "professionalized subject matter" — such as "Children's Literature," "School

---

[6] For those who have any interest in the matter, I might record the fact that data processing equipment turned out to be the most expensive and least expeditious way of making these tabulations. After an initial trial, I rejected it in favor of simple hand tabulation on mimeographed forms.

Health and Hygiene," "Science for Teachers," "Art in the Elementary School," and similar courses of a considerable variety. Many educationists are wont to claim such courses as "content," not methods, courses and often have them listed in the college catalogue as regular liberal arts offerings. This seems a poor rationalization. Such courses sometimes have a certain amount of liberal content, but it is extremely thin and clearly not on a par with regular liberal arts courses. "Children's Literature" may indeed include readings in Lewis Carroll, Mark Twain, or Hans Christian Andersen, but the focus is on the child's relation to such reading. (I would also note in passing that the bulk of reading in "Children's Literature" courses is in second and third-rate authors, or in those never heard of by anyone but the compiler of the textbook involved.) If any justification is needed for tabulating such courses in the "professional" column, I take my cue from the National Council for Accreditation of Teacher Education, an agency that would be inclined to give Education the benefit of any doubt in the matter. Its directions to accreditors, called "Standards and Guide," says: "In the elementary curriculum such courses as public school music and children's literature should be counted as professional education regardless of how they are listed in the catalog."

Table III (page 128) records the results for 26 items of information computed from the transcripts. One should realize that the averages reported in this Table are just that, *national averages,* and, like national averages of other kinds, can be misleading. In the field of teacher education, involving well over a thousand institutions and graduating nearly 150,000 teachers a year, it is somewhat unrealistic to talk about national averages. Many of the training programs in liberal arts institutions, for example, depart widely from these averages, as do those of teachers colleges. Thus it is more realistic and more useful if we compute averages separately for the major types of institutions now preparing teachers. One finds three such types, in

TABLE III

Academic Profile, Drawn from the Transcripts of Credit, for Recent Graduates of Elementary and Secondary Teacher-Training Programs. Asterisk indicates items not tabulated.	435 elementary teachers	446 secondary teachers of academic subjects
1. *Mean semester hours in professional Education*	*49.9*	*27.6*
2. *Mean semester hours in academic education*	*72.0*	*96.5*
3. *Per cent of total program devoted to professional Education*	*41.0%*	*22.2%*
4. *Per cent of total program devoted to academic education*	*59.0%*	*77.8%*
5. Per cent of time devoted to Education in an assumed 120-semester-hour program	41.3%	23.0%
6. Per cent of time devoted to academic education in an assumed 120–semester-hour program	58.7%	77.0%
7. Composite grade point average in professional Education	2.92	2.99
8. Composite grade point average in academic education	2.51	2.68
9. Mean semester hours devoted to practice teaching	8	7
10. Mean semester hours devoted to methods of teaching	12	*
11. Mean semester hours devoted to field of English (non-majors)	12	12
12. Mean semester hours devoted to field of mathematics (non-majors)	2	3
13. Mean semester hours devoted to field of science (non-majors)	9	11
14. Mean semester hours devoted to field of foreign languages (non-majors)	4	5
15. Per cent of transcripts showing no advanced work in any academic field(s)	50%	*
16. Per cent of transcripts showing 1-6 semester hours of advanced work in any academic field(s)	22%	*
17. Per cent of transcripts showing 7-12 semester hours of advanced work in any academic field(s)	17%	*
18. Per cent of transcripts showing over 12 semester hours of advanced work in any academic field(s)	11%	*
19. Mean semester hours in English for majors	*	34
20. Mean semester hours in mathematics for majors	*	30
21. Mean semester hours in science for majors	*	31
22. Mean semester hours in "general science" for majors	*	41
23. Mean semester hours in history for majors	*	31
24. Mean semester hours in "social studies" for majors	*	43
25. Mean semester hours in foreign languages for majors	*	31
26. Mean semester hours in major field for entire sample (including majors in "general science" and "social studies")	*	34

which there seem to be marked differences in the training programs: (1) liberal arts colleges, especially those that are confined to undergraduate work; (2) universities, usually with separate schools or colleges of Education; and (3) teachers colleges and so-called multi-purpose colleges that were formerly teachers colleges and still train teachers as their primary function. The first category accounts for a relatively small number of teachers. The second and third categories, in a ratio of about half and half, account for the vast majority. Dividing the 32 schools, then, into these three groups, and adding the classification of the United States Office of Education by highest degree and type of program, we get a picture like this:

Group I (Liberal Arts Colleges)

1.	Carleton College	II e
2.	Cedar Crest College	II e
3.	Concord College	II e
4.	Grinnell College	II e
5.	Oberlin College	III j
6.	Occidental College	III e

Group II (Universities)

7.	Boston College	IV k
8.	Drake University	III k
9.	George Washington University	IV k
10.	Indiana University	IV k
11.	Pennsylvania State University	IV k
12.	St. Louis University	IV k
13.	State University of Iowa	IV k
14.	Teachers College, Columbia University	IV k
15.	University of California, Santa Barbara	IV k
16.	University of Southern California	IV k
17.	University of Washington	IV k
18.	University of Wichita	IV k
19.	University of Wisconsin	IV k
20.	Washington University	IV k

Group III (*Teachers Colleges, Present and Erstwhile*)

21. Ball State Teachers College	III e
22. Danbury State College	III d
23. Eastern Illinois University	III e
24. George Peabody College for Teachers	IV k
25. Keene Teachers College	III d
26. Montclair State College	III d
27. San Fernando Valley State College	III e
28. Southern Connecticut State College	III e
29. State College of Iowa	III d
30. State Teachers College at Towson	III e
31. Troy State College	III d
32. Western Washington State College	III e

Four of the six institutions in Group I give only the bachelor's degree, and the other two give the master's; teacher education is not the main concern of any of them. Nor is it of any of the universities of Group II; Teachers College is the exception, of course, but for our purposes is considered part of Columbia University. Only four of the 12 schools in Group III have the word "Teachers" or "Education" in their titles, but the other eight are former teachers colleges and were normal schools before that; all train teachers still as their principal function. The great majority, that is, of the graduates of the Group III institutions have been put through the regular teacher-training programs of these schools; the single exception is San Fernando Valley State College, but even here about 60 per cent of the graduates are teachers.

There is a good deal of confusion in the field about what per cent of teachers are turned out by what types of schools. Generally the estimates given for teachers colleges, 15-20 per cent, are quite low, and those for liberal arts colleges and multipurpose institutions unrealistically high. The last reliable compilation (for the year 1956-57) put the percentage of new graduates who did all or most of their work at teachers colleges at 36 per cent, meaning schools that had the name "Teachers" or "Education" in their titles; graduates who did their work at universities were put at 34 per cent and those at liberal arts colleges at 25 per cent.[7] Even these figures are misleading, however, for the real differences in training programs for teachers are found between those institutions that still pursue teacher training as their main concern, whatever their titles may be, and those that do not. Data on this kind of division are not available at present, but an educated guess, which is all one can offer until better information is compiled, would be that perhaps half of the new teachers each year come out of institutions in which teacher training is still the principal function.

In many ways a more informative picture of things emerges when the data are rendered separately for these three groupings than when they are given as in Table III. Tables IV and V, on pages 132-133, contain the same quantitative information as does Table III, but rearranged according to the three groups of institutions. Groups II and III represent, as I have said, the types of institutions that prepare the great majority of American teachers. Group I institutions prepare relatively few. Thus there is, strictly speaking, no such thing as the national averages of Table III. Since there are sizable differences among the three groups, national averages depend on how one wishes to classify the 1,148 institutions that train teachers, and how one wishes to draw a sample of transcripts from these institutions after they are classified. Until there is an agreed-upon system of classifying schools that train teachers, a certain element of arbitrariness must be present in any sampling of transcripts. However, the 32 institutions I selected, and the three groupings made from them, represent a sample of the entire field of teacher education, a sample that reasonable men might agree is representative. I do not offer it as a "scientific" sample

[7] Ward S. Mason, *The Beginning Teacher,* U.S. Office of Education, Circular No. 644, 1961, p. 37.

TABLE IV

Academic Profile, Drawn from the Transcripts of Credit, for 435 Recent Graduates of *Elementary* Teacher-Training Programs.	Group I Liberal Arts Colleges	Group II Universities	Group III Teachers Colleges
1. *Mean semester hours devoted to professional Education*	36.7	49.6	55.0
2. *Mean semester hours devoted to academic education*	84.0	72.1	67.4
3. *Per cent of total program devoted to professional Education*	30.4%	40.8%	44.9%
4. *Per cent of total program devoted to academic education*	69.6%	59.2%	55.1%
5. Per cent of time devoted to professional Education in an assumed 120-semester-hour program	30.6%	41.0%	45.8%
6. Per cent of time devoted to academic education in an assumed 120-semester-hour program	70.0%	60.3%	55.1%
7. Composite grade point average in professional Education	3.00	2.97	2.84
8. Composite grade point average in academic education	2.57	2.50	2.54
9. Mean semester hours devoted to practice teaching	6	8	10
10. Mean semester hours devoted to methods of teaching	8	12	12
11. Mean semester hours devoted to field of English	13	13	11
12. Mean semester hours devoted to field of mathematics	2	1	3
13. Mean semester hours devoted to field of science	11	8	11
14. Mean semester hours devoted to field of foreign languages	7	5	1
15. Per cent of transcripts showing no advanced work in any academic field(s)	9%	42%	67%
16. Per cent of transcripts showing 1-6 semester hours of advanced work in any academic subject(s)	27%	25%	20%
17. Per cent of transcripts showing 7-12 semester hours of advanced work in any academic subject(s)	41%	15%	12%
18. Per cent of transcripts showing over 12 semester hours of advanced work in any academic subject(s)	23%	18%	1%

TABLE V

Academic Profile, Drawn from the Transcripts of Credit, for 446 Recent Graduates of Secondary Teacher-Training Programs in *Academic* Subjects.	Group I Liberal Arts Colleges	Group II Universities	Group III Teachers Colleges
1. *Mean semester hours devoted to professional Education*	*19.8*	*26.0*	*34.2*
2. *Mean semester hours devoted to academic education*	*104.1*	*98.0*	*90.1*
3. *Per cent of total program devoted to professional Education*	*15.9%*	*21.0%*	*27.2%*
4. *Per cent of total program devoted to academic education*	*84.1%*	*79.0%*	*72.8%*
5. Per cent of time devoted to professional Education in an assumed 120-semester-hour program	16.5%	21.8%	28.5%
6. Per cent of time devoted to academic education in an assumed 120-semester-hour program	86.7%	81.4%	75.0%
7. Composite grade point average in professional Education	3.07	2.98	2.95
8. Composite grade point average in academic education	2.68	2.66	2.71
9. Mean semester hours devoted to practice teaching	5	5	10
10. Mean semester hours devoted to field of English (non-majors)	12	14	10
11. Mean semester hours devoted to field of mathematics (non-majors)	2	2	4
12. Mean semester hours devoted to field of science (non-majors)	12	10	12
13. Mean semester hours devoted to field of foreign languages (non-majors)	10	6	2
14. Mean semester hours in English for majors	40	32	30
15. Mean semester hours in mathematics for majors	28	29	30
16. Mean semester hours in science for majors	31	30	30
17. Mean semester hours in science for "general science" majors	35	27	44
18. Mean semester hours in history for majors	32	31	29
19. Mean semester hours in "social studies" for majors	42	43	44
20. Mean semester hours in foreign languages for majors	37	31	34
21. Mean semester hours in major field for entire sample (including majors in "general science" and "social studies")	35	33	34

in any sense. It was not drawn according to the principles of mathematical statistics for the reasons just given. However, I *do* offer this sample and the results of this review of transcripts of credit as more reliable than anything else yet available.

Although Tables III, IV, and V are in general self-explanatory, some further comment may be in order on various items. Items 3 and 4 in all Tables were computed by adding items 1 and 2 to get the total mean hours for the program, and then dividing that figure into items 1 and 2 separately. The standard college program, however, has long been regarded as 120 semester hours; therefore items 5 and 6 were computed, for comparative purposes, by dividing 120 into items 1 and 2 separately. The composite grade point average, items 7 and 8 in all Tables, is simply the result of converting all letter grades from each transcript by the usual system: A = 4 points, B = 3, C = 2, and D = 1 — then computing each individual's grade point average, and then computing a mean for the whole group. "Advanced" work, or "upper division" work as it is sometimes called, was tabulated for elementary teachers; generally work beyond the introductory survey courses in academic subjects, which prevail during the freshman and sophomore years, was counted as advanced.

These Tables probably put the best light possible on the situation. If the transcripts for the entire group of new teachers in any given year were used instead of my sample, the results would probably indicate somewhat higher averages in the number of Education courses taken and lower averages in academic work. The reasons are several: my sample is concentrated on those institutions that are generally acknowledged to be among the better ones in the field; more transcripts than were proportionally justified were gathered from the liberal arts colleges (in order to have an adequate representation of their small graduating classes); no transcripts were used for graduates in such fields as home economics, physical education, industrial arts, business, art, and music — where the Education work tends to be a good deal higher than in academic areas; and in the tabulation process, the academic side of things was given the benefit of any doubt — that is, when there was some doubt as to whether a given course was academic or professional, as judged from the transcript entry and the catalogue description of the course, it was assigned to the academic column. For these and other reasons, the sample finally used in this survey probably yields the most favorable profile possible of Education programs.

In addition to the data recorded in the Tables, some other observations should be made about the transcripts:

(1) Since the data in the Tables are averages, it follows that a great many teachers went well beyond or below these figures in professional and academic work. The range, that is, was very wide in most categories. The greatest concentration of Education courses found among the elementary transcripts was 88 semester hours, or about 73 per cent of an undergraduate career; the lowest on the academic side, not for the same person, was 33 semester hours, about 28 per cent of an undergraduate career. Four of the institutions ranged into the 80's in semester hours of Education courses for their elementary teachers, three into the 70's, and nine into the 60's. For secondary teachers, the highest was 65 semester hours of Education work; the lowest for academic work was 48 hours. Two schools ranged into the 60's in semester hours of Education for secondary teachers, four into the 50's, and six into the 40's.

(2) For teachers of non-academic subjects, the average time spent in Education is even greater than for teachers of academic subjects. Although the non-academic transcripts were excluded from these tabulations, they were necessarily gathered in the course of drawing the sample from the 32 institutions. Teachers of art and music particularly, but also teachers of industrial arts, home economics, and physical education, regularly acquire a much narrower education than their aca-

demic colleagues; they get more work in Education, much more in their specialties, and much less in liberal arts. Teachers of art and music — who need, one would suppose, as much work in allied fields like literature, history, and philosophy as they could possibly manage — often spend between 70 and 80 per cent of their time, throughout their four years of college, in their specialties. This grotesque imbalance persists today in almost all the training programs in art and music. Whatever grasp of their fields teachers of these subjects may bring to the job, their education has scarcely been liberal.

(3) Grades awarded in Education courses were consistently higher than in academic. The consistency was absolute. This will be no surprise to those institutions whose registrars keep yearly tabulations of grades awarded in the various courses and by the various departments. Many registrars keep such records, sometimes distributing them freely on the campus, sometimes not. A typical example would be The George Washington University. Looking at its tabulation of all grades in all courses, averaged by each department for the 1959-1960 academic year, we find that, out of 44 departments or divisions of the University, Education gave the greatest percentage of "A" and "B" grades — 82% of *all* the grades it awarded — with one exception, Home Economics, which gave "A's" and "B's" 85 per cent of the time. The State University of Iowa, to use another example, which has what educationists regard as one of the stronger schools of Education in the country, computed the distribution of grades among its 43 departments or colleges for a 12-year period, 1948-1960. Results indicated that Education was fourth from the top in the number of "A's" awarded (preceded by Music, Physical Education for Men, and German) and was fifth from the top in the number of "B's" awarded (preceded by Museum Methods, Nursing, Child Welfare, and Physical Education for Women). And for comparative figures that cover more than a single institution, one might look at a report of two educationists who made tabulations of the grades

awarded over a period of four years in six large Midwestern state universities in Education and in the liberal arts and sciences divisions: Education was far ahead on every calculation, awarding 79 per cent of all its grades as "A's" and "B's," compared to 51 per cent in the liberal arts and sciences.[8] Educationists have often found reasons to deny the charge from academicians that Education courses were among the least rigorously graded on the campus. But the facts of my survey of transcripts would seem to support the charge quite well. The reasons for such a consistently high pattern of grading will be disputed, of course. My own conviction is that it is simply one more reflection of the low standards generally maintained in Education.

(4) There is a good deal of shopping around for schools indicated in the transcripts. Fully 82 per cent of the graduates of one large school of Education were transfer students. The average was 48 per cent for elementary teachers, many of whom had changed schools two or three times, and 36.3 per cent for secondary. Much of this shifting was from small, often denominational, little-known institutions that, judged from the point of view of faculty, financial resources, and general reputation, must be considered among the lowest ranks of American colleges. Although American students are a highly mobile group, this amount and type of transfer by future teachers suggests a certain amount of shopping around for cheap degrees. It also suggests that statistics about what per cent of new teachers are being turned out by multi-purpose colleges and by universities may not give the whole picture. It might be revealing to see what per cent of these graduates did what per cent of their work in second- or third-rate institutions before coming to the schools from which they were graduated. (The transcripts also reveal a heavy sprinkling of low grades in academic

[8] Robert M. Weiss and Glen R. Rasmussen, "Grading Practices in Undergraduate Education Courses," *The Journal of Higher Education*, March, 1960, pp. 143-49.

subjects and cases of probationary status; in a few instances even "F's" were counted toward the degree.)

(5) Also evident from the transcripts was the fact that a great many summer school courses, extension courses, and correspondence courses were taken for credit, as well as a good many courses at night, on Saturdays, and at other irregular times — all of which, as any educational administrator knows, is evidence of reduced academic quality. Teachers often have no choice but to take this kind of work, but that does not make the work any better; this kind of course is generally recognized to be less demanding, and often attended by less demanding students, than regular work taken in residence.

(6) The reason the national averages are so low in mathematics and foreign languages for elementary teachers is that so many teachers take no work whatever in these subjects. To understand the low state of mathematics and language instruction in the primary grades, one has only to look at the college records of the teachers. Nor do they take much science; a course in biology is frequently the whole of it. So "general" is their education that they often do not get beyond the sophomore survey level in any academic subject, while they ignore completely a large number of academic fields.

(7) Although secondary teachers get more academic work than elementary teachers (those, that is, who do not major in Education), too often their pattern of courses does not seem to make sense. It suggests a mere potpourri, even in the major field. Also, the major often fails to include work that teachers of the subject clearly need. English majors, for example, more often than not will show no work in advanced composition, advanced grammar (or any other kind), linguistics, or the phonetic alphabet. They usually show a collection of discrete courses in authors and periods that reveals no particular design and that leaves them with enormous gaps. History majors show no work in historiography and often none in sequential studies of periods or cultures that are most im-

portant to a high school teacher. If they major in social studies instead of history, as many of them do, their courses get little beyond the introductory or survey type in almost all subjects; they get, like the elementary teacher, a "general" education with a vengeance. They can be said to have had a "major" only by an unwarranted extension of the term.

Some Case Histories

There follow, as representative examples, ten fully reproduced transcripts of credit. They illustrate the various patterns of work characteristic of the training programs for elementary and secondary teachers. A number of further transcripts are reproduced in Appendix A as an extension of this section for those sufficiently interested in specific case histories. I have recorded directly from the transcripts each course by the name given it in the record, and the semester hours of credit awarded for it. The grade point average in Education and in liberal arts is also given for each transcript.

In order that the pattern may be evident to the reader at a glance, I confine each reproduced transcript to a single page. But since further information is important in each case, I group my comments on the ten examples together, as follows, after which the transcripts themselves appear, starting on page 144. Each example is from a well-established institution accredited by the appropriate regional association and by the National Council for Accreditation of Teacher Education:

Comment on CASE NO. 1 — This case illustrates how lopsided the education of an elementary teacher can be. Here is a recent graduate of one of our largest private universities, with a very large school of Education. For admission to this institution, the student brought from high school no work whatever in mathematics (not even "general mathematics," which is usually a review of arithmetic in the ninth or tenth grade), no physics, no chemistry, and one year of Spanish. The total of 113 semester hours listed for this graduate does not include the following courses, several of which are offered especially for teachers and which, properly considered, should be added to the Education column: "Physical Education Fundamentals," "Community Recreation Leadership," "Human Anatomy" [given by the Department of Physical Education], "Major Sports," and "Athletic Training." As the transcript indicates, the individual got no college work whatever in mathematics, in foreign languages, or in a number of other academic subjects, while his work in his native language consisted of the customary freshman English — itself a remedial course. This kind of case, although not typical of elementary programs today, is not at all rare. The individual is now fully certified and teaching in an Eastern state.

Comment on CASE NO. 2 — This is a reasonably typical case of those elementary teachers who get their education at a teachers college or at one of the state colleges that were formerly teachers colleges. Note that no fewer than half of her 61 semester hours of work in Education are in methods courses, while on the liberal arts side she gets no work whatever in a number of crucial subjects, including geography. She would not be qualified to take even an upper-division undergraduate course in many subjects and could not qualify to do graduate work in anything except Education.

Comment on CASE NO. 3 — This kind of preparation for elementary teachers is far more rare than its opposite as illustrated in Case No. 1. Only a handful of schools throughout the nation permit their elementary teachers to take a regular undergraduate major, or permit them to spend nearly 80 per cent of their time in liberal arts; and the number of teachers turned out of such programs, which are usually found in small liberal arts institutions, is negligible in relation to the total. Still, it demonstrates what can be done to turn out educated elementary teachers; it also demonstrates the ideological distance that often remains between the educationist and the academician.

Comment on CASE NO. 4 — Like Case No. 1, this illustrates, for secondary teachers of academic subjects, how lop-sided the training programs can and often do become. This kind of case is not typical, but it is plentiful enough. He came to the college with a poor high school record, was put on probation twice during college, did unpromising work in his major subject, mathematics, flunked several courses (including one in "Techniques of Make-up for Dramatic Production"), was permitted to follow an academic program that had no apparent rhyme or reason, was permitted to use up 44 semester hours in Education courses when he desperately needed not only far more work in his major field, in which he is clearly incompetent, but in about every other basic subject one could mention. Still, he was graduated in 1961 in good standing and is now a fully certified teacher in his state.

Comment on CASE NO. 5 — This kind of case occurs with great frequency, in both state colleges and university schools of Education. Note that English, the major subject, counting the course in "Effective Speaking" as part of it, is far from strong: it shows no advanced composition, no grammar, no work in any literary figure except Shakespeare, no classical literature in translation, no non-English literature of any kind, and no work in any literary period. Note also the serious amount of duplication between the academic and the Education courses: the student takes "General Psychology," "Abnormal Psychology," and "Juvenile Delinquency" on the one side, and then gets "Child Psychology," and a year of "Learning and Teaching" (which is educational psychology) on the other — 18 semester hours all told; he gets courses like "Man in Modern Society," "Social Movements," and "Social Control" on the one side, and then gets "Society and the School," and "The Family and the Modern Secondary School" on the other. There is, of course, no work whatever in mathematics, philosophy, economics, physical sciences, or in many other subjects.

Comment on CASE NO. 6 — This is a fairly representative transcript for a teacher in that most protean of fields, social studies, though this individual has had the advantage of more semester hours than is normal. Because the scope of this field is without any practical limit, the custom is for students to sample a bit of everything in history (in this case confined to a year's survey of American history!), economics, sociology, political science, and perhaps geography. Note the plethora of 3-hour introductory survey courses, meaning that the student becomes, not a specialist in anything, but a shallow generalist in half a dozen things. He necessarily suffers in knowledge and discipline from this pervasive superficiality; even so, it is a better education than that received by a great many secondary teachers.

Comment on CASES NO. 7 AND 8 —These illustrate the pattern of teacher training that characterizes most of the first-rate liberal arts colleges. These institutions stick close to the minimum state requirements in Education, but far exceed them in academic work and in the time devoted to the major. As is true with the elementary teachers, however, the number of secondary teachers turned out of these programs is extremely small. Whether the programs make up in influence what they lack in size, and act as a leavening on the programs in state colleges and in universities, is very doubtful; the liberal arts programs have been around a long time without having much noticeable effect on others. Quite the contrary, some of the liberal arts programs have been influenced in deleterious ways by the others.

Comment on CASES NO. 9 AND 10 — This is a matched pair that illustrates the differences often found within the same institution between secondary training programs controlled by the school of Education and those controlled by the liberal arts division. In this example, both teachers are majors in romance languages in the same institution, one the graduate of the liberal arts division of the university (No. 9), and the other the graduate of the Education division (No. 10). No. 9, as can be seen, got 15 semester hours of work, a full semester, more in the liberal arts than did No. 10, who got an additional 16 semester hours of Education courses instead. Moreover, No. 9 graduated *cum laude,* had four years of his specialty, French, in high school, permitting him to move into the reading of French masterpieces in his freshman college year, while No. 10 had two years of French in high school and begins with "3rd semester French." Also evident is the fact that No. 9 had 30 semester hours in foreign languages *other* than French, while No. 10 had 17 semester hours.

CASE NO. 1

Degree of Bachelor of Science in Education awarded August, 1960.
All work done at a large private university with a separate school
of Education. Major: Elementary Education.

Liberal Arts Courses (29 semester hours)

Communications (6)
Introduction to Aesthetics (2)
General Biology (3)
History of Western Civilization (6)

American History since 1865 (3)
American History, 1760-1865 (3)
General Geography (3)
Religions of the World (3)

Education Courses (84 semester hours)

Introduction to Educational Psychology (3)
Observations Public Schools (2)
Educational Biology (3)
Psychology of Learning (3)
School Health Education (3)
Arts and Crafts in the Elementary School (2)
History and Philosophy of Education (3)
Personal and Community Hygiene (2)
Indoor Group Games (1)
Combatives (1)
Child Growth and Development (3)
Use of Audio-Visual Aids (2)
Science in the Elementary School (3)
Physical Education Methods in Elementary School (3)
Speech Improvement [Education course] (2)

Elementary Education Laboratory (3)
Teaching of Reading (3)
Social Studies in the Elementary School (3)
Music Methods in the Elementary School (3)
Teaching Language Arts (3)
Methods of Teaching Arithmetic (3)
Methods in Health Education (3)
Student Teaching (6)
Art in the Elementary School (3)
Safety Education (3)
Educational Measurements (3)
Student Teaching (6)
Curriculum in Health and Physical Ed. (3)
Speech Improvement (3)

Further Information:

1. Per cent of total program devoted to Education   74.3%
2. Per cent of total program devoted to liberal arts   25.7%
3. Grade point average in Education   2.73
4. Grade point average in liberal arts   2.45

CASE NO. 2

Degree of Bachelor of Science awarded June, 1961.
All work was done at a state teachers college, lately renamed to delete "Teachers" from the title. Major: Elementary Education.

Liberal Arts Courses (64 semester hours)

Spoken Expression (3)
Fundamentals of Mathematics (6)
College Biology (6)
Introduction to Social Sciences (6)
U.S. History, 1877-Present (6)
Written Expression (3)
Music History and Appreciation (3)
English Literature (3)
Elements of Physics (3)

Modern British and American Lit. (3)
College Algebra (3)
Survey of Astronomy and Geology (3)
The U.S. as a World Power (3)
Music Theory (4)
Cultural Anthropology (3)
Genetics (3)
American Drama (3)

Education Courses (61 semester hours)

Human Development and Behavior (3)
Personal and Community Health (3)
Physical Education Activities (2)
Sophomore Orientation (1)
Art in the Elementary School (3)
Student Teaching (5)
Curriculum Materials: Reading (2)
Curriculum Materials: Language Arts (2)
Educational Psychology (3)
School Health Education (3)
Science in the Elementary School (3)

Children's Literature (3)
Personality and Adjustment (3)
Art Materials and Media (3)
Student Teaching (5)
Curriculum Materials: Arithmetic (2)
Curriculum Materials: Social Studies (3)
Music in the Elementary School (3)
Physical Education in the Elementary School (3)
History and Philosophy of Education (3)
Teaching of Reading (3)

Further Information:

1. Per cent of total program devoted to Education — 48.8%
2. Per cent of total program devoted to liberal arts — 51.2%
3. Grade point average in Education — 2.46
4. Grade point average in liberal arts — 2.34

CASE NO. 3

Degree of Bachelor of Arts awarded June, 1960.
All work done at a first-line private liberal arts college.
Major: Sociology and Anthropology.

Liberal Arts Courses (101 semester hours)

Freshman English (3)
Modern Europe (4)
Consumer Problems (3)
Intermediate French (6)
American Government (3)
Introductory Sociology (6)
Fundamentals of Speech (3)
Introduction to the Theatre (3)
Principles of General Biology (4)
Human Biology (4)
Introduction General Chemistry (3)
Survey of Literature (3)
General Psychology (3)
Introduction to Anthropology (3)
Cultural Anthropology (3)

The Community (3)
Marriage and Family (4)
Modern Novel (3)
American Writers (3)
Contemporary History (3)
History of Christian Thought (3)
Introduction to Philosophy (3)
Race Relations (3)
British History (3)
Criminology (4)
Social Analysis Research (4)
Greek and Latin Literature (3)
American History (3)
Independent Project [Anthropology] (2)
Social Theory and Application (3)

Education Courses (26 semester hours)

Educational Psychology (3)
Basic Skill Subjects [for the Elementary School] (8)
Problems in American Education (4)

Reading and Children's Literature (4)
Practice Teaching (7)

Further Information:

1. Per cent of total program devoted to Education 20.5%
2. Per cent of total program devoted to liberal arts 79.5%
3. Grade point average in Education 3.73
4. Grade point average in liberal arts 3.46
5. Total semester hours in major field(s) 35

CASE NO. 4

Degree of Bachelor of Science awarded June, 1961.
All work was done at a state teachers college.
Major: Mathematics.

Liberal Arts Courses (78 semester hours)

Composition and Literature (6)
Music Appreciation (2)
Biological Sciences (6)
Elements of Geography (6)
Fundamentals of Design (2)
Fundamentals of Speech (2)
English Literature (3)
College Algebra (3)
Fundamental Concepts of Arithmetic (3)
Physical Science (6)
History of Western Civ. (6)
American Literature (3)

Trigonometry and Analytical Geom. (4)
Statistics (2)
Art in the Culture (2)
Business Mathematics (3)
History of the United States (6)
Marriage and Family Relations (2)
Play Production (2)
Mathematics of Finance (3)
Music Fundamentals (2)
Concepts of Modern Mathematics (2)
Map Reading and Interpretation (2)

Education Courses (44 semester hours)

Individual and School Health (2)
Adolescent and His Community (1)
Introduction to Junior High School (4)
Developmental Psychology (3)
Audio-Visual Aids (3)
Directed Teaching (7½)
Language Arts in Secondary School (2)
Mathematics in Secondary School (2)

Science in Secondary School (2)
Core Techniques in the Public School (2)
Psychology of Adolescence (3)
Directed Teaching (7½)
Seminar in Education (1)
Psychology of the Exceptional Child (2)
Measurement in Secondary School (2)

Further Information:

1. Per cent of total program devoted to Education — 36.0%
2. Per cent of total program devoted to liberal arts — 64.0%
3. Grade point average in Education — 2.52
4. Grade point average in liberal arts — 2.19
5. Total semester hours in major field — 20

CASE NO. 5

Degree of Bachelor of Arts awarded June, 1960.
Three-quarters of work was done at the degree-granting institution,
a private university with a separate school of Education. Major: English.

Liberal Arts Courses (94 semester hours)

General Biology (6)
English Composition (6)
Health (3)
Modern European History (6)
Intermediate Spanish (6)
Art — Design (3)
Intro. to English Literature (6)
U.S. Civilization (6)
General Psychology (3)
Effective Speaking (3)
World Regions (3)
Introduction to Geography (3)

Abnormal Psychology (3)
Man in Modern Society (6)
Government of the U.S. (6)
Introduction to American Literature (6)
Juvenile Delinquency (3)
Social Movements (3)
Current History (1)
Introduction to Linguistics (3)
Shakespeare (6)
Social Control (3)

Education Courses (36 semester hours)

Child Psychology (3)
Introduction to Statistics in Education (3)
Learning and Teaching (6)
Society and the School (6)
Teaching Skills in Secondary School (3)

The Family and the Modern Secondary School (3)
Observation and Practice Teaching (6)
Teaching English (3)
Teaching Social Studies (3)

Further Information:

1. Per cent of total program devoted to Education   27.7%
2. Per cent of total program devoted to liberal arts   72.3%
3. Grade point average in Education   3.30
4. Grade point average in liberal arts   2.87
5. Total semester hours in major field   30

CASE NO. 6

SECONDARY TEACHER

Degree of Bachelor of Science in Education awarded June, 1961.
All work was done at a private university.
Major: Social Studies

Liberal Arts Courses (99 semester hours)

Biological Sciences (4)
College Algebra (3)
Trigonometry (3)
General Biology (4)
Mechanical Drawing (3)
Freshman English (6)
Analytical Geometry (3)
General Psychology (3)
Introd. to Social Sciences (6)
American Literature (6)
Development of Modern Society (6)
World Resources (3)
Elements of Geography (3)
Principles of Economics (3)
Introd. to Political Science (2)

American National Government (3)
Principles of Sociology (3)
Effective Speech (3)
English Grammar and Usage (3)
English Literature (6)
U.S. History (6)
Renaissance Literature (3)
Marriage and the Family (3)
Business and Government (3)
Conduct of American Diplomacy (2)
American Writers (3)
Governments of Russia and Neighbors (3)

Education Courses (29 semester hours)

Educational Psychology (3)
Introduction to Education (2)
Audio-Visual Materials (3)
Science Conservation [Education course] (3)
Principles of Secondary Education (3)

Planning Learning Situations (3)
Guiding the Adolescent (3)
Measurement and Evaluation of Pupil Growth (3)
Practice Teaching (6)

Further Information:

1. Per cent of total program devoted to Education   22.6%
2. Per cent of total program devoted to liberal arts   77.4%
3. Grade point average in Education   2.82
4. Grade point average in liberal arts   2.13
5. Total semester hours in major field(s)   46

CASE NO. 7

Degree of Bachelor of Arts awarded June, 1960.
All work done at a private liberal arts college.
Major: English

Liberal Arts Courses (106 semester hours)

Principles of General Biology (4)
Human Biology (4)
Freshman English (3)
Study of Literature (3)
Classical Literature (3)
Modern Europe (4)
Intermediate French (6)
Introduction to the Theatre (3)
American Writers (6)
Shakespeare (11)
Chaucer (4)
Social Institutions, Middle Ages (4)

College Mathematics (3)
General Psychology (3)
Introductory Sociology (3)
Studies in American Literature (8)
English Prose Style (3)
American History (6)
Old Testament Thought (3)
English Literature (4)
The Victorians (4)
Major British Writers (3)
Independent Project in English (2)
British History (6)
Contemporary History (3)

Education Courses (18 semester hours)

Educational Psychology (3)
Problems of American Education (4)
Secondary Curriculum and Methods (3)

Practice Teaching (6)
English for Teachers (2)

Further Information:

1. Per cent of total program devoted to Education — 14.5%
2. Per cent of total program devoted to liberal arts — 85.5%
3. Grade point average in Education — 3.33
4. Grade point average in liberal arts — 3.00
5. Total semester hours in major field — 54

CASE NO. 8

Degree of Bachelor of Arts awarded, *cum laude*, June, 1961.
All work done at a private liberal arts college.
Major: Social Studies

Liberal Arts Courses (102 semester hours)

Introduction to Art (3)
Elementary Astronomy (6)
General Zoology (8)
Principles of Economics (6)
Rhetoric (3)
Introduction to English Lit. (6)
American Literature (6)
History of the Modern World (6)
History of the U.S. (6)
American Studies Seminar (3)
History — the Twentieth Century (6)
England in the 16th and 17th Centuries (3)

Ancient Civilization (3)
History of Medieval Europe (3)
Middle Ages (3)
Russia since 1917 (3)
Age of Absolutism (3)
Spanish Prose (6)
Spanish Composition (4)
Principles of Ethics (6)
General Psychology (3)
Principles of Sociology (3)
Social Problems (3)

Education Courses (18 semester hours)

Principles of Education (3)
Teaching Social Studies (3)
Educational Psychology (3)

Student Teaching (6)
High School Teaching (3)

Further Information:

1. Per cent of total program devoted to Education	15.0%
2. Per cent of total program devoted to liberal arts	85.0%
3. Grade point average in Education	3.16
4. Grade point average in liberal arts	3.28
5. Total semester hours in major field	39

CASE NO. 9

Degree of Bachelor of Arts awarded, *cum laude,* August, 1960.
All work done in the division of Arts and Sciences of a large
private university. Major: Romance Languages.

Liberal Arts Courses (102 semester hours)

General Biology (6)
English Composition (6)
Principles of Speech (3)
American History (6)
Reading French Masterpieces (6)
General View of French Lit. (6)
Spoken French (6)
Advanced French Composition (3)
French Lit. of 18th Century (3)
Appreciation of Music (6)

Problems of Philosophy (2)
Introduction to Philosophy (2)
Physical Sciences (8)
Introduction to Government (3)
General Psychology (6)
Intermediate Spanish (6)
Elementary German (6)
Reading Spanish Masterpieces (6)
Spoken Spanish (6)
Elementary Italian (6)

Education Courses (17 semester hours)

Methods of Teaching in Secondary
  School (3)
Teaching of Romance Languages
  (2)

Psychology of Learning (3)
Student Teaching (6)
Educational Measurements (3)

Further Information:

1. Per cent of total program devoted to Education   14.3%
2. Per cent of total program devoted to liberal arts   85.7%
3. Grade point average in Education   3.70
4. Grade point average in liberal arts   2.98
5. Semester hours in major field(s)   54

CASE NO. 10

Degree of Bachelor of Science in Education awarded June, 1959.
Two years of work done at a major state university, and
two years in the Education division of a large private university.
Major: Romance Languages.

Liberal Arts Courses (85 semester hours)

English Composition (6)
English Literature (6)
Animal Biology (5)
3rd Semester French (3)
Elements of French Composition (4)
Survey of French Lit. (6)
Intro. to French Composition (4)
Introduction to Philosophy (3)
American Government (3)
Hebrew Studies (8)

4th Semester French (3)
Modern Drama (3)
Shakespeare (3)
Advanced French (6)
Spoken French (3)
Elementary Spanish (6)
Intermediate Spanish (3)
Spanish Literature (3)
Spanish Conversation (3)
Literature of Spanish Ideas (2)
Latin American Art (2)

Education Courses (33 semester hours)

Identifying Learning Problems (2)
Integrated Arts (2)
Fine Arts Elements (3)
School and Society (3)
Principles of Guidance (3)
Secondary Teaching Methods (3)

Teaching Romance Languages (2)
Educational Psychology (3)
Psychology of Learning (3)
Student Teaching (6)
Educational Measurements (3)

Further Information:

1. Per cent of total program devoted to Education   27.9%
2. Per cent of total program devoted to liberal arts   72.1%
3. Grade point average in Education   3.23
4. Grade point average in liberal arts   3.47
5. Semester hours in major field(s)   46

These ten cases, together with the other data from the transcripts, demonstrate the persistent differences in outlook between academicians and educationists. In the long-lived conflict over the quantitative problems of teacher education, the question, How much is enough? can probably never be answered in a way that will satisfy most of the interests involved. Like everything else in teacher education, the problem of quantity is not an isolated one; it depends on quality and on many other factors. If the quality of the Education faculty were higher, much more could be done in the typical Education course, thereby reducing the number of them; if the Education field had any inclination to transfer some of the material now covered in Education courses to the practice teaching program, this would likewise permit a reduction; if the field took a hard-headed look at its course requirements, with a view to eliminating what could not be justified by the substantive results produced, this could effect a great reduction and an accompanying increase in liberal arts courses for teachers. But since none of these revisions or others like them have much chance of happening, the conflict is likely to remain unresolved.

As mentioned at the beginning of this chapter, a number of forces have been at work in recent years to increase state certification requirements in academic subjects, though there seems to be no movement to reduce them in Education. The average requirements, as indicated earlier, are 23.4 semester hours in Education for elementary teachers and 18.7 hours for secondary. Considering all the realities of teacher education today, these requirements will seem to many people to be reasonable enough. But the crucial fact to remember is that these are minimum state requirements; they are almost always exceeded, as we have seen, by the institutions.

Educationists who have investigated via college catalogues the question with which this chapter deals — the quantitative aspects of teacher education — arrive, not surprisingly, at the conclusion that all is well and that the proportion of time devoted to Education and to liberal arts is wholly suitable. McGrath and Russell, for example, whose study was cited earlier, after determining that elementary teachers average 36 per cent of their four years in Education courses and secondary teachers 17 per cent (both figures being low), move directly on to such *ex parte* and unsupportable assertions as:

> Those who observe elementary school teachers at their work realize that special training is the *sine qua non* of success in this demanding occupation. . . . Secondary teachers too must acquire the basic skills of teaching. . . . Prospective teachers, like individuals preparing for other careers, need to acquire the techniques and practical knowledge of their vocation. Without specialized knowledge of their chosen work, and without the skills needed to perform these exacting tasks, teachers would be as ill-equipped for their work as a surgeon would be for his if he had studied only the basic sciences and none of the skills required to put such knowledge to practical use. If institutions of higher education have accepted the responsibility of preparing teachers, they must *ipso facto* provide the appropriate professional training.[9]

Apart from the tired and irrelevant medical analogy here, the authors offer no support beyond their private opinions for the other assertions and for their general conclusion that training programs are satisfactory now in their quantitative aspects. In addition they present data derived from school catalogues about certain other professional fields and again come to the rather curious conclusion that, because vocations like nursing, music, or pharmacy require even more hours in professional work than does Education, teacher training must be in good shape. They merely reflect in these sentiments the consensus of the Education field.

The number of Education courses now required or permitted

---

[9] Earl J. McGrath and Charles H. Russell, "Are Teachers Illiberally Educated?" published for the Institute of Higher Education by the Teachers College Bureau of Publications, 1961, pp. 4-5.

in the undergraduate programs of future teachers is, I believe, indefensible. When one considers the thin and elusive substance of these courses, as I have discussed it in previous chapters, and the failure to relate this professional training to the quality of teaching actually done by graduates, the educationist asks a great deal to be allowed to consume 40 or 50 per cent of the elementary teacher's four years and 20 or 30 per cent of the secondary teacher's. Especially is this true when we contemplate the kind of liberal education most teachers get, or fail to get. The elementary teacher who never gets beyond the sophomore survey level in any academic subject, while at the same time accumulates half a hundred semester hours in Education, has been turned into a technician, not an educated person. The secondary teacher who spends more time in Education than in the subject he intends to teach has been deprived of the preparation that is most truly "professional" and that would prove of greatest use to him as a teacher and a person.

The McGrath-Russell kind of argument, echoed by most educationists, has a specious plausibility: teaching is such a complex activity and so much is known about how to deal with this complexity, that it is not possible to reduce the time devoted to Education much below current practice. Teaching *is* a complex act, to be sure, but whether this is a complexity best mastered in the doing or in the passive and enervating milieu of the typical Education class is another question. Moreover, as we have seen, the amount of reliable knowledge about this complexity which has been formalized and which can be conveyed to inexperienced persons in a way that will allow them to make actual use of it seems extremely limited. Finally, it is manifestly not true that Education courses cannot be reduced below their present levels. If the excess fat that one finds in most of them were rendered out, and the multiple duplication of courses and content eliminated, and several other kinds of waste corrected in the process, the number of courses in the average program could be reduced by at least

50 per cent and still accomplish everything the theorists say must be accomplished in professional training.

Much progress could be made if institutions would simply stick to the state requirements. This would mean for elementary teachers an average of about 24 semester hours in Education, which would give them ample time for work in educational psychology (building on a course in general psychology on the liberal arts side), history and philosophy of education, for work in methods that cannot be done in any other way but by courses, and practice teaching. It would also mean that the elementary teacher could devote about 80 per cent of her own education to work in the liberal arts, and might even be able to enjoy the experience of pursuing a field of liberal knowledge to at least the depth of a weak major. It would not leave room for separate courses in "Physical Education in the Elementary School," "Personal and Community Hygiene," or "Arts and Crafts for the Intermediate Grades." For the secondary teacher, it would mean spending 18 semester hours or so, about 15 per cent of the time, in Education. Again, this would be ample room, as has long been demonstrated by the good liberal arts colleges, in which to cover the ground thought to be essential in educational psychology, history and philosophy of education, perhaps a methods course in the major field (provided a competent instructor could be found, which is rare), and practice teaching. It would not leave room for separate courses in "Orientation to Teaching," "Core Techniques in the High School," "Community Relations," or "Audio-Visual Aids." It would leave room for a major of some depth and in many cases for a considerable amount of work in related fields.

This is what might be done if institutions would limit the professional work to that required for state certification. It is not ideal, it is only an improvement over present practice. For the secondary teacher of ability, 18 hours in Education is still needlessly large, as is 24 hours for many a bright elementary teacher. But more important than any talk about the quantity of courses in teacher education is, of course, their quality; for only when that critical element is dealt with are we in any position to consider the question of quantity. Thus I leave further discussion of these points to the concluding chapter, where I shall bring together a number of recommendations. Suffice it here to say that the transcripts of credit seem to indicate with impressive regularity that the amount of time devoted to Education courses is excessive, and that it frequently precludes the elementary teacher's attaining anything like a liberal education and the secondary teacher's attaining anything like an adequate grasp of his teaching field.

CHAPTER VI

Masters and Doctors of Education

The chief wonder of education is that it does not ruin everyone concerned in it, teachers and taught.

— Henry Adams

Graduate Education in Brief

SOMETIMES, as one contemplates the vast expanse of graduate work in Education, the comment of Henry Adams, only partly facetious as he reflected upon his own miseducation, takes on a certain relevancy. It is at the graduate level that some of the real excesses of the field are found; the characteristic deficiencies of the undergraduate programs seem to be even more exaggerated when practiced at advanced levels.

To begin with, the theory that underlies graduate work in Education is even shakier than that of the undergraduate work. Such rationale as there is reflects a narrowly conceived utilitarianism, which produces school administrators who may often have accumulated a myriad of courses in such subjects as "The Dynamics of Large and Small Conferences," "School Bus Management," and "Educational Promotion and Fund-Raising," but who are woefully ill-educated men. Graduate programs given over to such work are apt to turn out schoolmen, as well as future professors of Education, who are the antithesis of the liberally educated person, who have but scant acquaintance with the intellectual heritage of which they are presumably custodians in the public schools.

Suggestive of the impoverished condition of graduate Education is a controversy that took place recently in one of our major cities over the appearance of two books on the supplementary reading list for high school seniors in the city's schools. The books were George Orwell's *1984* and Aldous Huxley's *Brave New World*, two of the most eloquent anti-totalitarian statements to be produced in the West in modern times. An irate mother who discovered the word "exotic" in *Brave New World* and was suspicious of *1984*, protested to the school principal. He, it turned out, had never heard of the books, but promised to investigate. He took the matter up with the superintendent of schools, who had never heard of the books either; but he asked the curriculum director, who was responsible for the books' appearance on the reading list, to look at them. The curriculum director decided that the books were indeed "trashy" and had them removed from the reading list. Subsequently, an enterprising reporter asked the then Commissioner of Education for the United States, an educationist of some reputation, to comment on the incident. The Commissioner declined to comment because, as he explained, he had never heard of either of the books in question.

An isolated incident? No. There are numerous such revelations on the record. A meaningless incident? Hardly. One might even ask whether ignorance of such books on the part of a modern schoolman is not *prima facie* evidence of incompetence. A symptomatic incident? Probably. When one examines the education of school administrators, their reading habits, the journals they subscribe and contribute to, and the general caliber of their intellectual activities, such an incident becomes wholly understandable. There is little in the academic background of the graduate of the typical master's or doctor's program in Education that would encourage a wide and discriminating reading or a cultivated, intellectual life.

The theory of graduate work in school administration, for instance, one of the largest segments of the field, is that it should include instruction in all the tasks and responsibilities, however trivial, that are required of school administrators. As one history of Teachers College puts it:

. . . the faculty has been committed always to teaching everything the successful educator needed to know. It was a favorite saying of the elder Russell [James Earl Russell, dean of Teachers College for nearly 30 years] . . . that if the surgeon needed to sew, the medical school taught sewing; and there was no question of graduate credit or whether sewing was truly a "liberal" discipline.[1]

The prevalence of this "commitment" among schools of Education and the grotesque logic behind it naturally create a curriculum in which no system of priorities is possible and in which little room for genuine education can exist. Since there are hundreds of day-to-day tasks that Education graduates, or anybody else, must do on the job, it follows that schools of Education must create an unlimited number of graduate courses to cover these tasks for their students. Abraham Flexner, who was a strong defender of the best of progressive education and whose suggestions in 1915 led to the founding of the progressive Lincoln School of Teachers College, had a low tolerance for the anti-intellectualism he found developing in the graduate programs in Education. Surveying some of these programs in 1930, especially the voluminous course offerings of Teachers College, Flexner was reminded of "A Negro preacher in a popular play [who] declares: 'The Lord expects us to figure out a few things for ourselves'; but Teachers College seems to be organized on the opposite principle." Looking at the Teachers College catalogue for 1930, Flexner comments:

In education, there are things that require doing, but it does not follow that it is the business of the university to do them all. The members of the first teachers colleges in the United States were themselves scholars; but scholars and scientists are now scarce, very scarce in these faculties. In their place, one finds hordes of professors and instructors possessing meagre intellectual background whose interests centre in technique and administration viewed in a narrow *ad hoc* fashion. The staff of Teachers Col-

[1] Lawrence A. Cremin, *et al.*, *A History of Teachers College*, Columbia University Press, 1954, p. 272.

lege, Columbia University, requires 26 pages for mere enumera-
tion: the roster contains 303 instructors; the catalogue lists over
19,000 students of one kind or another. A few instructors offer
courses in educational philosophy, in foreign or comparative education; problems of elementary and secondary education are not
slighted. But why do not these substantial and interesting fields
suffice? Why should not an educated person, broadly and deeply
versed in educational philosophy and experience, help himself
from that point on? Why should his attention be diverted during
these pregnant years to the trivialities and applications with
which common sense can deal adequately when the time comes?
Most of the 200 pages, filled with mere cataloguing, are devoted
to trivial, obvious, and inconsequential subjects, which could
safely be left to the common sense or intelligence of any fairly
well educated person. Atomistic learning — the provision of
endless special courses, instead of a small number of opportunities
that are at once broad and deep — is hostile to the development
of intellectual grasp.[2]

Teachers College still expects its graduate students to figure
out but few things for themselves. A look at the current catalogue indicates that the faculty has grown a bit since Flexner
added it up, that the enrollment has markedly declined, but
that the course offerings have remained roughly the same. In
the 1960-1961 year, Teachers College had a faculty of 342, an
academic-year enrollment of 5,452 (plus a summer enrollment
of 4,404), and offered 900 different courses; it actually gave
715 different courses! What is chiefly suggested by such a
Gargantuan smorgasbord is the lack of any clearly defined
purpose at all in graduate Education.

Of course, the fragmentation of knowledge in Education is
no longer the responsibility of Teachers College, though the
institution still has much to answer for in making the field what
it is today. It still receives more inquiries from employers each
year than does any other school, and probably places over a

[2] *Universities: American, English, German,* Oxford University Press, 1930,
pp. 99-100.

thousand of its graduates and alumni in new jobs each year; it has about 125,000 living alumni, many now the administrators and senior professors of other schools of Education. Harold Rugg, staunch progressive and member of the Teachers College faculty for over 30 years, recorded in 1952 at the end of a 14,000-mile trip he had made visiting schools of Education around the country that he found in them

> . . . the devotion to the problem of rethinking and reconstructing [professional] education, and the burning enthusiasm and dynamic spirit which had characterized the best of the child-centered schools in their youthful days immediately after World War I. I confess I came back to my own Teachers College with a deep nostalgia for the exciting months of the Depression Thirties when my colleagues foregathered in the Main Hall around Heard Kilpatrick and created the *Social Frontier*, and the John Dewey Society, and the new Division I of the College — Social and Philosophical Foundations of Education. The spirit and the unity are both gone from our center now, but much of it has come alive again in Illinois and Florida, in Troy and San Francisco and Cheney and Drake and Wayne and a dozen other places. And that is good. That is exactly as it should be.[3]

One need not share Mr. Rugg's reverence for permissive education, or the rosy naïveté with which he looks at the field of Education, to appreciate the ramifying influence exerted by Teachers College through both its graduates and its prestige in Education. Such influence is the logical consequence of the College's prolonged monopoly on graduate programs. While no one can calculate this influence in any precise fashion, it is plainly very great. Although Teachers College remains the colossus of graduate Education, it is no longer unique, as it was for many years. Other schools, such as New York University, Harvard, Chicago, and Stanford, and some state institutions like Illinois, California, Ohio, and Wayne State now rival it in many ways. They offer numerous degrees and hundreds

---

[3] *The Teacher of Teachers*, Harper, 1952, p. 206.

of courses in the fructifying specialties and sub-specialties of professional Education. It should bear repeating that this growth, more than anything else, reflects the history of slovenly administration that has characterized graduate Education, the manufactured professionalism that has obsessed educationists for many years, and the disgraceful abdication of responsibility by the academic faculty. However the responsibility is to be parceled out for the unhappy condition of so much of graduate Education today, the results of the condition are clear enough: the production of, as Flexner put it, "hordes of professors and instructors [and, he might have added, school administrators] possessing meagre intellectual background whose interests centre in technique and administration viewed in a narrow *ad hoc* fashion."

As for the actual conduct of graduate courses in Education, it is often weaker than the undergraduate, having atomized content even further. Professors find it even more expedient than at the undergraduate level to rely on students themselves to carry on the courses through "workshops," "field studies," "projects," and other applications of group dynamics. While such methods may be useful with truly advanced students capable of independent investigation of important subjects, one quickly reaches the limits of their usefulness with poor students and superficial subject matter.

To take, for illustrative purposes, just one subject among many in graduate Education, one might consider the course work commonly offered in "Guidance," an administrative specialty that has come into its own in recent years through the help of the Federal government and the general controversy over American education. Everyone agrees that public school students need some guidance, sometimes curricular, sometimes emotional or disciplinary, sometimes in occupational matters or questions of college admissions. Hopefully, students get most such guidance, or ought to get it, at home. Actually, many students don't, and so, as in many other areas of neglected parental responsibility, the school takes over. This eventually creates, in strict accordance with the laws of Parkinson, a new administrative specialty which in turn creates graduate programs that prepare people for the new job. In something like this fashion, we now have a field with the redundant name of "Guidance Counseling" in which one can earn both a master's and a doctor's degree. But nobody knows what either degree should stand for, since nobody knows what guidance counseling is, can be, or ought to be; there is as yet no accepted "theory" of guidance counseling. But there is agreement among educationists that the field is very important, that it represents an expanding market, and that schools of Education must give courses and degrees in it. Schools of Education now commonly give anywhere from two or three to fifteen or twenty courses in this "subject."

In the graduate courses in Guidance which I visited, I was particularly struck by several recurring phenomena: there is a spurious and irresponsible use of material, such as case studies from the medical sciences and clinical psychology. Cases of disturbed individuals ranging from deep psychoses to mild neuroses are often discussed by instructors and certainly by students who have no competence in the subject and no business toying with it. The effect is to suggest to students, most of whom will not go beyond the master's degree, that they have some right to engage in psychological diagnosis and perhaps even therapy in public schools. Other and less rarefied jobs that guidance people do in schools, such as administering and interpreting standardized examinations, advising students about job possibilities in various industries, or about requirements for admission to various colleges, are too often neglected. The utterly nebulous nature of the entire field of guidance counseling encourages an amateurish attempt in the course work to probe into areas of human motivation, guilt complexes, sexual adjustment, and the like, in search of the true reason why Johnny sassed his teacher.

Also, there is a distressing lack of respect in these courses for the rights of privacy of both parent and student. Too much time is spent in fruitless and questionable attempts at the psychological analysis of student behavior, as well as impudent speculations about parents and home life. Case studies are held up as models in which detailed "anecdotal records" are kept by teachers and guidance counselors containing their interpretations of human behavior. For instance, a hypothetical case study used for discussion in a guidance course in one of our most respected universities presents a problem of a teacher who comes to the school guidance officer complaining about one of her students and asking the guidance officer to do something. Promptly, according to this mimeographed case history, the guidance officer looks up the student's folder, complete with its "anecdotal records," and finds, in part:

> Glancing over his folder you find: he is 14 — has a sister, 11, in the 6th grade, doing well — father, 43, a very bright and promising scientist, professor, industrial consultant, researcher, etc. — mother, 34, a busy suburban housewife, in many community activities, genial, eager to appear at least nearly as intelligent as her husband — (the parents are noted in the folder as "cooperative," "objective," and "pride themselves on using reason in their relations with the children and the school.")

No member of the class objected or raised the obvious question of what business any teacher or school official had making and recording in school records the judgment that a housewife was "eager to appear at least nearly as intelligent as her husband"; or for that matter what the propriety was of the school's deciding and entering on a student's record the condescending note that his parents "pride themselves on using reason in their relations with the children and the school." Unhappily, the incident is far from an isolated one; it reflects the typical approach of the new "guidance counselor." The mentality that sees nothing wrong with this is the same mentality that encourages teachers to use "sociograms," an instrument for determining the social and personality stratification of a class by having each student write down the names of his fellow students that he likes most and those he likes least — so that the teacher can plot the answers on a sociometric diagram. It is the same mentality that promotes personality and projective tests in public schools in which unsuspecting students are asked such questions as whether they like their mothers better than their fathers, how they like their home life in general, and whether, how much, and how often, they feel certain kinds of emotions. Whatever value such invasions of privacy may have in appropriate medical hands, "guidance counselors" in public schools would seem to be rather poorly qualified to conduct them.

Apart from the question of ethics involved in course work in guidance is the question of whether this kind of training prepares anybody to do useful and important work in a public school, as well as the question of whether the master's and doctor's degree ought to be awarded for it. Guidance courses are now without any apparent boundaries or validity. As a measure of their fluidity, consider another class being conducted in another of our renowned graduate schools of Education: The guest speaker for the day (another variation on the ways to dispose of the time available in Education) happens to be the chief medical officer of the university, who is to discuss the counseling of high school students as it looks to the world of medicine and university counseling practice. But the first half hour of the doctor's lecture turns out to be a partisan political speech, in which he tries to link various kinds of mental ills with the political atmosphere created by right wing extremists; he describes such persons as George Sokolsky and Fulton Lewis, Jr., as "lower than a snake's belly" and accuses them and their ideological fellows of creating a highly divisive force in society. No student, whatever might be his opinions of Messrs. Sokolsky and Lewis, objects to the proceedings, nor is any useful connection ever made between the doctor's lengthy editorial and the subject of guidance in public schools. Perhaps this suggests one danger of offering course work in subjects before there are subjects.

It must be said for those who teach guidance courses that they too are aware of the lack of substance involved, for a good deal of the class time is devoted, as it is in many other areas of Education, to introspective discussion; that is, to the exploration of what work in the subject of guidance ought to be. Thus the real subject of the course often becomes, not guidance counseling, but what a course in guidance counseling might become.

A few years ago a Canadian educationist and psychologist, traveling under a foundation grant, visited a number of American universities to survey the kinds of important research being done in Education. He did not find a great deal, but he

> . . . gained the impression that a surprising number of [Education] courses in many institutions were very much depleted in intellectual content. Guidance, for example, struck me as a hybrid mélange of watered-down child psychology, mental health, tests and measurements, and non-practical clinical psychology. The subject never struck me as having any academic significance and its existence presupposed that the teacher was a fool. The less distinguished the institution, the greater was the proliferation of courses in guidance. Often instructors in education would explain the dilution as a product of the poor quality of the student in education.[4]

Weak as are guidance courses in Education, they deserve no special distinction. I discuss them merely as an example of graduate work in Education in general. One could just as well use Educational Administration and its flowering sub-specialties as an example, or Curriculum Supervision, or half a dozen other degree-awarding areas of Education.

[4] Charles C. Anderson, "A Canadian Critic on Teacher Education in Western U.S.A.," *School and Society*, April 23, 1960, p. 204.

The selection of students for graduate work in Education is often poorer, ironically, than it now is at the undergraduate level. Many students are admitted by the mere possession of an undergraduate degree, though they could not be admitted to present undergraduate programs in the same institution. Graduate Education draws large numbers of public school teachers who seek to qualify for the better-paid and less onerous jobs of school administrators or professors of Education. They are more often motivated by a desire to escape the rigors of the public school classroom than by an attraction to the rigors of the higher learning. True, some "screening" is usually done for admission to candidacy for the graduate degrees, but it is not very effective. The degrees are still awarded, not to those who have been "selected," but to those who have merely persisted; and these persons are likely to be found, as discussed in Chapter II, near the bottom of the academic barrel.

All of these factors — the low quality of the Education faculty, the low quality of the graduate student, the ludicrous excess of course offerings, and the lack of any clearly defined purpose, all coupled with a studied disregard for the fundamental intellectual disciplines — interact and reinforce one another to perpetuate the low status of graduate work in Education, the same as they do the undergraduate work. Once again, there are numerous exceptions to these generalizations. When courses are limited to the fundamental areas, they can be very worthwhile; the quality of teaching is occasionally first-rate. But the generalizations nonetheless abide.

Five-Year Plans and Master's Degrees

One of the exceptions to these strictures are the Master of Arts in Teaching degrees, sometimes called fifth-year programs, that have been increasingly in evidence over the last decade. Characteristically, the programs admit persons with regular liberal arts undergraduate degrees who did not prepare for teaching and thus had no work in Education as undergraduates. Although Harvard boasts of having had the first MAT program, beginning in 1936, it was under the impetus of the Fund for the Advancement of Education that such programs developed on any scale. The Fund saw in them an answer to the teacher shortage and one way of attracting into teaching the more capable student who was often repelled by the orthodox training programs:

> Many of the brightest and most able college students . . . were rejecting teaching as a career not only because of low salaries and diminishing status, but because conventional teacher-training programs were heavily weighted with courses in professional education, the content of which was frequently incapable of interesting them or capturing their imaginations. For this reason, the Fund has supported a large number of projects designed to help reduce the emphasis on professional courses and increase the emphasis on liberal education, on supervised teaching, and on the subjects to be taught.[5]

Between 1951 and 1960, the Fund together with the Ford Foundation spent about 27 million dollars supporting fifth-year programs, and since then has spent a good deal more. Generally these grants have gone to private colleges and universities, which have created programs that vary widely in their details but that have important characteristics in common: they admit only students with good academic records, usually with a Bachelor of Arts degree; they involve some kind of internship whereby the student is paid for what amounts to full- or part-time practice teaching under superior supervising teachers in public schools; they include work of varying amounts in the major academic field of the student together with a moderate number of more-or-less orthodox courses in Education (often plus a professional seminar or two); they often involve the

---

[5] *Decade of Experiment*, published in 1961 by the Fund as a review of its activities since 1951, the date of its creation, p. 28.

active collaboration of the liberal arts and the Education faculty.[6] Although the Fund's initial experiment with the fifth-year idea, in Arkansas in 1951, ran afoul of many vested interests and was bitterly criticized by educationists, it did serve as an important proving ground for ideas that went into subsequent programs around the country. Since then many educationists have been caught between their desire for grants and their dislike of the conditions necessary to get them. The fact that so many fifth-year programs are now under way is perhaps a sign of increasing flexibility on the part of state certification officials and those who run teacher-training programs. In the fall of 1962, the Ford Foundation launched with three and one-half million dollars its most ambitious fifth-year program to date. While embodying the main features of the customary Master of Arts in Teaching degree, the program is unusual in that it is built upon a state-wide effort (in Oregon) to coordinate more closely than has ever been done before the work of the state department of Education, the public schools of the state, and the majority of Oregon's colleges and universities. If successful, this program could eventually have a substantial impact on teacher training in other states.

On balance, these programs can be considered nothing but a gain, an important gain, for the education of American teachers. They have done much to bring academicians and educationists together, they have demonstrated that superior people can be attracted to teaching in substantial numbers through improved training programs, they have brought a certain balance into the professional-academic course equation, and most of all they have encouraged those in charge of training teachers to examine the old assumptions, reconsider the traditional programs,

---

[6] Those programs supported by the Fund are described, in addition to statements from the individual schools involved, in Paul Woodring, "New Directions in Teacher Education," The Fund, 1957; and in *The High School Journal* for February, 1960, which issue is given over entirely to the topic, "Utilizing a Fifth Year in Teacher Preparation." Additionally, several journal articles and several compilations of data on fifth-year programs have been done, the most complete being one by the U.S. Office of Education.

and try some new ideas. They have been a happy development.

Naturally, they also have problems. They are expensive, and the question of whether schools are going to continue them at full speed when foundation support runs out is not yet answered. They usually concentrate on teachers for the secondary schools, ignoring the equally pressing problems of improving the elementary programs. And they sometimes stray a good deal from the original ideas and fall back into the old programs in which a fifth year becomes simply that — a fifth year of work in which Education courses predominate and disorganization and lack of focus are evident. They frequently incorporate Education courses that are merely copies of the undergraduate courses, taught by the same people with the same textbooks and methods, which is one of the reasons why students in them, while favoring the program as a whole, voice the old familiar criticisms of Education course work.

How soon the time will or should come when all teachers will have five years of preparation is an open question. The tendency is strong toward making this a state requirement for certification; three states now require five years for initial certification, and nine require it within a given number of years after certification. Thus a number of programs are becoming, not "fifth-year" programs enrolling liberal arts graduates, but programs in which the last three years of a five-year college career are integrated into a teacher-training curriculum. This usually means an excessive amount of time spent in professional courses and a general weakening of graduate work.

In addition to that problem, the creation of a five-year requirement for new teachers imposes an enormous burden on an already overtaxed system of higher education in America. And most of all, it takes the pressure off the undergraduate programs of teacher training. The easiest answer in any field to the conflict between the demands of the academic and of the professional components of preparatory programs is to increase the time available. This allows everyone to continue doing what he did in the past, only more so. A worthier aim might be to see how much time can be saved through overhauling existing four-year programs. In teacher education, as this book has tried to show in a number of ways, four years would be enough to prepare competent people if the programs were what they can and should be. If the water were squeezed out of both the academic and the professional curricula, if admission to the programs were restricted to able students, and if the caliber of instruction were what students have a right to expect, four years would be ample. It would not be ideal (what would be?) but it would be ample. Of course, it would be nice for all new teachers to have five years of preparation, or six, eight, or ten. But the conditions of society at any given time are the determining factor, and these conditions now seem to me to call, not for putting all new teachers through a fifth year simply because of their diluted undergraduate programs or because it would improve the professional "image," but for seeing how much time can be salvaged from that now available and putting it to the best possible use. Mandating a fifth year may well insure the perpetuation, if not the increase, of those weaknesses of training programs that we have discussed in previous chapters.

Quite distinct from the Master of Arts in Teaching degrees are the other master's degrees given in Education — the Master of Arts in Education, the Master of Education, the Master of Science in Education, and various others. These degrees, taken by some classroom teachers but especially by administrators, are concentrated in such professional areas as "Guidance," "Elementary Education," "Secondary Education," "Administration," and the like.

The sampling of transcripts of credit discussed in Chapter V also included a large group of graduate degrees in Education. A total of 481 transcripts from 26 institutions were used in the tabulation of master's programs in Education. Of these, 178 were for Master of Arts in Teaching programs, or other master's programs for classroom teachers and subject-matter majors; the remaining 303 were for administrative specialties. This sample was drawn in the same way at the same time as that for the undergraduate degrees: by taking every second, third, or fourth name, depending on the total number involved, from the most recent commencement roster of the institutions and reproducing the transcripts. Sometimes inferences had to be made about the purpose for which the degree was taken, since it was not always recorded on the transcript. Most of the time the pattern of courses indicated clearly enough whether the individual was taking the degree to improve as a classroom teacher or taking it to become or continue as an administrator. Here are some of the results:

1. For the entire group of 481 cases together, the average number of semester hours devoted to academic courses was 9.
2. For the entire group of 481 cases together, the average number of semester hours devoted to Education was 26.
3. For the 178 cases of teachers and academic majors, the average number of semester hours devoted to academic courses was 17 and to Education courses was 18.
4. For the 303 cases of administrative programs, representing a number of sub-specialties, the average number of semester hours devoted to academic courses was 4, and to Education courses was 30.
5. The range of work for the whole group in academic courses was 0-32 semester hours; the range for Education was 5-44.
6. A thesis was required in 21 per cent of the cases, in contrast to the prevailing practice in liberal arts fields, where a master's thesis is a standard requirement.
7. A foreign language was required in 4 per cent of the cases.

Or, to look at the results another way, let us pick at random a dozen master's transcripts from one of the large, prestige graduate schools of Education and compute averages, including the undergraduate work, for the whole group. We find that these dozen cases represent six different administrative specialties, and that:

1. At the *undergraduate* level, the average number of semester hours devoted to academic courses was 92, and to Education courses was 31.
2. At the graduate level, the average number of semester hours devoted to academic courses was 5, and to Education courses was 32.
3. For the entire academic career of the dozen people, all holders of the master's degree, the average number of semester hours devoted to academic courses was 97, and to Education courses was 64; about 40 per cent of all their work, that is, was in Education.
4. In no case was a master's thesis or a foreign language required.

Because the undergraduate transcripts were not always available for each graduate in the sample, there was no way of determining averages for the whole group in academic and professional work done as undergraduates. But it is obvious that, with the exception of the relatively few Master of Arts in Teaching transcripts, the overwhelming majority of the group were already teachers or administrators at the time they enrolled for graduate work and had done considerable work in Education as undergraduates.

In other words, the graduate programs for administrators and special school personnel were building on a base of professional work already done and professional experience already accumulated, often a substantial amount of it. Yet they consistently reveal a thoroughly one-sided approach to the further education of such people. As indicated above, the average master's program in these fields includes what amounts to one course for one semester in some liberal arts field, while it piles up an additional nine or ten in Education. The nine or ten often overlap not only themselves, but the undergraduate work already done, as can be seen later in this chapter when sample transcripts are reproduced. Moreover, these master's transcripts, as noted earlier with the undergraduate records, are freighted with courses taken at night, in the summer, on Saturdays, and by extension and correspondence; such times are convenient for teachers, to be sure, but the courses are inevitably inferior in the quality of faculty and of student performance to that in regularly scheduled courses in residence. Not infrequently, such courses are the *only* kind on the transcript and stretch over a period of five or ten years, until enough credits are accumulated for the student to qualify for a master's degree. In such cases, as well as in many others, there seems to be no logical connection between the courses taken; rather, they seem to be a mere conglomeration reflecting the student's particular whims at any given point. Here, for instance, is the graduate record of a person who, over a period of five years, took nine courses, *all* of them by extension:

> Principles of Guidance
> Curriculum Development
> Organization of a General Metals Shop
> Visual Aids
> Supervision in Schools
> Alcohol and Narcotics Addiction
> Opera and Dramatic Music
> Astronomy
> Graduate Project

At the completion of the last course of this salmagundi, he was awarded a master's degree in educational administration. Or, consider this typical example of the master's degree in administration, earned over a period of three summers by a student who as an undergraduate in the same institution had taken a total of 37 semester hours in Education courses; his graduate record included no work in any liberal arts subject, but instead consisted of 30 more hours in Education, as follows:

Social Foundations of Education (also taken as an undergraduate)
State and Local School Administration
Supervision in Education
Educational Evaluation and Guidance
Curriculum Construction in the Secondary School
Psychological Foundations of Education (also taken as an undergraduate)
Curriculum Construction in the Elementary School
Principles of School Administration
School Finance

In elementary education, the master's degree results in an even narrower graduate. Here is a representative case: The student arrives in 1960 for graduate work at the school of Education of a large Midwestern university with a Bachelor of Science degree in elementary education taken in 1952 at a state teachers college. The transcript shows 54 semester hours of work in Education as an undergraduate and 64 in academic subjects. The school of Education proceeds to give the student 33 more hours in Education, as follows:

Human Relationships and Group Guidance
Philosophy of Education (also taken as an undergraduate)
Methods in Educational Research
Introduction to Tests and Measurements
Mental Hygiene
Sociological Foundations of Education (also taken as an undergraduate)
The Learning Process (taken several times, under other names, as an undergraduate)
Visual and Auditory Aids (also taken as an undergraduate)

Elementary School Supervision
Principles and Practice of Guidance

Another favorite specialty, as already indicated, at the master's level is guidance, recently given a considerable impetus in schools of Education by the National Defense Education Act of 1958. In view of the job that "guidance counselors," as they are unfortunately named, are presumed to be doing in high schools, one might assume that a considerable acquaintance with the academic subjects of the secondary school would be essential; but this is not the view of the educationist. To him, guidance is an *administrative* specialty, attractive to teachers who want to get out of the classroom, and as such must be developed solely as a graduate program in Education. Thus a typical case goes like this: A high school teacher of mathematics arrives in 1961 at a state college for his master's degree in guidance, bringing with him a bachelor's degree taken in 1955 at a state teachers college. The school proceeds to give him 16 two-hour courses and one 4-hour course in Education, and then his master's degree, as follows:

Principles of Mental Hygiene
Principles and Techniques of Guidance
Teaching Reading in the Secondary School
Advanced Educational Psychology
Educational Measurement
Social and Moral Guidance
Vocational Guidance
Organization of Extra Curricular Activities
Group Guidance and Counseling
Methods of Research
School Administration and Community Relations
Foundations of Algebra (student was a math major as an
    undergraduate)
Curriculum and Teaching Junior High School Mathematics

Workshop in Curricular Problems of Mathematics
Methods of Research
Educational Guidance
Seminar in Guidance

In the various Master of Arts in Teaching programs, the idea of striking a balance between the academic and the professional in graduate work is often lost sight of. Although many persons do manage to keep something like a half-and-half relationship between the two, many do not. With one of the oldest and best known of the Master of Arts in Teaching programs, for example, the pattern of course work often looks like this: A girl reports to the graduate school of Education with a bachelor's degree from Stanford and a major in English, and no work in Education. The school gives her 8 semester hours of survey work in American literature, which duplicates much of the work she did at Stanford, and 24 hours of work in Education, far more than she needs for state certification, and she is awarded the Master of Arts in Teaching degree. Or take the case of a man who wishes to become a history teacher: he reports to the school with a bachelor's degree from Northeastern University, a major in history, no work in Education. The school gives him 8 semester hours in history and 26 in Education. In such cases, there is little to distinguish the Master of Arts in Teaching degree from the run-of-the-mill Master of Education degree.

In general, then, the master's degree in Education is not only a markedly inferior degree in quality, but possibly does a good deal of harm in public education. The staffing of key administrative posts in public schools with persons whose academic training sometimes stops after the sophomore undergraduate year in college and rarely extends to graduate work in any liberal arts field is hardly the way to strengthen the intellectual life of these schools; indeed it is an excellent way to enfeeble it.

The Doctorate in Education

From about a hundred institutions, the field of Education turns out over 1,500 doctors a year, which is around 18 per cent of all the doctor's degrees conferred in all fields by American institutions and a good many more than conferred in any other single field. In addition to the sheer size of this operation, the doctoral programs in Education are a crucial factor in the kind of training that classroom teachers get and in the entire conduct of the public education system. Doctors of Education now occupy practically all the important school superintendencies, many of the lesser ones, many of the principalships, and countless other administrative positions in public education. They also staff state departments of Education, professional associations at national and local levels, the United States Office of Education, and accrediting agencies; and they constitute the principal faculty of schools, departments, and colleges of Education. In short, doctors of Education exercise an enormous amount of power and influence (the subject of the next chapter) over the quality of the American system of public schools. In turn, the quality of *their* education becomes a rather important matter.

If the master's degree programs in Education exhibit but little interest in the liberal arts, the doctoral programs exhibit less. Programs for the doctorate in Education suffer from all the deficiencies we have already discussed with the lower programs, and add a number of their own. While a very few Ph.D. programs can be found of consequence in Education, most of the programs for both the Ed.D. and the Ph.D. in Education represent a kind of nadir of utilitarianism and triviality. As usual, much of the weakness of these degrees is a reflection of the quality of the faculty and the standards for admission.

Also, a good many of the reasons for the low state of the Education doctorate must be ascribed to the creation and growth of the Ed.D. degree. For many years, the principal degree in Education was the customary Ph.D., and a few schools still restrict themselves to it. But with the coming of progressivism and the "professionalizing" of school administration, pressures from the field against the rigor and alleged narrowness of the Ph.D. made themselves felt. What was needed, said the new educationist, was a "field-oriented" doctorate for educational administrators not concerned with original research but with practical school problems and with the application of research findings to concrete situations. With Harvard, California, and Temple University leading the way, a new doctorate to satisfy these demands was inaugurated, and by the end of the 1930's was solidly established in about 25 institutions. Since then the number of institutions giving it has more than tripled; together they turn out over a thousand new Ed.D.'s a year — about twice the number of new Ph.D.'s in Education. Teachers College can serve as well as any school to illustrate the growth of the new degree. It began giving the Ed.D. in 1934-35, when it awarded five of them, along with 69 Ph.D.'s; in 1938-39, it gave 38 Ed.D.'s and 47 Ph.D.'s; by 1941-42, the Ed.D. had overtaken the Ph.D. and had pulled ahead. In 1950-51, Teachers College gave 203 Ed.D.'s and 60 Ph.D.'s; in 1960-61, it gave 234 Ed.D.'s and 32 Ph.D.'s (plus 194 "Professional Diplomas," signifying two years of graduate work and coming in status somewhere between the Master of Education degree and the Ed.D.).

The reasons for the popularity of the Ed.D. are plain enough. It is an easier degree than the Ph.D. Course work for it is often entirely in Education (the Ph.D. used to be attacked as narrow!), it carries no foreign language requirements, it usually carries no dissertation requirement, and control over it is usually vested entirely in the Education division of the university — meaning that advisors from the academic departments are not involved in the candidates' programs and that the doctoral standards of the arts and sciences division do not have to be met. At Teachers College, for example, the Ph.D. often requires, among other things, that academic faculty from Columbia University approve doctoral dissertations and participate in doctoral oral examinations. This creates onerous problems, for the University representatives often feel that they cannot in good conscience accept the low standards of either the dissertation or the oral exam, in contrast to the Teachers College representatives who are anxious to accept both; on the other hand it is extremely awkward to flunk numerous doctoral candidates at that stage, more especially if the indications are that the candidate would not be able to improve the second time around. In the past, humanitarianism, if it can correctly be called that, has won more often than not, and the candidate has been approved, but there have also been a number of flunks and a lot of friction. It did not take the Teachers College faculty or students long, however, to learn that it was much safer and easier to go the Ed.D. route, along which there were few encounters with the University faculty, with the result that Teachers College now gives 7 or 8 Ed.D.'s for every Ph.D.

As for the theoretical distinction between the two doctoral degrees — the Ph.D. for research and college teaching, and the Ed.D. for public school administration — practice has long since lost sight of it. A glance at the faculties of any school of Education is enough to dispel the myth that the Ed.D. is for practical men "out in the public school field," for almost all such faculties are heavily staffed with Ed.D.'s. The dean of Education is likely to be an Ed.D., as are his administrative assistants. Even more important is the fact that in a great many areas of the Education doctorate, substantially the same courses are taken by both the Ed.D. and the Ph.D. candidate. There was never very much validity in the rationale for a second doctor's degree in Education, and what little there may have been has disappeared in practice. The Ed.D. continues to grow in popularity and will for the foreseeable future because of the comparative ease with which it can be earned.

In the case of either the Ed.D. or the Ph.D., however, the quality of the degree is notably below that of the arts and sciences doctorate. Course work, as has been mentioned, is even more fragmented and inflated than at the undergraduate level. A recent survey of the field found no fewer than 80 specialties in which the Education doctorate can be earned: it can be earned in 11 aspects of educational administration alone; in six aspects of guidance and counseling; and in six aspects of educational psychology. The Education doctorate can even be earned in such disciplines as "Intergroup Relations," "Audio-Visual Aids," "Human Relations Education," "Safety Education," and "Camping." [7] So far as the caliber of those who take the doctor's degree in Education is concerned, the latest study, as cited in Chapter II, indicated no difference between the recent holders of the Ed.D. and the Ph.D. — both are on the bottom of the graduate ranks of the universities.

Transcripts of credit for recent doctors of Education reveal the same pattern of infirmities as do the master's transcripts. They show, with a few exceptions in which a good deal of work in academic departments is included, an almost complete devotion to Education courses, despite the fact that candidates for the degrees have accumulated a large number of such courses before embarking on the doctorate and despite the fact that such candidates are preparing for educational jobs where, presumably, some depth of liberal learning would be essential. The doctor's transcripts show an incredible amount

[7] Laurence D. Brown and J. Marlowe Slater, *The Doctorate in Education, Volume I — The Graduates,* published by the American Association of Colleges for Teacher Education, 1960, p. 93. This is the first volume of a 2-volume report of the survey, the data for which were gathered from questionnaires sent to all persons who received the doctorate in Education during the period, 1956-58, and from other questionnaires sent to all the institutions that gave the degrees. A third volume, called *Conference Report,* contains summaries of the two volumes plus other papers. This study is by far the most complete available on the Education doctorate and is replete with pertinent information. Its chief limitation is that which always inheres in questionnaires, and in asking those in charge of an educational program to assess the program.

of duplication in courses; they often show poor performance in the undergraduate work and low or non-existent admissions standards to the graduate programs. They show grades of "C" with some frequency, particularly in the scattered academic courses ("C" is universally considered below graduate standards); the Ph.D. sometimes shows no foreign language passed, and often only one language; almost all of the transcripts show a great deal of summer work; they show a range of 3-20 years needed to complete the degree; they often show, even where languages and dissertations are indicated as mandatory in the school catalogue, that the candidates were "excused" from these requirements; they show course patterns that are "programs" only by courtesy of the name, but that lack any sort of coherence or sequential relation; they show a good deal of work done at odd times out of residence; they show that candidates are close to forty years of age at the end. In a word, they more often than not show a weak candidate put through a weak program by a weak faculty to earn a weak degree. The graduate then goes out to administer a school or a school system or to join another Education faculty.

When one examines the kind of doctoral dissertation commonly done in Education, it is hard to feel that much is lost in that a like performance is not required of most Ed.D. and some Ph.D. candidates. Those that are done are often so trifling as to contribute little to the candidate's education and nothing to human knowledge. It is true that the dissertations in many fields are apt to be less than inspiring. One recent and perceptive critic of graduate education cites the general trend throughout higher education:

> More attention should be paid to dissertation subjects. The unsuitability of some topics and the triviality of others are matters of great concern to thoughtful educators. If they are the criteria by which American higher education is to be judged, they constitute a sad commentary upon it. Some subjects require an ac-

cumulation of detailed facts; others, a report on a piece of mediocre research; and still others, an array of specialized facts and
figures to prove an hypothesis that was not worth investigating in
the first place.[8]

Following its usual custom, Education extends the general
problem, exaggerates and caricatures it. If dissertations in
academic areas are vapid, Education's will be more so. The
dissertations in Education, reflecting the problems of the field
itself, seem to concentrate on obvious and inconsequential subjects that should not be the business of the dissertation in any
field, and attempt to invest them with impressive substance
and scientific authority. Educanto is a great help in doing so.
Here are some examples, among hundreds, or thousands, accepted by American institutions in the last few years:

"The Effects on Non-Target Classmates of a Deviant Student's
Power and Response to a Teacher-Exerted Control Technique."
Translated, this means a study was made of how a teacher's
use of discipline against a misbehaving student affects other
students in the same class. Accepted for the Ph.D. in Education.

"A Study of the Emotions of High School Football Players."
The investigator, using a "galvanic skin resistor," discovered,
among other things, that "emotional levels" of high school football players before an important game are high. Accepted for
the Ed.D.

"The Interpersonal Evaluation Structure of a Selected School
District." The investigator, using the "Semantic Differential,"
identified and illustrated the "interpersonal evaluation structure, one administrative sub-structure, and nine staff sub-struc-
tures." Meaning an analysis was made of the ways in which

[8] Oliver C. Carmichael, *Graduate Education: a Critique and a Program*,
Harper, 1961, p. 153.

the staff of a school district reached opinions about one another. Accepted for the Ed.D.

"A Study of the Relationship Between Certain Aspects of Clothing and the Ability to Handle Selected Clothing Construction Tools with the Developmental Levels of Early Adolescent Girls." The author measured the ability of certain girls to use things like shears and needles and compared the results with the girls' declared interests in clothing. Accepted for the Ed.D.

"A Study to Determine the Relationship Between the Position of Teachers on the California F. Scale [a "Scale" to measure "authoritarianism"] and Their Disposition toward Teamwork." Accepted for the Ph.D. in Education.

There is also a universal reliance upon the questionnaire or the opinionnaire as dissertation material, no matter how remote or unimportant the subject being surveyed is. For example:

"Administrative Practices which Promote Effectiveness in Pupil Transportation Programs." The author sent "a free response questionnaire" to selected professors of Education and to school districts to ask about "good practices in pupil transportation," then put the answers together and made a chart of the good practices. Accepted for the Ph.D. in Education.

"A Study of Chief School Administrator Opinion Regarding Human Relations Behaviors of Public School Superintendents." The investigator polled 110 administrators in New York asking them what the "behaviors are that public school administrators need to exhibit in order to operate effectively in their human relations with teachers." Accepted for the Ed.D.

"A Course of Study in Audio-Visual Education Based on an Opinion Poll." The author sent his questionnaire to professors of visual aids and to their students, found that they both thought the same things were important in "audio-visual education," and made a list of 113 items that should be included in such courses. Accepted for the Ed.D.

The reliance on questionnaires and the distorted scientism that one finds everywhere in the dissertations is only the smallest part of the problem. The real trouble lies in the inability of either advisors or candidates to dredge up from the slithery bog of graduate Education some really important subjects that doctoral candidates can deal with and that can represent a genuine advance either for the student or the field. There *are* important problems in the basic areas of Education — in history, philosophy, and psychology — but they cannot easily be isolated when the field is divided into 80 doctoral specialties; nor can serious problems be attacked by graduate students who have a thin academic background. Until graduate Education is willing to take a far more critical look at itself than it ever has, it will doubtless continue to delude students into believing they have done something of consequence when they have finished dissertations like the following dozen, all of which have been accepted in the last few years by American universities for the Ph.D. in Education or the Ed.D.:

"Recruitment, Selection, and Training of Custodians in Selected Public School Systems."

"An Experimental Study of the Effect of Soothing Background Music on Observed Behavior Indicating Tension of Third Grade Pupils."

"A Performance Analysis of the Propulsive Force of the Flutter Kick."

"Public School Transportation Practices in Jackson County, Mississippi."

"The High School Student's Perception of Most-Liked and Least-Liked Television Figures."

"The Relative Effect of Mental Practice and Physical Practice on Learning the Tennis Forehand and Backhand Drives."

"The Relationship Between Personality Traits and Basic Skill in Typewriting."

"A Study of Little League Baseball and Its Educational Implications."

"A Study of Factors Influencing Selection and Satisfactions in Use of Major Household Appliances as Indicated by Three Selected Groups of Married Women Graduates of the Ohio State University."

"An Experimental Investigation into the Effect of Format on Following Written Directions."

"The Cooperative Selection of School Furniture to Serve the Kindergarten Through Third Grade Program in the Garden City Public Schools."

"Speak Up for Education — the Use of the Speech Arts in Promoting Better Schools and Colleges."

To the incredulous reader, I would emphasize that these examples are not particularly unusual, as a short time spent in any library reading abstracts of dissertations accepted by American universities will show. If doctoral candidates in Education and their senior professors can find nothing more important in their field than such topics as these, this fact in itself says a great deal about the field.

Neither the dissertation nor the course work for the doctorate in Education would have to be a watered down exercise in busywork if the degrees were genuinely controlled by the liberal arts division or by academicians and educationists together. If academicians took their responsibilities seriously, a major overhaul of the doctorate in Education would be made in most institutions. The Ed.D. would be eliminated or, if not, the rationale for it would be more clearly outlined than it now is and the distinction between it and the Ph.D. more clearly preserved. Both degrees might then require far more work in academic areas and far more important topics for dissertations; and both degrees might involve the academic faculty on program, examination, and dissertation committees. Academicians, however, will probably fail to take these steps just as they failed in the past to prevent Education's becoming what it now is. In a few institutions, control over the Education doctorate, especially the Ph.D., is really exercised by the liberal arts division, which tries to insist on standards comparable to those for its own Ph.D.; but most of the time, even in institutions where the school of Education does not have explicit autonomy in the doctorate programs, it enjoys a *de facto* autonomy, due to the failure of the academic contingent to exercise its given powers. Academics may sit on "all-institution committees" to advise on the doctorate or other programs in Education, but the fact is that they often fail to take the job seriously or they find it easy and time-saving to rubber-stamp most of the proposals from Education. When they do take their job seriously, personality conflicts and other quarrels develop which consume time and energy. The result is that most schools of Education, whatever may be the paper arrangements within the university, are pretty much free to do as they wish in their graduate programs; certainly they are free to make the major components of these programs what they want them to be. And what they want them to be is no compliment to higher education in America.

The chances of changing graduate Education are not very good. In view of the abdication of responsibility by the academicians, any important improvements will have to emanate from educationists themselves. The closest they have come in recent years to recognizing the need for reform was in the 1960 *Yearbook* of the American Association of School Administrators, the most powerful department of the NEA. It is called "Professional Educators for America's Schools," and it takes a refreshingly frank look at the education of school administrators. It found that most schools of Education "practice admission rather than selection" of candidates for graduate work, that the master's work is often a "tasteless potpourri" of "administrivia," that no provision is made for culling out the incompetents, that the "mediocrity of programs" called for a "drastic overhauling," so as to attract to them "men with big minds." The Yearbook is as sharp an indictment of graduate Education as any "outsider" has ever penned. But the AASA's reasons for dissatisfaction with the graduate programs were much different from those one might suppose; and its suggested remedies for the ills which it cogently points up come as a shattering anticlimax: the AASA proposed and voted at its 1960 convention the following resolution:

> Beginning on January 1, 1964, all new members of the American Association of School Administrators shall submit evidence of successful completion of two (2) years of graduate study in university programs designed to prepare school administrators and approved by an accreditation body endorsed by the Executive Committee of AASA.

Thus it turns out that all the AASA was really worried about was, not the intellectual quality of graduate Education, but only the AASA's professional "image." Two years of work in a program designed by most of our schools of Education for administrators might qualify people for admission to the AASA's closed shop after 1964, but it is not going to improve the caliber of school administrators. Additionally, the AASA's Executive Committee later endorsed, for the purpose of accrediting graduate programs for school administrators, an organization called the National Council for Accreditation of Teacher Education; this is an extremely important and powerful agency almost wholly controlled by educationists whose approach to the education of teachers and administrators is very different from the academician's. (This agency is discussed in Chapter VII.) With the AASA's blessing, this agency now examines and accredits graduate programs in Education for school administrators; the kind of program it recommends as ideal for administrators would require about

75 per cent of the student's work to be in Education courses, and the other 25 per cent in subjects that have some direct, practical application to his job, such as courses in public finance and sociology.

As with so many other programs in Education, there is no theoretical base for the training of school administrators. The inevitable result, as suggested by these accreditation standards and by the multi-million-dollar investment of the Kellogg Foundation in the Cooperative Program in Educational Administration, is the development of training programs dedicated to applied tricks of the trade and made up of "field work," "laboratory experiences," "internships," "case studies," and reminiscences of erstwhile school administrators; but very little, if any, work in fundamental academic subjects that would contribute to the student's intellectual perspective and perhaps give him the wherewithal to become a genuine intellectual leader in his community, as well as the ability to learn on the job whatever tricks of the trade he needs. It is safe to say that neither the AASA nor the National Council for Accreditation of Teacher Education, nor the Kellogg Foundation envisions what might be called major reforms in graduate Education; they hope to make some small improvements without disturbing the existing structure.

What is obviously missing from the AASA's Yearbook, and from the entire field of graduate Education as we have outlined in this chapter, is any understanding of or interest in the training of educated, cultivated men as school administrators. Instead, the training programs worship at the altar of vocationalism and attempt to teach all the "skills," however mundane, that administrators need, apparently on the assumption that the individual is powerless to learn such things for himself. If the administrator needs to schedule buses or maintain reasonable relations with the community, he must have a course in "School Bus Scheduling" and in "School-Community Relations"; if the curriculum specialist needs to keep abreast of new developments when he gets on the job, he must have courses in new developments, plus a seminar in curriculum research methods, and maybe a "practicum" in revising course syllabi, not work in history, literature, languages, or science; if the future professor of Education must know something about teacher training when he becomes a teacher of teachers, he must have courses in teacher education, in new practices, and several in current issues in teacher education, not advanced work in those subjects that men have always found most fruitful in liberalizing their intelligence and extending their view.

Naturally, doctoral programs in Education find it impossible to prepare students for all the contingencies that might confront them on the job. So far their answer to this impossibility has been, not a radical condensation of courses, but an attempt to create more and more sub-specialties of administration, the trivia of which can then be covered more thoroughly. Until those who run the doctoral programs in Education recognize that the professional competence most needed by their graduates — in contrast to that of professional fields which have proven, well-developed and indispensable bodies of professional knowledge to be conveyed — lies chiefly in the liberal disciplines, just so long will their doctoral programs continue to be among the shallowest in higher education, and just so long will schools of Education continue to send out second-rate people to manage the vast public education establishment or to reproduce themselves by running other doctoral programs in other schools of Education.

Some Case Histories

As indicated earlier, my sample of transcripts of credit included a large number of graduate records. In the final tabulations, 481 transcripts at the master's level were used, and 218 at the doctoral level. A graduate record is most significant when the undergraduate record is also available, for it is then, when examining the student's entire academic background, that one can see the problems and practices of professional Education most clearly. Therefore, the ten case histories that follow (see Appendix A for additional ones), six for the master's degrees and four for the doctorate, either reproduce the undergraduate record entirely or indicate various totals from it. These cases can be considered highly representative of the programs that are among the most popular in graduate Education. Even more than with the undergraduate records, the excesses of professional Education are strikingly demonstrated in the transcripts from the graduate programs. The duplication of courses, the duplication of work done in the undergraduate programs, the triviality of courses, the extreme narrowness of the program as a whole, the conspicuous lack of academic work and in particular *advanced* academic work — all are painfully evident. The intellectual deterioration implicit in these records is so self-evident that there seems to be no point in my offering further comment on each case separately, as I did with the undergraduate records.

CASE NO. 1

MASTER'S DEGREE IN EDUCATIONAL PSYCHOLOGY, 1961

Undergraduate Record — Major: Elementary Education

Liberal Arts Courses (56 semester hours)

Art Appreciation (2)
Biology (2)
English Grammar and Composition (6)
American Literature (6)
World Literature (4)
Problems of Consumers (3)
Public Speaking (4)
World Geography (3)
American History (6)

History of Civilization (2)
American Government (3)
General Psychology (2)
Lit. of New Testament (3)
Rural Sociology (2)
History of the American Negro (4)
English Literature (2)
Science Survey (2)

Education Courses (79 semester hours)

Rural School Management (2)
History of Education (2)
Principles of Education (2)
Arithmetic for Teacher (3)
Public School Music (2)
Arithmetic and Methods (2)
Nature Study (2)
Drawing and Methods (2)
Penmanship (1)
Elementary School Curriculum (2)
School Hygiene (2)
Child Psychology (2)
Methods in English (2)
Geography and Methods (2)
Practice Teaching (6)
Educational Sociology (2)

Children's Literature (4)
Methods in Social Studies (3)
Tests and Measurements (3)
Methods in Health Education (1)
Educational Psychology (2)
Public School Music (2)
Home Economics for Teachers (3)
Practice Teaching (4)
Art Projects (4)
Problems and Practices of Elementary
  School (5)
Guidance (4)
Philosophy of Education (3)
Rural Trends (1)
Audio-Visual Aids to Instruction (4)

Graduate Record

Liberal Arts Courses (0 semester hours)

Education Courses (32 semester hours)

Teaching the Slow Learners (2)
Development of Children, 6-12 Years
  (3)
Work of the Teacher (3)
Development of Children to 6 Years
  (3)
Psychology of Family Relations (3)
Health Care of Children (2)
Psychology of Late Adolescence (2)

History of Education in American
  Culture (3)
Mental Hygiene (3)
Audio-Visual Materials and Methods
  (2)
Psychology of Early Adolescence (3)
Teaching and Remedial Work in
  Reading (3)

CASE NO. 2

Undergraduate Record — Major: Elementary Education

Liberal Arts Courses (43.4 semester hours)

Arts and Crafts (3)
Principles of Composition (4)
Literature of Our Times (6)
Speech Making (2)
Introduction to Geography (3)
American History (1.4)
Economic History, U.S. (4)
Contemporary Europe (3)

American Frontiers (3)
History of [State] (3)
American Government (2)
Psychology (1.7)
Personal Relationships (1.3)
Introduction Sociology (3)
Science in Conservation (3)

Education Courses (78.2 semester hours)

Audio-Visual Aids in Education (3)
Introduction Principles of Education (3.3)
Principles of Secondary Education (3)
Introduction to Guidance (3)
Creative Dramatics for Children (3)
Public School Problems (2)
Principles of Method (3.3)
Advanced Teaching of Reading (3)
Special Problems in Education (2)
Remedial Development in Elementary School (3)
Child Psychology (2)
Problems in Child Development (3)
Psychology of Pupil Adjustment (3)
Education of the Gifted (3)
Individual Mental Testing (3)

Measurement and Evaluation (3)
Introduction to the Exceptional Child (3)
Management and Measurement (3.3)
Workshop Remedial (3)
Rural School Problems (1.7)
Supervision of Rural Elementary School (2)
Nature Study (3.3)
Public School Music (3)
Plastics and Crafts (1.3)
Improvement of Instruction (3)
Speech Correction (3)
Diagnostic Education in Basic Skills (3)
Physical Education Activities in Elementary Schools (3)

Graduate Record

Liberal Arts Courses (0 semester hours)

Education Courses (33 semester hours)

Elementary School Administration (3)
School Administration (3)
Supervision of Instruction (3)
Elementary School Curriculum (3)
Philosophy and Principles of Guidance (3)
Problems of Secondary Teaching (3)

Psychological Foundations of Basic Skills (3)
Mentally Retarded Child (3)
Seminar in Educational Research (3)
Thesis (3)
Social Trends in Education (3)

CASE NO. 3

Undergraduate Record — Major: Physical Education

Liberal Arts Courses (42 semester hours)

Composition and Rhetoric (3)
Inorganic Chemistry (4)
Survey U.S. History (6)
Introduction to Psychology (3)
American Literature (3)
Public Speaking (3)

General Biology (8)
Introduction to Sociology (3)
Systematic Botany (4)
American Federal System (3)
Elementary Genetics (2)

Education Courses (29 semester hours)

Introduction to Educational Psychology (3)
Community Health (2)
Health Education (2)
Secondary Education (2)
Safety Education (2)
Principles of High School Studies (2)

Audio-Visual Aids (2)
Advanced Educational Psychology (2)
Pupil-Personnel Administration (2)
Principles of Secondary Teaching (2)
Methods in Physical Education (2)
Student Teaching (6)

Physical Education Courses (46 semester hours)

Apparatus and Tumbling (1)
Baseball (1)
Football (1)
Basketball (1)
Intro. to Physical Education (1)
Wrestling and Boxing (1)
Minor Sports (2)
Camping (2)
Track and Field Activities (1)
History of Physical Education (2)
Athletic Training (2)
Swimming and Life Saving (1)
First Aid (2)
Ballroom Dancing (1)
Officiating (3)

Recreation (2)
Service Program Management (1)
Games (1)
Folk Dance (1)
Group Work in Recreation (2)
Theory of Coaching Football (1)
Theory of Coaching Basketball (1)
Kinesiology (5)
Intro. to Health in Physical Ed. (2)
Theory of Coaching Track (1)
Theory of Coaching Baseball (1)
Corrective Activities (3)
Administration in Physical Education (3)

Graduate Record

Liberal Arts Courses (0 semester hours)

Education Courses (33 semester hours)

Secondary Education (6)
Techniques of Counseling (3)
Evaluation in Education (3)
Teacher and School Supervision (3)
Contemporary Problems in Education (3)

Teacher and School Administration (3)
Secondary School Management (6)
Education of Slow Learners (3)
Methods of Educational Research (3)

CASE NO. 4

Undergraduate Record — Major: Sociology

Liberal Arts Courses (80 semester hours)

California Trees (2)
Mythology (3)
Economics (6)
English (9)
Speech (2)
Drama Laboratory (1)
Geology (2)
History (6)
Spanish (4)
Music (2)
Physical Science (4)
Political Science (7)

Psychology (3)
Life of Jesus (3)
Intro. to Sociology (3)
Social Psychology (3)
Family as a Social Institution (2)
Personality Leadership (3)
Race Relations in the U.S. (3)
Social Cultural Origins (3)
Juvenile Delinquency (2)
Small Groups (3)
Industrial Sociology (2)
American Civilization (1)
A Cappella Choir (1)

Education Courses (18 semester hours)

The Teacher and the School (4)
Class Use of Audio-Visual Materials (2)
The School Society (2)

The Learning Process (2)
The Learner (3)
Child Behavior Problems (3)
Education (2)

Graduate Record

Liberal Arts Courses (3 semester hours)

Folk Culture of Mexico

Education Courses (32 semester hours)

Organization-Administration of Public Ed. (2)
Curriculum Making — Secondary Schools (2)
Principles and Techniques of Guidance (3)
Problems of the Junior High School (2)
Secondary Education (3)

Methods of Directed Teaching in Social Studies (9)
High School Methods (2)
Practicum in Secondary Education (2)
Introduction to Educational Measurements (2)
Master's Project Seminar (3)
Geography Education (2)

CASE NO. 5

Undergraduate Record — Major: Secondary Education

Liberal Arts Courses (83 semester hours)

Art Appreciation (2)
Biological Science (3)
Principles of Economics (6)
English Composition (6)
Survey English Literature (6)
Advanced Composition (3)
Growth and Structure English Language (3)
Fundamentals of Public Speaking (3)
American History (6)

Modern Europe (6)
Intermediate French (3)
Advanced French (6)
Survey French Literature (6)
French Conversation (4)
French Phonetics (2)
College Algebra (3)
Music Appreciation (3)
Physical Science (3)
Orientation to Social Science (6)
American Race Relations (3)

Education Courses (38 semester hours)

Educational Psychology (3)
Adolescent Psychology (3)
High School Methods (3)
English Grammar for Teachers (3)
School Health Education (2)
Tests and Measurements (3)
English in Secondary Schools (3)

French Secondary Schools (3)
Problems of Guidance (4)
Directed Teaching — English (3)
Directed Teaching — American History (3)
Introduction to Education (3)
Supervision of Games (2)

Graduate Record

Liberal Arts Courses (0 semester hours)

Education Courses (32 semester hours)

Secondary School Curriculum (3)
Psychology of Early Adolescence (3)
Improvement in Reading (2)
Education and Society (3)
Problems of Jr. and High School Teaching (3)
Teaching English in Secondary Schools (2)

Language Arts in Childhood Education (3)
Teaching Slow Learners (2)
Survey Principles of Guidance (3)
The Study of Language (3)
Group Discussion (2)
Audio-Visual Materials and Methods (3)

CASE NO. 6

Undergraduate Record — Major: Junior High School Education

Liberal Arts Courses (79 semester hours)

Fundamentals of Design (3)
Biology (6)
Principles of Economics (6)
Composition and Literature (6)
English Literature (3)
Speech (2)
American Literature (3)
English Grammar (2)
Elements of Geography (6)
History of Europe (6)
History of U.S. (6)

History of England (2)
History of France (2)
Far East in Modern Times (2)
General Mathematics (3)
Survey of Mathematics (3)
Music Literature (3)
Physical Science (6)
General Psychology (3)
Introduction to Sociology (3)
Social Problems (3)

Education Courses (36 semester hours)

Introduction to Education (1)
Library Instruction (1)
Principles of Teaching Junior High School (3)
Teaching Core in Junior High School (3)
Social Studies in Junior High School (2)
Language Arts in Junior High School (2)

Mathematics in Junior High School (3)
Science in Junior High School (2)
Directed Teaching Junior High School (16)
Human Growth and Development (3)

Graduate Record

Liberal Arts Courses (0 semester hours)

Education Courses (33 semester hours)

Contemporary Problems in Education (6)
Learning and Teaching (6)
Secondary Education (6)
Adult Education (3)

Educational Research Methods and Procedures (3)
School Administration (3)
School and Community (3)
Guidance in Secondary School (3)

CASE NO. 7

Undergraduate Record

Liberal Arts Courses (101 semester hours)

Education Courses (19 semester hours)

Graduate Record

Liberal Arts Courses (0 semester hours)

Education Courses (86 semester hours)

Administration of Secondary Education (3)

Curriculum of Secondary School (3)

Supervision of Secondary Education (3)

Research in Education (3)

Public School Administration (3)

Records and Reports in Education (3)

History of Education [in the state] (3)

Introduction to Guidance (3)

Audio-Visual Education (3)

Survey of Curriculum Literature in Ed. (3)

Organization and Administration Guidance Program (3)

Organization and Administration of Physical Ed. Program (3)

Guidance for the Slow Learner (2)

Educational-Occupational Information Guidance (2)

Contemporary Secondary Education (2)

Business Administration of Schools (2)

Contemporary Philosophy of Education (3)

Introduction to Educational Measurement (3)

Advanced Educational Psychology (3)

Personality-Mental Hygiene (3)

Principles of Curriculum Organization (2)

Research Seminar in Education (3)

Research in Education and Supervision (2)

Techniques of Administrative Leadership (2)

Research in Educational Psychology (2)

Advanced Statistical Method (3)

Vocational Guidance in Secondary School (4)

Elementary School Supervision (2)

Elementary School Administration (2)

Legal Aspects of School Administration (2)

Teaching of Reading (2)

Curriculum Making in Elementary School (2)

Teaching Social Studies in Elementary School (2)

CASE NO. 8

DOCTOR OF EDUCATION IN GUIDANCE, 1960

Undergraduate Record

Liberal Arts Courses (91 semester hours)

Education Courses (29 semester hours)

Graduate Record

Liberal Arts Courses (3 semester hours)
Survey of Clinical Psychology (3)

Education Courses (87 semester hours)

Personality Mental Hygiene (3)
Workshop in Composition (2)
High School Music Organization (2)
History and Philosophy of Education (3)
Curriculum Development (3)
Advanced Study of Child Development (3)
Seminar in Elementary Education (2)
Language Arts in the Elementary School (2)
Social Studies in the Elementary School (2)
Reading in the Elementary School (2)
Audio-Visual Aids (2)
Graduate Project Education (2)
Graduate Project Education (1)
Practice Mental Testing (3)
Advanced Practice Mental Testing (3)
Exceptional Children (3)
Principles and Techniques of Guidance (3)
Educational Statistics (3)
Advanced Educational Psychological Development (3)
Contemporary Philosophies of Education (3)

Educational Sociology (2)
Tests in Counseling and Guidance (2)
Group Guidance (2)
Resources of School Guidance Worker (2)
Readings Educational Psychology-Guidance (2)
Organization-Administration Guidance Services (2)
Methods of Training the Mentally Retarded (3)
Individual Diagnostic Reading (2)
Research Educational Supervision — Administration (2)
Research Educational Psychology — Guidance (2)
Advanced Laboratory in Counseling and Guidance (4)
Advanced Laboratory in School Psychology (5)
Research Seminar (3)
Research Educational Psychology — Guidance (2)
Principles Curriculum Organization and Development (2)

CASE NO. 9

Bachelor's and Master's Degrees Taken in Physical Education,
1953 and 1954

Graduate Record

Liberal Arts Courses (o semester hours)

Education Courses (90 semester hours)

Guidance and Student Personnel Administration (4)

Group Activities in College and Secondary School (3)

Supervision of Student Residence Halls (3)

Field Work in Guidance-Student Personnel Administration (4)

Psychology of Family Relations (2)

Critical Study of Research in Guidance (3)

Introduction to Group Development (3)

Issues and Trends in Guidance (4)

Improvement of Reading (2)

Purposes and Policies of Higher Education (3)

Religion and Education in Contemporary Education (3)

Project Conference and Seminar in Guidance (3)

Expressive and Projective Techniques (3)

Organization and Administration of Higher Education (3)

College Personnel Policies and Practices (3)

Introduction to Philosophy of Education (3)

Case Problems in Guidance (2)

Psychological Differences Bright and Dull Child (2)

Vocational Testing (2)

Role of Teacher in Guidance Program (2)

School Health Education (3)

Community Recreation Resources (3)

Research Problems (3)

Student Personnel Work (3)

High School Curriculum (3)

Public School Administration (3)

Advanced Education (9)

Problem Construction (3)

Personal Development (3)

CASE NO. 10

Undergraduate Record

Liberal Arts Courses (126 semester hours)

Education Courses (6 semester hours)

Graduate Record

Liberal Arts Courses (13 semester hours)

Explication de Textes (6)

Shakespeare and His Times (3)

French Literature of Renaissance (3)

Art Appreciation (1)

Education Courses (86 semester hours)

Educational Psychology (4)

Teaching of French in Secondary Schools (3)

Measurement in Secondary Education (2)

Composition for French Teachers (6)

Educational Foundations (4)

Administration of Secondary Schools (3)

Supervision of Secondary School Instruction (3)

Fundamental Course in Educational Administration (3)

Educational Statistics (2)

Principles of Curriculum Construction (2)

Personnel Problems of Teaching Staff (2)

Organization of the Elementary School (2)

Guidance in the School (2)

Materials and Methods of Teaching of Reading (2)

Techniques of Guidance (2)

Audio-Visual Aids in Education (2)

Administration of Elementary Education (3)

Teacher and School Supervision (3)

Education Administration as Social Policy (4)

Function and Administration Junior High (3)

Structure and Administration School Finance (3)

School Building Planning (3)

Materials and Methods in Parent Education (3)

The Cooperative Movement (2)

Fundamentals of International Education (3)

Seminar and Project Conference in Administration (2)

Current Problems and Trends in Administration (3)

Seminar in Secondary School Organization (3)

School Plant Administration (3)

American Secondary Schools (2)

Research in Secondary School Administration (2)

CHAPTER VII

The Exercise of Power in Teacher Education

"The question is," said Humpty Dumpty, "which is to be master — that's all."

— Lewis Carroll

The Establishment

THE EXERCISE of power in the field of professional Education, and thus in the matter of training teachers, is an old and important controversy. The authority to make policy, define aims and programs, and to enforce standards in Education has a direct bearing on the quality of teachers, administrators, and educationists graduated from the training programs, who in turn set the standards in public schools. For many years this authority has been a highly concentrated and exclusionist one, being reposed in all significant matters in the educationist and his several professional organizations. As is true of any other conflict in professional Education, controversy exists in this area because of widespread dissatisfaction with the results of teacher-training programs. If educationists, that is, were doing an outstanding job in these programs, nobody would worry much about what system of controls was in operation or how narrow it might be. But when this performance is as poor as it is, the question of how control is exercised in the field must be considered.

Most of the ailments of teacher education as we have explored them in previous chapters are the natural result of narrowly concentrated power protecting accumulated professional orthodoxies. Although educationists have been willing from time to time to admit that too much power is exercised by too few hands in Education, they generally reject the charge that the field is controlled by "an interlocking directorate" of educationist agencies or that there is any kind of orthodoxy to be perpetuated. Perhaps it is only the terminology, not the idea, that troubles them. Whatever words one chooses to characterize the hierarchy of controls in Education, an excessive concentration of power *does* exist in the field, and an entrenched orthodoxy *is* very much in evidence.

At every point in his preparatory career, a teacher or administrator is governed by policies created and enforced, not by the liberal arts faculty (except in a perfunctory sense), or by the larger field of higher education, but by the professional educator working through his various state and national agencies. I do not suggest that any vast conspiracy of educationists has been operating in subversive ways to bring about this unfortunate condition, but I do suggest that an Establishment obviously exists in professional Education, that it suffers from all the customary disabilities of large and monopolistic bureaucracies, and that its most characteristic stance is athwart the road to reform in teacher education. Educationists "who worship their own gods," as one eminent dean of Education pointed out years ago, "without admitting their colleagues of other faculties (now especially the faculty of arts and sciences) into their congregation, are in danger of becoming fanatics . . ." [1]

The major components of this Establishment are the state departments of Education, the accrediting associations, the professional associations, and the institutions themselves — all complementing and reinforcing one another and all staffed by persons who are themselves graduates of the advanced training programs in Education and who share the same basic educational views. Let us look briefly at the role of each.

The institutions are collectively the most potent source of

[1] Henry W. Holmes, "Shall Teachers Be Scholars?" *Occasional Pamphlets of the Graduate School of Education of Harvard University*, No. 1, October, 1937, p. 14.

policy and power in the field. They employ by far the largest number of people in the Establishment, over 20,000 full-time faculty members scattered through 1,148 colleges and universities. Although individually the preparing institutions are impotent in policy matters, especially if they happen to be interested in unorthodox policies, any large group of them, and certainly all of them together, can pursue just about any course they wish to pursue, and with the help of the rest of the Establishment. Of course, groups of institutions, not to say the whole field, rarely get actively together on much of anything in higher education, but a consensus is reached among teacher-training institutions, if only passively, on most important matters of policy. The institutions are by no means hamstrung, as they sometimes claim, by state certification or by accreditation requirements, which they themselves have much to do with formulating. If they felt themselves handicapped by such regulations, they could, acting in concert, make whatever changes seemed to them desirable. In short, the fundamental locus of power in the Establishment, itself a locus of power, is the institutions; and they must therefore accept the principal responsibility for the state of teacher education at any given time. It is within their power to make the training of teachers and other school personnel what they want it to be; the corollary fact is that the state of that training at any particular point reflects the consensus of the institutions.

The state departments of Education constitute a second powerful arm of the Establishment. They exercise the only legal authority related to licensing teachers and accrediting their training programs. While they usually do not take their accreditation function very seriously, they do take seriously their function in certifying individual teachers. The original rationale for state certification regulations was that they afforded the public a measure of protection against frauds and incompetents, the same as state licensing requirements did with other professional and semi-professional groups, and against the capriciousness or low standards of local school boards. For a time they probably did do this. In the process, however, they seem to have created more problems than they solved, and it is an open question whether their total contribution to teacher education has been negative or positive. Certification officers have applied the rules with such singular inflexibility as to negate many of the gains they might otherwise have made; state certification has now become one of the classic examples of administrative rigidity. The certification process in most states involves the mere mechanical adding up of the credit hours the applicant has had in Education and in other subjects, no matter what their quality might be. If he is short of the stipulated amounts, regardless of any other possible qualifications, he cannot be certified (except in some cases as an "emergency" or "substandard" teacher). Thus are created those legendary and amusing anomalies of certification: the fact that Einstein could not be licensed to teach third-grade arithmetic, or that a learned Frenchwoman could not be admitted to teach French in any American public school, or that Leonard Bernstein would not be competent to teach music to any public school student, or that many professors of Education, those who teach teachers how to teach, could not themselves be licensed to teach in any public school.

There is no very precise way of measuring the deleterious effects of the obtuse administration of certification laws, but a good deal of individual testimony exists, for what it is worth, to the effect that the brightest students find these laws a severe deterrent to entering teaching, as do many mature people who could bring to the classroom a lifetime of experience and accomplishment but who happen not to have any Education courses on their record and who cannot face the prospect of getting any. How well the licensing laws still fill their original function of saving the schools from incompetent teachers is not clear. The incompetent teacher today is a great deal more competent, with a great deal more education, than was the incompetent teacher in the early days of certification, when he might have no work beyond high school and often not that much. Today incompetence means chiefly the lack of Education courses. In view of the quality of teachers who *are* often certified today with a full complement of Education courses and then some, and in view of the quality of person who is often not certifiable despite a first-rate liberal education and demonstrated intellectual achievements — one wonders just what kind of incompetence public schools are now being saved from by the state departments of Education, whose laws have been appropriately described by A. Whitney Griswold as "the icicles of the old system of pedagogy. And behind these laws stands a militant organization with branches in every state and elaborate headquarters in Washington." [2]

Fortunately, several forces are now in play that will ultimately reduce the stultifying influence of the certification process. More and more, state departments of Education are relying on the *accreditation* of schools and of programs in teacher training to take the place of *certification* of the individual graduates of these programs. When the state department, that is, has approved the program of a given college, it may certify the graduates of the program automatically and without a review of the individuals' records. This in effect takes the certifying authority away from the state and gives it to the preparing institution. Also important in tempering the traditional problems of certification is the growing movement for state "reciprocity." This allows the graduates of institutions that enjoy certain kinds of accreditation to move among the reciprocating states without going through the usual certification procedure, which in the past often involved picking up additional Education courses. Both these tendencies are in some ways just as bad as what they are supplanting, as will be

[2] In an interview on the subject of the American university, conducted at the Center for the Study of Democratic Institutions, Santa Barbara, California, 1962.

seen later in this chapter, but they at least get away from the iron-fisted rigidity of the old certification process. Even so, the state departments of Education remain a very powerful voice in the Establishment and will continue to be for the foreseeable future.

Another government agency not to be overlooked is the United States Office of Education. Although it has little formal power over the states, it is able to exert a good deal of influence through its grants of money for research and its disbursements of Federal funds under the National Defense Education Act of 1958 and other Federal aid legislation. For many years the Office of Education, staffed almost completely by educationists, has acted like an arm of the Establishment within the Federal government. For reasons that are not very compelling, the United States Commissioner of Education has customarily been an educationist and a member in good standing of the Establishment. This unhappy tradition (is there some reason why the nation's highest official representative in educational matters should not be a scholar and a man of intellect?) was broken in 1961 with the appointment of an academician, Sterling M. McMurrin, who was no Establishment man. His instincts were strongly in the direction of the liberal arts and toward changing the life-adjustment orientation of the United States Office. He resigned the commissionership 17 months after his appointment. Whatever the future course may be of this Federal agency, its record has been one of solid support for the Establishment.

A third important component of the Establishment are the voluntary accrediting agencies. As noted above, the states have the only legal accrediting function in the Education field, and usually carry out this role rather superficially through the state departments of Education, which make routine visits to colleges within the state, and occasionally outside, and accredit the programs for preparing public school personnel in those institutions. The voluntary accrediting agencies, however, have broader though extra-legal power and cover much more territory. Most important for higher education are the six regional accrediting associations that cover the 50 states and some territories. These agencies accredit both secondary schools and all types of institutions of higher education. They accredit the institution as a whole, not specific programs such as those for teachers. However, they make only infrequent visits to their member schools and do not conceive of themselves as "policing" organizations; they regard their function as one of "stimulation" for their members, who now include about 90 per cent of all colleges that train teachers. Being membership agencies, they depend as much for continued support on their constituencies as the constituencies depend on their continued stamp of approval. Because of the low standards tolerated by the regional associations and because of their timorous attitude toward their own role, they simply become another supportive arm of the Education Establishment.

In addition to the regionals, there are numerous specialized accrediting agencies, arms of professional associations, that accredit particular programs in such areas as music, library science, nursing, social work, psychology, physical education, and others related to programs that prepare teachers. And finally there is a national agency that is by far the most powerful in the field of teacher education, the National Council for Accreditation of Teacher Education. This is a relatively new organization that promises to become one of the strongest in higher education. Because it is best examined in the light of specific case histories, I discuss it at some length in the last section of this chapter. Suffice it here to say that this agency is a crucial part of the Establishment and a force to be reckoned with in the exercise of power in teacher education.

A fourth component of the Establishment are the professional associations in Education. While having no direct responsibility for the training of teachers, they exert an enormous influence on the field. The primary organization is, of course, the National Education Association. It is, to use its own words, "the largest professional organization in the world and the only over-all national professional association for teachers in the United States." More than a hundred years old, the NEA now counts a little over half the nation's 1,500,000 public school teachers as members (even the AMA is not able to do much better than this, commanding about 60 per cent of the nation's doctors as members), a good many of whom are members because of the coercive activities of school superintendents and other individuals and agencies of the Establishment. The NEA boasts, at the latest count, 64 state and 7,501 local affiliated associations, 33 departments, 13 divisions, and 26 commissions and committees. It spends over eight million dollars a year to further its interests, and constitutes one of the most potent lobbies in many a state legislature; it also constitutes one of the largest, if not most effective, lobbies in Washington. Many of its departments and commissions have an active interest in teacher education, and at least two of them make it their principal concern. These are the American Association of Colleges for Teacher Education, and the National Commission on Teacher Education and Professional Standards. The former agency counts a total of 609 member institutions, which train the vast majority of teachers and administrators. In previous years, the AACTE carried on an accrediting function among its member schools, but has relinquished it to the organization mentioned above, which it helped create, the National Council for Accreditation of Teacher Education. The present role of the AACTE is very much like that of any other organization of colleges or universities: to promote these institutions and, in this case, their programs for training teachers. As the only agency of its kind in the field, operated wholly by educationists, it carries a good deal of weight in the Establishment.

The National Commission on Teacher Education and Professional Standards was created by the NEA in 1946 with the general mandate to promote the professional status of teachers, the selection of them, the certification of them, and the training programs for them. It has pursued this goal through conferences, reports, the creation of affiliated state committees, and cooperation with other professional agencies. While its function is purely advisory and hortatory, its influence has been considerable.

All of these agencies, in complementing and reinforcing one another, compose, I submit, a monolithic Establishment in which academicians and noneducationist organizations have very little voice, though they have the largest stake in the education of American teachers. The Establishment, not the learned world, dictates the fundamental orthodoxy of today's teacher training, with its devotion to the *status quo* and its insistence upon only one system for the preparation of public school personnel. There are, of course, frequent disagreements within the Establishment and departures from the common mold in minor ways; but the Establishment has, like bureaucratic orthodoxies everywhere, an extremely low tolerance for basic dissent either inside or outside its ranks. As I. L. Kandel accurately comments, after a long lifetime of observation and involvement in professional Education: "The more professionalized the administration of education has become, the greater has been the tendency among its practitioners to become complacent and to resent criticism from any source." [3]

In response to criticism the Establishment is apt to invoke cant-ridden slogans: "We want professional teachers for *all* American youth," as though its critics wanted something else. Or it is wont to deal in tired but unexamined ideas: "Certification requirements are essential protection to the tax-paying public against incompetence in the classroom;" but it fails to come to grips with the problem of why so many incompetent teachers are fully certified people offering no "protection"

[3] *American Education in the Twentieth Century,* Harvard University Press, 1957, p. 7.

whatever to the public. Or it will indulge in *ad hominem* attacks upon its critics, impugning their character or motives or sometimes their mental stability, and attempting to draw distinctions between what it calls "constructive" and "destructive" criticism, never failing to make the pious claim that it welcomes the one but deplores the other and never bothering to define or illustrate either one.[4]

The Establishment sometimes responds to vigorous criticism in bizarre ways. It is apt to shout "Enemies of the public schools!" at its individual critics, or to try intimidation or boycott when it is criticized by groups or by the mass media. A few years ago, for example, one of the major departments of the NEA, the National Association of Secondary School Principals, representing around 20,000 of the nation's educational administrators, displayed the characteristic hysteria of the Establishment when public education is criticized in mass-circulation magazines. Reacting to some educational articles in *Time* and *Life* magazines with which it happened to disagree, the NASSP's leadership sent out a secret letter to its entire membership urging school principals to write irate letters to *Time* and *Life* warning them that if they did not stop criticizing education these magazines would be removed from school libraries and school subscriptions would be cancelled. The letter added the cautionary note that the recipients should not let it be known that the nation's school principals had been urged to write such letters. One can hardly avoid drawing conclusions about a professional association, backed by the NEA, whose leadership could indulge in such an incredibly stupid and totalitarian act (the NASSP has been known in times past to inveigh mightily against "book-burners" of one sort or another!). The letter immediately became public, of course, and

---

[4] I have often asked educationists to name some examples of "constructive" criticism, but they seem able only to name examples of "destructive" criticism, which turn out to be just about anything that criticizes contemporary education. What they regard as "constructive" criticism would not be recognized by anyone but themselves as critical of anything.

was widely reprinted. If the incident were not so dangerous, *Time* and *Life* might well have said, with Voltaire: "I have only made one prayer to God in all my life, 'God, make my enemies ridiculous.' And God granted it." But the fact is that Education can bring enormous pressure to bear on magazines and other mass media, and rarely seems to bring it to bear on behalf of anything but its professional "image." Nor is the *Life* and *Time* incident an isolated one; the Establishment, especially the NEA, has exercised its capacity for censorship on numerous occasions, with such magazines as *U.S. News and World Report,* the *Reader's Digest,* the old *Collier's,* and with many newspapers and lesser journals. Unfortunately, it frequently succeeds in intimidating the press.

Another of the Establishment's major weapons in its fight against the critical discussion of educational issues is the NEA's pompously named Commission for the Defense of Democracy Through Education,[5] a body which devotes itself to "investigating" school boards, citizens groups, and other persons or agencies, who allegedly mistreat school personnel, especially administrators. In addition to these often repressive activities, the Defense Commission spends a lot of time worrying about critics of the Establishment. At considerable expense, it maintains, oddly enough for defenders of democracy, a secret file of dossiers on persons or organizations who criticize education anywhere in the nation, and stands ready to send out summaries of this intelligence to any beleaguered educationist in the field. Nor is it overly fussy in its methods for gathering information: at least one of its principal officers has been known, in the course of his gumshoeing travels, to misrepresent himself as a member of a university faculty pursuing quite a different mission from his true one. Others of its administrative officers have been known to indulge in semantic and typographical tricks in order to associate critics of the Estab-

[5] Recently given the less insolent title of the National Commission on Professional Rights and Responsibilities, but with no substantial change in function.

lishment with various kinds of extremist political and social groups.

It is significant that the Defense Commission, in all of the cases it has investigated of abused school administrators (in which it almost invariably finds the administrator the innocent victim of powerful, malign forces) has been less ready to come to the defense of a teacher, not to say a layman, who has been abused by the Establishment. Despite the fact, for example, that a number of cases of administrative blacklisting of individual teachers (who have been too critical of modern education or of the Establishment) are on the record, the Defense Commission has never seen any point in investigating such matters. To some observers, phenomena like the Defense Commission are too ludicrous to be taken seriously, but to others their potential for mischief is rather great. In either case, such phenomena reveal the preoccupation of the Establishment with silencing critical discussion and with maintaining an orthodoxy that has been a-building for half a century.

And yet in all of this the Establishment is neither insincere nor sinister, except in isolated cases. It merely acts out of what it conceives to be its legitimate self-interests. Thus it instinctively opposes every new idea, especially those coming from "outside," in the training of teachers which threatens to diminish the Establishment in any way — which might entail the reduction of Education courses, endanger jobs or status, or introduce some much-needed checks and balances into the exercise of power in teacher education. For decades the Establishment has fought against every such proposal that has been made. There are naturally exceptions to this rule, both individuals and institutions, but the general rule remains: the Education field and its various agencies have a solid history of opposition to new ideas in teacher education and have had the power to make their opposition prevail. This negative stance has been the despair of those who feel that new approaches in the education of American teachers are urgent, and those who feel that the Education field at the least should be conducting significant experiments that depart radically from the orthodox programs.

Regrettable as is this attitude toward innovation in teacher education, even more so is the continued failure of the Establishment to support the intellectual and combat the non-intellectual in *present* programs. Although this failure is evident in numberless ways, as detailed in previous chapters, it is most apparent with those agencies of the Establishment whose specific function it is to maintain standards in teacher education — the state departments of Education and the accrediting organizations. The state departments rarely invoke their legal accrediting powers to sanction or police in any important way the training programs of teachers colleges or schools of Education within universities, or programs that are controlled by fellow educationists; but they are apt to use their full power against any liberal arts college or other institution whose program seems to put too much emphasis on academic excellence and too little on Education courses. The Connecticut State Department of Education, as one example among many, can harass and threaten to shut down the excellent Master of Arts in Teaching program at Yale University, which it regards as too heavily academic, but has no trouble approving the training programs of the state's four teachers colleges (now alleged, by virtue of a change of name, to be general purpose colleges), which are academically mediocre. Likewise, the Texas Education Agency can give Rice University's teacher-training program, combining the minimum number of Education courses needed for certification with a strong emphasis on the liberal arts, a very difficult time, while it continues to smile upon the anemic training programs of state-controlled schools run by members of the Establishment. Just how far state departments can permit educationists to go in watered-down programs is nowhere better illustrated than in the story of one university's graduate school of education and its relations during the last few years with the state department of education, which I describe in the next section of this chapter.

The same ambivalence prevails in the work of the National Council for Accreditation of Teacher Education, which talks a great deal about intellectual excellence in teacher training but which often uses its enormous power in precisely the opposite direction. It accredits some of the weakest schools to be found in the country, when their training programs are controlled by educationists, but can refuse accreditation to some of the strongest, whose programs may be controlled by academicians. This curious condition is nowhere better illustrated than in the case of Carleton College and its relations with the National Council for Accreditation of Teacher Education, which I detail in the last section of this chapter.

The moral of both these cases, as well as of this chapter, is that the principal power in teacher education is exercised almost completely by an Establishment representing only one segment of the larger field of education that prepares teachers; and that, in pursuing its own self-interests, narrowly conceived, it far more often blocks than supports the reforms and improvements most needed in teacher education. The liberal arts representatives and the professional associations of the learned world would need to have a major voice, perhaps a controlling voice, in the education of American teachers before such debacles as "Metropolitan University's," and such grim comedies as Carleton College's, could be obviated. Until the liberal arts are solidly represented in the Establishment, the exercise of power in teacher education will remain dangerously exclusionist. Whether this crucial problem, replete as it is with political, emotional, and economic considerations, can be resolved is doubtful.

The Case of Metropolitan University

A school which I shall call Metropolitan University — for my interest is in the lessons it offers to higher education and not in holding it up to ridicule by properly identifying it — provides an illuminating study of controls in teacher education and of the reasons that they frequently fail to operate.

Like many other schools, Metropolitan University began growing rapidly after World War II, establishing first one new school and then another, in social work, medical sciences, mathematical sciences, and in other fields. In 1957 it officially launched its Graduate School of Education with 185 students enrolled in a teacher internship program, supported by the Fund for the Advancement of Education, and leading to the Master of Arts in Teaching degree. Meeting with success in this, the GSE soon decided to expand its operations and to create numerous programs that would attract a large enrollment, including programs leading to the Ed.D. degree and to the Ph.D. in Education. In March of 1958, the President of Metropolitan appointed as Dean of the GSE a man who brought to his new job an impressive record of work in educational journalism, of books on education, of conferences attended and speeches made, honorary degrees and other marks of esteem in the world of professional Education.

Under his management the GSE prospered fantastically. In September of 1958, six months after his appointment, enrollment went to fully double what it had been a year earlier, and doubled again in September of 1959, when it reached a count of 1,320! Such an unprecedented growth rate, especially at the graduate level, was due mostly, everyone seems agreed in retrospect, to the new Dean's astonishing promotional abilities and his equally astonishing educational policies.

The truth is, to come to the heart of the matter at once, that the GSE under the leadership of its new Dean soon became a little-known but incontestable disgrace: its intellectual standards were non-existent; its administrative incompetence was absolute; its general operation was as bad as, one would suppose, a university could get by working at it.

Its new doctoral programs, presumably the epitome of the

GSE's academic strength, illustrate general conditions as well as anything. Established as an "experimental" school, to "break through intellectual sterility," as the Dean put it at one faculty meeting, the GSE's doctoral programs were assuredly original. The GSE's "standards" for these degrees could only be considered spectacular, even in a field not known for the rigor of its doctoral work. For instance: Candidates for the Ed.D. and Ph.D. degrees at the GSE were allowed to teach a wide variety of *graduate* courses for which they had no significant training. Such doctoral candidates were allowed to accumulate doctoral credit by taking courses from one another. Doctoral candidates were allowed to serve on one another's doctoral committees and advise on one another's doctoral dissertations. Doctoral candidates were allowed to sign one another's course registration cards and approve one another's total program for the doctor's degree. Doctoral candidates were allowed to take practically all of their course work from two or three teachers, who themselves might be candidates for the degree, and were allowed an incredible amount of duplication of course content. Doctoral candidates were allowed to give themselves course credit for courses *they themselves* were teaching.

A few doctoral candidates (how many nobody really knows) were allowed to engage in "a gentlemanly interchange of credits." This means that some candidates recorded grades and gave course credit, in courses they were teaching, to other candidates who never attended their courses, which credits were then reciprocated. In short, fraudulent credit. In one case, a candidate wrote the Dean explaining that he had given credit to another candidate who had never appeared in his course. He had done it at his colleague's request "when turning in grades for the summer session under the impression that this practice was standard, had the Dean's approval and was designed to facilitate record keeping"! At the bottom of the letter, the Dean replied, thanking him for the letter and saying simply: "I do appreciate the information contained in your letter. You may rest assured that this will be kept confidential."

Doctoral candidates were allowed to give each other "Directed Study." "Directed" or "independent" study is commonly given in graduate schools by senior professors to advanced students, wherein the student does a piece of independent research under the professor's general supervision, and produces a manuscript of some consequence to prove it. A perfectly respectable and valuable practice. But Metropolitan is perhaps the only case on record where candidates for a degree gave independent work to each other! No manuscripts from such "courses" seem to be available for examination at Metropolitan.

Unfortunate as these blind-leading-the-blind, or learning-by-doing practices were, they are eclipsed by others that were not so picturesque but that had an even more fundamental effect on the doctoral offerings. While Metropolitan used many part-time teachers, some of them distinguished in their fields, the full-time faculty was incredibly small in relation to enrollment. During the 1959-60 academic year, when the School encompassed eight major departments plus a psychological clinic and had an enrollment of 1,320, 60% full-time students, its full-time faculty consisted of 29 persons, including several administrators who taught only partial loads or none. This student-faculty ratio of forty-five- or fifty-to-one is probably unique in the history of graduate education.

Equally unfortunate was the lack of any coherent and clearly defined programs for the astonishing numbers of doctoral candidates drawn to the school. One must assume that such numbers were attracted by the excessive promotional efforts of the administration and by the evident ease with which the doctorate in Education could be completed. In January of 1960, one of the chief administrative officers of the GSE forecast with pride that enrollment for the 1960-1961 academic year, less than three years after the inauguration of this graduate school and less than two years after the inauguration of the GSE's doctoral degrees, would reach a minimum of 2,000 students, with no fewer than 500 of them doctoral candidates. The entire field of Education, including such giants as Teachers College and New York University, turns out only about 1,500 new doctors a year, and all of American higher education together turns out only about 10,000.

Admission to doctoral study at the GSE was for all practical purposes automatic. One had only to present an undergraduate degree, whatever its quality and wherever awarded. It even happened on occasion that a candidate could complete his doctoral requirements at the GSE without ever having furnished the School with an undergraduate record. There was no significant evaluation of graduate credit transferred to GSE, incoming students being allowed to transfer practically any amount of graduate work from other institutions; nor was there any time limit on transfer credit (about seven years is customary), some students being accorded graduate credit for a course in, say, educational psychology taken thirty years ago. This may not have been a bad policy, when one considers the content of some of the GSE's courses, but it was in violation of its application to the state department of education and of stipulations in its own catalogue. There were in practice no residence requirements for the doctoral degrees, though the School's catalogue stipulates a minimum of one year in residence beyond the master's degree.

Nor were there any checkpoints along the aspiring doctor's way at which his record was scrutinized and the next leg of the journey planned. Consider, for example, the record of Mr. "X". His career at the GSE is neither the best nor the worst case that could be used. Bringing a master's degree with him in the summer of 1958, Mr. "X" enrolled at the GSE as a candidate for the Ph.D. One year later he had completed virtually all of Metropolitan's requirements for the degree, while holding down a full-time job on the outside. During the two semesters and one summer session he was at the GSE, and fully employed elsewhere, he completed ten graduate courses, worth 33 hours of doctoral credit, in such subjects as, Principles of Guidance, Audio-Visual Aids, Methods of Teaching Physical Education, Family and Personality Development, Human Relations in Teaching, Principles of Guidance (II), and Crucial Issues in American Education. Of the ten courses that he took, two were taught by full-time faculty members, two by part-time teachers from outside the GSE, and the remaining six by other students at the GSE.

Or consider the composition of the Committee on Doctoral Studies, theoretically the chief supervising body for all doctoral candidates at the GSE: it had only one person sitting on it with an earned doctorate himself; the rest were *candidates* for the degree. Doctoral degrees were offered in major fields in which the School had no full-time faculty whatever. Comprehensive examinations for the doctorate, a major crisis and turning point in other graduate schools, were simply not given in numerous cases at Metropolitan; if the student had taken the Graduate Record Examination, normally one of the requirements for mere admission to graduate study, his score on the exam, which might be as low as 350, was frequently deemed tantamount to passing his comprehensives. And in at least one instance where the candidate was simply not able to write an acceptable doctoral dissertation, and I leave it to the reader to surmise what an acceptable dissertation would have been at the GSE, two faculty members undertook to write it for him.

One could go on ticking off such malpractices, but perhaps these suffice to illustrate life at Metropolitan's Graduate School of Education. Here is the way some faculty members and students have characterized the GSE to me during interviews:

"an educational bordello"
"to describe it as a 'slum' or a 'dictatorship' would be an understatement"

"a cesspool"

"a sick pedagogical situation on a level with agencies that sell ghost-written theses"

"not only its doctoral programs but its much-touted teaching fellowship program was a sham"

"a school that has become a satire on itself"

One should pause at this point to make it clear that neither the faculty nor students at the Graduate School of Education can be indicted as a group. The faculty could count some persons of thorough competence and integrity, as could the student body. Some in both groups were sickened by the conditions of the School and either fought against them or simply left. But it must also be said that a substantial part of both groups followed the lead of the Dean and lent him the support without which he could hardly have effected the policies that led the School to catastrophe.

It is one thing for a Dean to say, for example, as Metropolitan's did in a faculty meeting in February, 1960, that, so far as the dissertation for the Doctor of Education degree went, "an article suitable for publication in the New York *Times* or a professional journal such as *School and Society* would satisfy our requirements"; or, in answer to a question, "Yes, the Doctor of Education degree will become like the master's degree"; or to dismiss all critics of his anti-intellectual programs as mere "academicians" and "traditionalists." But it is another thing to put such grotesqueries into practice: one must have substantial faculty support to do so.

Fortunately, there was also substantial faculty opposition, and this in the end proved the undoing of the Dean, of the GSE, and of Metropolitan University. The end came about through the protestations of various faculty members, but of one in particular, who, after repeated and fruitless attempts to get remedial action by the Dean, the President, and the Trustees, finally released a memorandum in the fall of 1959 to the education editor of a large newspaper containing a series of specifications and charges against the Dean and President of incompetence and malfeasance. He released it at the same time to the state department of education and to the appropriate regional accrediting association of colleges and secondary schools, both of which had accrediting responsibility for approving the educational program at Metropolitan. Thereafter, the editor, while making nothing public, began asking the state department of education about its intentions regarding the charges contained in the memorandum and kept asking them until the spring of 1960 when the state took action.

Its action came in the form of a letter to the President which in effect censured Metropolitan and the GSE for unprofessional practices in its doctoral programs — a traumatic and extremely rare experience for any university. Shock and dismay engulfed many friends and donors of Metropolitan and that part of its faculty not already aware of conditions at the GSE. The President "allowed" the Dean to resign, for the State's letter had suggested that Metropolitan might want to make "provision for additions to and possibly changes in the administrative staff . . . [of the GSE in order] to bring about increased confidence in the academic leadership of the school." He also appointed a committee made up of four of Metropolitan's other deans to investigate. The Deans Committee worked hard to uncover the truth — for itself, of course, not for the public — and to enact at least the beginnings of reform by the summer of 1960, by which time it had to report its progress to the state department of education. The State was happy with the report, gave the University a vote of confidence, and now seems pleased with the way in which the GSE is going about the re-building of its shattered reputation.

It would be well if Metropolitan's case were merely a bit of educational curiosa, but the facts are different. In the failure of key persons and agencies to control the situation at the GSE, the case, though dramatized by publicity, is highly instructive. Let's look at how these persons and agencies deported themselves in the face of clear evidence of educational malpractice which it was their duty to oppose.

First, the faculty of the GSE, the most important point of control over quality. A substantial part of it not only failed to protest the subversion of academic standards but actively aided and abetted the process. Low standards made for large enrollments which made for large receipts which made for high salaries and rapid promotions and other good things of academic life. A smaller part of the faculty did protest, a few violently, but the influence of those who did not quit or get fired was neutralized through discriminatory gimmicks in budgetary matters, class scheduling, committee assignments, etc. In short, such unqualified support of the GSE administration was demanded of the faculty that it was impossible for individuals to genuinely disagree with administrative decisions.

That being true, the next stop within the University was the President, who had ultimate authority and responsibility for doing something. He was aware from the beginning of the kind of operation being run by the administration he had appointed to the GSE; he was apprised of the situation early and on many occasions. Obviously, he was aware of the enrollment figures and receipts of the GSE, which were so explosive as to demand in themselves some investigation. The President was requested, indeed entreated, to restrain the GSE administration long before it became too late. That it was his clear duty to do so cannot be doubted. But there is no record of his having taken significant steps in that direction until the publicity accompanying the State Department's letter of censure, after which it was, of course, impossible to maintain the *status quo*. In justice it must be said that the President's role is not wholly negative. It is simply ambiguous. Under his administration Metropolitan has established several outstanding schools and has accomplished other notable things. But one gets the impression in discussing the GSE matter with him that, for reasons which never become quite clear, he simply found himself unequal to that particular situation. In any event, his inaction was disastrous. As for the University's Trustees, they naturally played a part similar to the President's: they were advised directly on various occasions of conditions at the GSE, but failed to take significant action or to direct the President to do so.

Since no controls were being exerted within Metropolitan, the possibilities of control moved outside the University. What about the academic profession at large and its associations? In contrast to other fields such as medicine and law, there is no professional society in education, and certainly none in professional Education, that is able to prevent, correct, or even influence such a condition of academic anemia as prevailed at the GSE, though all professional societies have a clear stake in the maintenance of high professional standards. They have no precedent, no funds, no machinery, and probably no desire to attempt to exercise control within the profession. Higher education has nothing that even approaches the ubiquitous controls exercised by, for instance, the AMA in the field of medicine. While agencies like the American Association of University Professors interest themselves in certain types of unethical practices, especially on the part of an administration, they avoid the hornets' nest of professional and educational standards. Whether one regards this as a blessing or an evil, the effect is to leave education wide open to malpractices of many kinds.

One then turns to whatever other agencies there are whose function is to affect educational quality. These are the regional accrediting association and the state department of education. Both agencies have accrediting responsibilities, and both are staffed by educationists. The regional association, a quasi-legal agency like the other five regional accrediting associations covering the rest of the United States, made its routine "visitation" to Metropolitan in the fall of 1958, examined the entire establishment, and sent a team of educationists into the GSE to gather information and make a recommendation to accredit or not. "Accreditation," says the association, "signifies that the institution offers commendable programs leading to the achievement of its own particular objectives. It indicates that all its work is conducted at a satisfactory level, in the judgment of [this] Association, but not that it is necessarily of uniform quality." The GSE team of inspectors was apprised in some detail by faculty members of the abuses of the administration, just in case they did not uncover them for themselves. Despite this knowledge, the regional association renewed Metropolitan's accreditation. Thus one more agency of control proved unequal to the job.

The last agency that presumably could influence GSE's operation, the state education department, turned out to be the one agency that did, in fact, do something. But even here there are large questions.

The state department had approved in the fall of 1958 the very programs its letter censured 18 months later. It approved the programs on the basis of its own "visitation" to the GSE and upon the school's application. An interesting question is, What kind of evaluation could the state department have conducted that could possibly have justified approval in the first place? If it gave approval with full knowledge of the facts, and it was given a good many of the facts during its "visitation," then is not the state's accreditation meaningless? If it gave approval in ignorance of the facts, is not its evaluation incompetent?

For that matter, there remains a question as to whether the state would have taken as decisive action as it did, or if it would have taken any action at all, had it not been for the pressure exerted by the editor of the newspaper in the form of embarrassing questions. The state commissioner of education was made aware of the press's interest in the Metropolitan question in February of 1960 when it was suggested to him by the editor that a newspaper story about the GSE would be forthcoming in the near future and that his department might not look good sitting on its hands. Six weeks later the state issued its letter to the President, which it knew would also be demanded and scrutinized by the press. Still, the state says it would have taken substantially the same action had the press not been aware of the situation at all.

Whether it would have or not, the fact is that the record of the accrediting bodies in the Metropolitan matter is an obvious failure. There is no reason whatever to think the record is any better in other situations. The accrediting associations, despite the aura of respectability they seem to cast over their member institutions, possibly do more to lower standards in colleges and universities (and also in the secondary schools they accredit) than to raise them: they have never saved the country from the more aggravated assaults, such as Metropolitan, on academic quality; having once accredited an institution, they almost never disaccredit it no matter how far downhill it may have traveled since the original rating; their elaborate sets of "standards" and "criteria" for judging institutions have "no perceptible relationship," as Henry Wriston once observed, "to that inner drive for excellence which marks a worthwhile institution." Yet American education foolishly persists in looking to them to exercise a kind of control over educational standards which they are incapable of.

Ideally, educational control should be exercised entirely by the faculty of a college or university, which would have both the power and the will to maintain the intellectual life of the establishment at the highest possible level. But in reality the faculty often has neither the power nor the will; and when the administration is equally pusillanimous, and the state and other accrediting agencies ineffective, such cases as Metropolitan's should not be a surprise. The surprising thing is that they do not happen, or at least that they do not come to public attention, more often.

The Metropolitan situation is perhaps as good a measure as any of how reluctant the Establishment is to exercise its great power to combat anti-intellectualism and low standards in its own ranks. Such controls as are alleged by the Establishment to exist in teacher education fail more often than not to operate in the interest of anybody but the Establishment.

The Case of Carleton College

Still another incident revelatory of the ways in which the Establishment exercises its powers over teacher education is in the relations of Carleton College with the National Council for Accreditation of Teacher Education. This Council, known in the trade as NCATE and pronounced "N-kate," has been superimposed over the last dozen years on several other accrediting bodies that have more restricted roles in controlling the teacher-training programs of our colleges and universities. Although NCATE has been well supported by educationists and is considered a major part of the Establishment, it has been held strongly suspect by representatives of the liberal arts, whose disaffection has reached something of a crescendo in recent years. The basic conflict is simple enough. It is over the question of whether NCATE, as it is presently operating, can fulfill the function it has assigned itself: to make significant improvements in the education of American teachers through accreditation. Most educationists do not doubt that it will, but a good many of their academic colleagues feel that it will not only fail in its mission but may do incalculable harm in the process. Before discussing the Carleton case specifically, let us explore this often embittered conflict over NCATE's general operation by looking as dispassionately as possible at the more important grounds upon which it is based.

NCATE was created in 1952 by various organizations in the field of professional Education, notably the American Association of Colleges for Teacher Education. AACTE, as mentioned earlier, had been accrediting its limited list of member institutions for some time prior to NCATE, but wanted to see a more representative and more powerful agency in operation. NCATE inherited the 284 member institutions of AACTE, considering them automatically accredited, and has now added about 90 new ones, bringing its total membership to 374 schools which train over 70 per cent of all new public school teachers. It is adding new schools and revisiting the AACTE ones as rapidly as possible. It has been recognized by the National Commission on Accrediting[6] as the principal accrediting agency in the field of teacher education.

Through the smoke and swirl of controversy, one can isolate at least six major reasons that move much of the academic community to view NCATE with considerable alarm.

First: the efficacy of accreditation itself, as an instrument for improving the education of teachers, is not self-evident, whether done by NCATE or any other group. The question of whether some kinds of accrediting do more harm than good in higher education is a complex one upon which much evidence pro and con can be mustered; and it is a question, say many academics, that should have been explored at length by all the principal interests concerned before the creation of any national agency to accredit programs or institutions in this field.

Second: assuming that accreditation *is* a good way of improving the training of teachers, who should make policy about how to do it? Who, that is, should run the operation? The governing body of NCATE, itself called a "Council," is made up of 19 persons, 13 of whom are appointed by departments of the National Education Association; one more is appointed by the Council of Chief State School Officers; and still another by the National Association of State Directors of Teacher

---

[6] A sort of accreditors' supreme court that now rules over all accrediting agencies and whose job it is to regulate the industry, mediate disputes, give official recognition to one organization in each field, and if possible keep the number of proliferating agencies within reasonable bounds. The NCA was organized in 1949 by a group of college and university presidents who were unhappy about "the conflicting demands and unnecessary expenditures" being inflicted on their institutions by the myriad of accrediting agencies.

Education and Certification — bringing the tongue-twisting total to 15 members out of 19 representative of the field of professional Education, and running heavily to educational administrators. To the academic eye, this concentration of Education specialists has, to say the least, an insular look. It may also serve to emphasize and perpetuate the customary separation of educationists from the liberal arts faculty.

Third: NCATE attempts to accredit only the professional part of a teacher's education, and relies on the six regional associations to insure adequate quality in the liberal arts work and in everything else about the institution. While it is obvious that NCATE in its present form is incompetent to accredit the academic program of future teachers, it seems equally clear that the use of the regional associations for that purpose is ill-conceived. Such a schizophrenic accreditation process might work well enough for the training of optometrists, podiatrists, or foresters, but the dangers of it for accrediting programs that educate teachers are great. As we have seen at Metropolitan University as well as in other aspects of teacher-training programs, it is debatable whether the regional associations, which have now become mere "advisory" bodies to their member institutions, have managed to secure any significant degree of academic quality in higher education. A glance at the accredited list of any of them suggests that, whatever other virtues may inhere in the regionals, academic rigor isn't one of them. Yet NCATE must rely on what would be widely regarded as the meaningless approval of the regionals for assuring quality in the most important part of a teacher's education, the liberal arts.

Fourth: NCATE has developed a set of seven standards that constitutes the instrument with which it measures and judges institutions. They cover matters of faculty, admissions, administrative machinery, library resources, and the like. These standards appear to many an academician decidedly like a way of replacing the old rigidity of state certification requirements with a new and equally invalid, but more dangerous, rigidity of their own. They are based on two extremely controversial assumptions: that the way to get good teachers in public schools is to look chiefly at what goes *into* the training programs and not at what comes out; and that the things which should go into these programs are well known, agreed upon, verified, and that they can be measured. Because little supporting evidence can be presented on either of these counts, NCATE's set of standards will no doubt continue to draw critical fire.

Fifth: NCATE is naturally committed to the idea that there is one and only one permissible preparation for teaching — exposure to an orthodox program of courses in pedagogy in a college or university, preferably one accredited by NCATE. This commitment makes it impossible for institutions to experiment with other ways of training teachers, such as internships and apprenticeships involving little or no course work in Education. It also makes impossible the exploration or development of qualifying examinations as an alternate route to the teaching certificate, one that makes very good sense to the academician. It freezes teacher education into one pattern, the pattern that NCATE happens to think is the "correct" one and the one that it exists to accredit.

Sixth: the most serious charge against NCATE is that it threatens to become a vast academic cartel that will ultimately prevent the employment of any person for any job at any level in any public school, and perhaps in any private school as well, who has not been through an NCATE-accredited program. NCATE calls itself a voluntary agency, but is rapidly becoming, like any accrediting agency when it has accumulated enough power, coercive. Within the professional fraternity, more and more groups are "endorsing" NCATE and using its accreditation as a weapon to exclude schools or persons from one or another function in public education.

Twenty-four states now practice NCATE reciprocity, allow-ing graduates of NCATE-accredited schools to move to new teaching jobs without having to go through the same certification procedures as everybody else; the next logical step is for the state departments of Education to begin *requiring* graduation from an NCATE school for any kind of certificate to teach. State teachers organizations as well as national associations like those within the NEA talk frankly about the time when NCATE will furnish the only acceptable entree to the public schools. For an idea of how exclusionist the future may be in teacher education, one has only to refer to Chapter V of the 1961 publication of the National Education Association's "TEPS" Commission, one of the founding groups of NCATE, which still appoints 6 of the 19 members of NCATE's governing Council. It is called *New Horizons for the Teaching Profession,* the report of a "task force" of well known educationists containing their recommendations about numerous problems in teacher education. Here is outlined a complete plan for making graduation from an NCATE-accredited institution a prerequisite for membership in any kind of professional association or for the freedom to do much of anything in the field of public education. Or, consider a policy adopted recently (and referred to in Chapter VI) by the American Association of School Administrators, the most potent of the NEA's departments, which will prohibit anyone from joining its ranks after 1964 who has not been through two years of graduate work in an NCATE-accredited program for school administrators — which programs, according to NCATE's proposals, should consist of at least 75 per cent Education courses.

The good liberal arts colleges are apt to see in NCATE a genuine threat to their teacher-training programs. Many of these programs are in conflict with NCATE's standards, which means that, when the pressures for accreditation become strong enough, either these programs will have to change or these schools will have to get out of the business of preparing teachers. In short, the course of empire seems to academicians to have been rather plainly mapped out by NCATE, and it presents a cheerless prospect to the first-line liberal arts colleges and to other high-quality institutions.

Other points at issue, such as the kinds of people who make up NCATE visiting teams, their qualifications and training for the job, the large number of years between NCATE visits to member schools (ten years), and the wide range of scores that graduates of NCATE schools make on standardized teacher examinations, are too numerous to survey here. I cite the above points only to indicate something of the range of controversy involved. A look at how the organization has actually performed in the field is perhaps the best way to assess it. I will therefore choose for illustration two institutions that have been visited in recent years by NCATE and that represent sharply different approaches to the job of educating teachers: Carleton College at Northfield, Minnesota, which NCATE rejected; and a school that, for propriety's sake, I will call Crossroads State Teachers College, which it accepted.

NCATE made its "visitation" to Carleton with a team of five educationists in 1960. (Accreditors, it seems, never make just plain visits. Like supernatural beings, they make only "visitations.") Crossroads State Teachers College was "visitated" in 1958. Below I record various kinds of facts, and my interpretations of the facts, about each school as of the time it was evaluated by NCATE.

Carleton is, of course, one of the elite among America's private colleges, usually classed with institutions like Amherst, Oberlin, and Williams. Nearly a century old, it has built an enviable record for high-quality undergraduate liberal education. Traditionally, Carleton trained large numbers of qualified teachers for Minnesota and other states, often as much as 30 per cent of its graduating classes. A precipitate decline in these numbers became evident late in the Thirties and again after World War II. In 1954 Carleton began to give some organized attention to the problem. It held a much-noted series of faculty seminars that year addressed specifically to the question of what colleges like Carleton might best do in the preparation of secondary teachers. Among other results of these meetings was the appointment of a standing committee to propose new programs for Carleton's prospective teachers, to maintain liaison between the Education department and the academic departments, and to promote in general the education of secondary teachers at the College. It turned out to be a hardworking and extremely effective committee that guided the development of the teacher education program as it is now to be found at Carleton. In other words, Carleton led the way in doing precisely what NCATE and other groups of educationists have been saying is indispensable to improving and accrediting teacher education programs: effecting a continuous institution-wide involvement in, and support for, the education of teachers.

At the time of the NCATE visit, Carleton had an enrollment of 1,175 students and a faculty of 103. Sixty-four per cent of the faculty, about twice the national average, had the Ph.D. degree, mostly from first-rank, prestige universities. Many members of the faculty were solidly established scholars with wide reputations in their fields. Carleton's entering class in 1960 came overwhelmingly from the highest quintile of their high school graduating classes; 30% of them clustered in the 700's on the SAT examination, most of the others in the 600's; 30% qualified for scholarship help.

Those enrolled in Carleton's teacher education program, according to the transcripts of credit, took an average of 105 semester hours in academic work and 18 hours in professional Education. An English major, for example, got about 40 semester hours in English and 65 hours in other academic areas, a history major got about 34 and 69, a science major about 34 and 75. Everyone, regardless of field, got substantial work in a foreign language. Near the end of his career at Carleton, each student passed a comprehensive examination in his field, consisting of a six-hour written exam and a one-hour oral. And throughout his career there, he associated and competed with students following many different academic programs, some terminal, many others pre-professional.

The fourth important component of an institution of higher education, besides the caliber of the faculty, of the students, and of the curriculum, is the library and the institution's general resources. Carleton's library contained about 175,000 volumes in 1960, the principal holdings and special collections reflecting the school's traditional emphasis on the liberal arts. Building on this base, it spent $25,000 that year for new books (and currently spends $50,000). Carleton owns about a thousand acres of land, is handsomely housed, and generously endowed.

NCATE's Committee on Visitation and Appraisal, meeting in 1961, found Carleton unqualified to be training teachers and denied it accreditation. This Committee is a wholly separate body from the "visitation" teams and makes its decisions on the basis of two written reports from the teams. One report goes both to NCATE and to the institution and is supposed to be a more or less objective description and not an evaluation of the school. In Carleton's case, this report was strongly favorable. The second report, the existence of which most schools are unaware, is secret, goes only to NCATE, and is the team's evaluation of the school. NCATE's present appraisal committee, having too little time to review each case itself, has been split into a number of regional divisions. Carleton was in the domain of a western division, which also has too much work to do, and therefore assigned Carleton to a subcommittee. Thus the evaluation of Carleton was made by a subcommittee, no member of which may ever have seen the institution, of one of the divisions of the committee within NCATE charged with the responsibility of accepting or rejecting institutions.

The Committee cited five reasons for rejecting Carleton: 1) the institution-wide committee on teacher education that grew out of the faculty seminars was not continuously in operation overseeing the program; 2) no formal procedures were in operation for screening out of the program those students, if any, who had emotional or personality problems; 3) the faculty teaching Education courses did not itself have enough work in Education to handle the "scope" of Carleton's program (the scope was limited to secondary teachers, of which Carleton turned out about 25 a year); 4) the Education courses, as taught by Carleton's regular faculty, were too theoretical, not practical enough; and 5) not enough time was spent in "professional laboratory experiences."

Our scene shifts to Crossroads State Teachers College. It has been in operation about half the time of Carleton, beginning as a normal school in 1909 and offering its first baccalaureate degree in 1928. At the time of its NCATE visit, it had a faculty of 57 persons and an enrollment of 751. Two members of the faculty had the Ph.D. degree and five more held the Ed.D. degree. Most of the faculty degrees at all levels were from second-rank institutions, or lower. The teaching load was 15 hours. For admission, the school required students to be in the upper half of their high school graduating class — which, in this particular state, is meaningless — or to reach a score of 50 on the Armed Forces Institute Tests of General Educational Development.

About a quarter of the students at Crossroads were enrolled in the home economics or industrial arts programs. Those in programs for high school teachers of academic subjects took, as stipulated in Crossroads' report to NCATE, 43 semester hours in professional education. Most of them took between 85 and 95 hours in academic work. Crossroads also trained many elementary teachers, who took an average of 54 hours of Education courses and 69 of academic.

It was impossible at Crossroads, and still is, for students to major in several of the academic subjects taught in high schools. One could not major in history, for example, but had to do so in "Social Studies." Here the minimum program consisted of 24 hours of work: a year's course in world history, one in economics, one in U.S. history, and a semester each of geography and sociology. Most "Social Studies" majors took more work than 24 hours in this highly amorphous area, but this was all that was required for Crossroads' degree and NCATE's approval. Nor could one major in *a* science, only in science, which course also consisted of 24 hours as a minimum: one year each of biology, inorganic chemistry, organic chemistry, and physics. Although Crossroads offered a major in languages, almost nobody took it; the great majority of its graduates, both secondary and elementary teachers, had taken no work whatever in a foreign language.

Although 80% of the regular faculty had taken their highest degree in Education, and often their undergraduate degree as well, many were teaching the academic courses. "It is doubtful," as Crossroads with disarming frankness says of itself in an official report to its regional accrediting association, "if there are any real [sic] unique or distinctive features of the curricula." Students at Crossroads, being a homogeneous group all following a teacher preparatory program, were deprived of the bracing and invaluable experience of associating and competing with students preparing for a variety of graduate and professional schools and for many occupations.

The library at Crossroads in the year of NCATE's visit reported holdings in the areas of the school's major programs. It reported, for example, 1,273 titles in literature, 1,044 in science and mathematics combined, 4,461 in social sciences (including not only the field of Education as such, but a multitude of other fields subsumed under this heading in the Dewey Decimal System), and 120 titles in languages. That year it spent a total of $5,500 on new and replacement books. The library undertook most acquisitions on its own, but was able to buy within that budget everything the faculty asked for! A visit to Crossroads' library quickly indicates that a plethora of dead-wood is badly in need of pruning, that the holdings run substantially to anthologies and similar collections, that its titles in major authors are either non-existent or extremely thin, and that many of its books have not been checked out for years.

Other items: Crossroads' physical plant occupies about 18 acres; the school has no endowment, few esthetic assets, and is obviously ill-supported by the state. Its bookstore, when I visited it, was the size of a tobacco shop, with *no* hard-cover books for sale except textbooks, only a handful of paperbacks, no out-of-town newspapers, no "little" magazines, no academic quarterlies.

NCATE's Committee on Visitation and Appraisal gave full accreditation to all of the undergraduate programs, both elementary and secondary, of Crossroads State Teachers College. It also gave provisional accreditation for a *graduate* program in Education that Crossroads had been running for some years and hoped to expand.

All this, I emphasize, is not to declare that Crossroads, *which is no different from many other institutions on NCATE's accredited list,* does not deserve its accredited status; nor is it to cast any aspersions on Crossroads' faculty; nor do I offer any judgments about the quality of teachers turned out by Crossroads. Perhaps the school does the best it can with what it has. "I simply record the facts," as Mencken used to say, "in a sad, scientific spirit."

NCATE's performance at Carleton and Crossroads would seem to throw considerable light on the major issues outlined earlier. The basic question with which we began — will NCATE in fact improve the education of American teachers? — becomes sharper. And other questions press for answers: If all teachers in the United States were prepared in NCATE-accredited programs (over 70% already are), would there be any discernible improvement in public schools, which is of course the point of it all? Will NCATE respond to the wide-spread criticism of its standards and procedures and transform itself into a less coercive, more representative organization? If no important changes are made, will first-line liberal arts colleges as well as others of academic distinction be driven out of the business of preparing teachers? The answers to these and many related questions are in the not-too-distant future; and they will have a lot to do with the quality of public education.

The foregoing presents the Carleton case up to spring of 1961, when, in view of NCATE's denial of accreditation to Carleton, the College, following the strong urging of its Dean, decided to make itself a test case and to appeal the decision. This meant the preparation of an answer to the alleged short-comings of the program and a return visit to the campus of one or more members of the original NCATE visiting team. It also meant the presentation by Carleton of a defense and general exposition of its teacher-training program before NCATE's Appeals Board in April, 1962. Subsequently, this Board reported to NCATE itself and made a recommendation. On the basis of the Appeals Board report, NCATE in May, 1962 reversed its original decision and awarded full accredita-tion to Carleton, effective as of the date of NCATE's original evaluation. Thus Carleton now enjoys equal status with Cross-roads State Teachers College.

What this reversal signifies about NCATE's future work is not yet clear. It may suggest a more favorable attitude than in the immediate past toward teacher preparatory programs of the Carleton type; it may also suggest the possibility of NCATE's responding to some of the criticisms that have be-come increasingly evident against it — which it has shown little sign of doing up to now. Carleton's decision to use itself as a test case rather than accept NCATE's rejection may have set a most valuable precedent, and other liberal arts colleges, most of which have not yet applied for NCATE accreditation, may find themselves very much in Carleton's debt when they choose to make such application or are forced by circumstances to make it. Still, the fundamental issues of whether special accreditation for teacher-training programs is a useful instrument for improving public education, and, if so, what kind of agency ought to carry it out, how much power the agency should have, and what standards it should use in judging schools — these issues abide. As does the problem of bringing some balance, some substantial academic participation, into the exercise of power in teacher education.

CHAPTER VIII

The Future — Past or Prologue?

People are always telling me to make PRACTICAL suggestions. You might as well tell me to suggest what people are doing already, or at least to suggest improvements which may be incorporated with the wrong methods at present in use.

— Rousseau, in his preface to *Émile*

Speculations

BY NOW it must be clear that the education of American teachers is trapped in a series of circular problems that makes reforms extremely difficult. A weak faculty operates a weak program that attracts weak students. Strong students are deterred by these weaknesses from entering the field and ultimately forcing improvements. Graduate programs in Education put large numbers of incompetent persons through a variety of incompetent degrees, and these persons then become school administrators who hire teachers, or they become professors of Education who train teachers and who run other graduate programs to train other administrators and professors of Education. Standards in Education are set and enforced by an Establishment of centripetal powers which has been alienated from the learned and academic community and whose alienation feeds upon itself, thus reinforcing the exclusionism of the Establishment and preventing the exercise of the academic influence that could modify it. How one breaks out of, or into, these circles is the fundamental issue in today's teacher education.

The point of greatest potential leverage in the reform of teacher education is the one most often ignored. That is the local school districts, which hire the graduates of the training programs and establish the conditions of their work. Through their hiring policies, local school boards could, if they chose, exert more pressure on the training programs than any other single agency. Through the simple device of refusing to hire ill-educated teachers and administrators, they could eventually effect a vast transformation in the Education field. But of course the time is a number of light-years away when school systems in any numbers will adopt, or will be in a position to adopt, such a policy. Like an elephant chained to a peg in the ground, school systems dance to the tune of the educationist, while they could, if they but knew their strength, break away with ease to freedom.

School systems generally delegate to administrators the basic responsibility for hiring teachers and in doing so often abdicate their responsibility for defining the qualifications they want their teachers to have. The administrator in effect becomes the hiring party and the one who decides what the qualifications will be. As a graduate himself of the professional Education system, he is not likely to have unorthodox ideas about how teachers should be educated or about where to go to find them. The result is that the most potent source of pressure for reforming Education, the employer, is neutralized.

Employers do establish some conditions, particularly the matter of salary, that indirectly affect the training programs for teachers. Indeed, most educationists regard the salaries paid teachers by school boards as the principal obstacle to improvement in teacher training. Although teachers' salaries are a large and complex subject, not to be dealt with very satisfactorily in a brief space, any analysis of teacher education must recognize some connections between teachers' salaries and prestige and teacher education; for it is obviously true that the conditions of work in a given field affect the kinds of people attracted to the field and the kind of training they get.

The chief difficulty with most discussions of teachers' salaries by teachers themselves and by educationists is the underlying and, I believe, untenable assumption upon which they are based. Which is that salaries for today's teachers should compare favorably with those in other professional and semi-professional fields. However much one might like to see public school teaching truly a profession, and however much educational associations may assert that it is a profession and demand all the accompanying rights and privileges, the facts of the matter still seem otherwise. Although there are no precise criteria defining when a field is or is not a profession, the condition of the teaching field today does not even measure up to such gross standards of professionalism as these: exercising significant control over the caliber of people entering the training programs, establishing standards for admission to professional associations, policing its own ranks and guarding against abuses, administering qualifying examinations to graduates of approved programs before admission to the field or creating some other means for insuring minimum competency on the part of its members. When one looks closely at the Education field, at the caliber of the faculty and students and training programs, and when one looks at the conditions under which public school teachers actually teach — with the myriad of incredibly trivial and demeaning tasks that administrators create and inflict upon their staff, anything from punching time clocks to collecting the milk money to taking tickets at school football games — it becomes rather obvious that whatever else teaching is, it is not yet a profession. Perhaps it is gradually becoming one and may one day achieve that happy status, but it is not there yet.

Educationists, not to say teachers themselves, further assume that salaries for a nine-month working year, with many vacations, should compare favorably with salaries for the 12-month working year that is standard in practically all other fields. Now teaching, done well and conscientiously, is very hard work which makes large demands on one's energies, and the summer and other vacations bring the teacher a most welcome rest. But teaching done badly and perfunctorily, as it very often is, makes for an extremely leisurely life all year long, which, in working hours a year, might not come to half that of most occupations. In either case, there is no readily apparent reason, though it may be heresy to say so, why people whose "productivity" covers three-quarters of a year should receive a salary comparable to that received by people who "produce" all year long. If some teachers work a 50-hour week and more for their nine months, so do many other people for their 12 months in those fields where educationists are wont to compare salaries; if the pressures of teaching 30 students in four or five classes a day become heavy for the nine months, so do the pressures in other fields for the 12 months, where they may be very heavy indeed; if teachers need lengthy vacations in which to do advanced work and to keep up with their subjects, so do people in other fields, where they usually are expected to keep up without extended vacations and as a normal part of their work.

All of which is not to say that teachers are well paid, but merely that discussions of salary ought to be carried on in recognition of the job teachers actually do, the training required, and the caliber of people who actually fill the job. To compare, as the NEA and other agencies of the Establishment are continuously doing, the salaries of teachers with those of accountants, engineers, doctors, and people in similar fields is hardly realistic. These fields are able to attract people from the upper academic ranks, who should not, in fairness to either group, be compared with people from the lower. If comparisons must be made, one might with more justice look at such fields as nursing, social work, or perhaps forestry or pharmacy and various kinds of government employment. The NEA reported, for example, that the average salary of classroom teachers in the United States for 1961-1962 was $5,527. Although comparable data nation-wide are not available in most other fields (no other field studies the matter with the assiduity of the NEA), we can look at some typical instances of salaries in, say, nursing, which is perhaps one of the other fields that teachers might logically enter if they were not in teaching. The Department of Labor's "Occupational Wage Surveys" of particular cities are perhaps as reliable as anything for current salaries in various occupations. They reported, for example, that registered industrial nurses in Dayton, Ohio, in 1962 were earning $105 a week, which is $5,760 for a 12-month working year; in York, Pennsylvania, in 1961 they were earning $4,289 for a 12-month working year; in Des Moines, Iowa, $4,810; and in the San Francisco area, $5,408. Other comparisons: the average salary in 1959 of new librarians with a master's degree was $4,862; the average salary of social workers, a field that now requires two years of graduate work, in 1960 was $4,590 for women and $5,060 for men; chemists with a bachelor's degree started in private industry in 1960 at $5,880; occupational therapists with a bachelor's degree started in 1959 at something between $4,200 and $4,700. In public school teaching, the average salary of all elementary teachers in 1959-1960 was $4,835, and for all classroom teachers was $5,025; for the 1961-1962 school year, as mentioned, the average salary of all classroom teachers was $5,527, ranging from California's high of $7,325 (Alaska excepted, where the average was $7,650) to Mississippi's low of $3,675.[1]

Statistics about salaries in teaching and in other fields are even more difficult to deal with fairly than are most statistics. Comparisons of national averages are not very satisfactory,

[1] The NEA seems to have the only machinery for gathering up-to-date statistics on salaries in public schools. It publishes them in an annual compilation called "Rankings of the States," of which I have used the 1960 and 1962 editions, and in its "Research Bulletins" and numerous other publications. The "Occupational Wage Surveys" are conducted regularly in many cities by the Department of Labor, and reported in separate leaflets, of which I have used the four indicated, picked more or less at random; and I have used the massive compilation of the Department of Labor called *Occupational Outlook Handbook*, 1961 edition, which presents detailed information about current conditions in 650 different occupations.

for they lump together the infinite variety of communities, living standards, and other factors that affect conditions of work and salary. What is needed, if this kind of comparison for teachers is to continue as a means of agitation for higher salaries, is a systematic comparison of salaries by cities or labor areas, which would use some formula for equalizing such matters as the educational level required in the occupations being compared, the salary differences between beginning and experienced personnel, and the number of weeks or months actually worked during the year. If statistics of this kind were available for, say, 20 different occupations, including teaching, in several dozen representative areas around the country, it is highly probable, I believe, that teaching would be found a good distance from the bottom, and in the early years of work might well be near the top. Until such data are available, it will continue to be possible for any partisan to select and interpret statistics to "prove" about anything he wishes to prove concerning teachers' salaries and how they compare with those in other fields.

I am not suggesting that all teachers are adequately paid now. I am suggesting that they are not grossly underpaid in relation to their talent, their educational level, and the amount of time they devote to their job. For beginning teachers especially, in view of the salary they might command in other fields that they might enter if they were not in teaching, current salary levels seem decently competitive. The real trouble is at the top, where salaries are not competitive in most systems and where capable people find their greatest deterrent from entering or remaining in teaching. The lid should be taken completely off teachers' salaries, I believe, or substantially raised, so that the best people now in the classroom will remain there and so that better students can be attracted to the training programs. Certainly this should not mean higher salaries all around for today's teachers, a procedure naturally advocated by the Establishment, but one that, by rewarding alike the incompetent, the mediocre, and the excellent, would merely aggravate and perpetuate a poor salary system; instead, it should mean that the same incentive which exists in most occupations, especially in the professional areas, would exist in teaching: that the individual's talent and performance on the job would become the primary criteria in the determination of his salary. The educational world calls this unoriginal idea "merit" pay, or often applies a variety of euphemistic or pejorative terms to it. While school boards themselves generally favor paying teachers the way that most other people in our economy are paid, according to ability, teachers themselves and their professional associations are generally against it and go to great lengths to explain why such a system would not work.

One should recognize that paying teachers by their ability instead of on a kind of union scale does have complicating factors, having mostly to do with who is to do the judging and how. Teaching ability, so the argument goes, cannot be judged on the same basis as performance in other fields. The vehemence with which teachers attack the competence of their supervisors to judge their teaching is no compliment to graduate training programs in Education; there is much to be said for their position. Also it is true that no generally accepted method of making judgments about teaching ability has yet been formalized. But it is also true that such judgments are constantly and of necessity being made throughout our educational system at all levels, all the way from the individual school district's decision to hire one kindergarten teacher instead of another, to the department chairman's decision about how Professor X is performing with his doctoral students. Judgments about teaching ability are everywhere made, because they must be made. Also, they are supposed to be the heart of any teacher-training program: the *raison d'être* of teacher education, after all, is that we know how to select good future teachers, how to train them, and how to judge whether and when they have a sufficient ability in teaching to be graduated as teachers.

The criterion that common sense suggests as the best single basis of judging teachers and paying them is the progress that students make under them. But again, despite the fact that the assessment of student progress is universally used for *other* purposes in education, educationists find a thousand reasons why it cannot be invoked for the assessment of teaching. Granted that teaching ability cannot be judged solely by how well or poorly students do under a given teacher, and granted that this criterion is not as precise as one could wish, still it is the best and most precise one now available and is surely as reliable as are the means employed in other imprecise fields to determine advancement. It also avoids the teachers' fears about the capriciousness or incompetence of their administrators. And it is one of the major steps that teachers need to take before teaching can make any just claims to professionalism. The hardest and safest test of a teacher's quality, as Gilbert Highet observes in *The Art of Teaching,* is the pupils he produces; teachers are the first to take the credit for good results — as determined by the progress students have made under them — but the last to accept responsibility for poor results.

Until school boards face up to this whole matter and begin to pay their teachers, not according to a set schedule wherein the worst are paid as well as the best, but on the basis of individual performance, teaching will continue to be a field that fails to attract high-quality people and put them through demanding programs. Meanwhile, the agitation of professional groups for higher across-the-board pay might be regarded with some reservations. Certainly the more extreme demands which often claim that teachers' salaries should now be in the range of 12-15 thousand dollars a year for a nine- or ten-month year are not to be taken seriously; *all* teachers would first need to be immeasurably better than *most* teachers now are. The more restrained and authoritative demands of the Establishment, as set forth by the NEA, claim that an average teacher salary of $9,710 will be necessary by 1970 if we are to staff public schools with "highly trained professionals." This would represent an across-the-board raise of 75 per cent in seven years. No one can say how such a figure will compare in 1970 with salaries in other fields (which will undoubtedly continue to require 12 months of productive work, not nine) similar to teaching. But the chances are that other fields will not experience quite such a good fortune. If American teachers are to average $9,710 a year by 1970, they will probably be among the best-paid people in the country in relation to training, talent, and time spent on the job.

In brief, then, the local school boards are by far the greatest point of potential leverage in raising the level of teacher education, through their hiring and salary policies. Unfortunately, they have never exercised this power intelligently, and are unlikely to get together in the future on any plan to do so. Instead, they will probably continue to yield on these crucial matters to the Establishment.

A good speculative case could probably be made for giving local boards complete freedom in staffing their schools, as is the practice in the private schools of most states. If public schools did have such freedom, they would worry a good deal more than they now do about a prospective teacher's substantive qualifications and less about his formal qualifications; and they would worry a good deal more about developing a method for the regular assessment of their teachers' performance. They would have an enormously enlarged field, indeed all of society, in which to search for good teachers, and might well undertake their own on-the-job training programs. In private schools, which labor under a necessity not imposed on public schools — producing results or losing the customers — freedom in staffing has clearly been a major point in their success. One outstanding headmaster, with a strong affinity for the best of progressive education, typifies the experience of the better schools as he recalls the early efforts of private schoolmen to staff their classes with the best possible teachers to handle the "new education." They found that the

> . . . best and most successful teachers came neither from the teachers colleges (at that time called normal schools) nor the graduate schools of education, but from the liberal arts colleges. It was obvious that what was essential for our type of teaching was young men and young women who were vigorous, enthusiastic, intelligent personalities in their own right, who knew about life and living with others, who were keenly interested in children and anxious to help them, and who were well grounded in their subject and had great faith in its value to their pupils and in the world ahead of them. This we had not found as frequently among the graduates of the other two types of institutions.
>
> We had found that we could take promising products of the better liberal arts colleges and train them on the job, inadequately as we were equipped to do it, with better results in the end than we had had with graduates of the other two. . . . The results have been most gratifying. After almost twenty years I am more convinced than ever that the solution to the problem [of getting good teachers] lies along these lines.[2]

It will be objected that if school boards had this kind of freedom to choose their teachers, they would often hire them for reasons other than promise and ability and would often get extremely poor people. Many boards undoubtedly would. Community pressure might then come into play for improvement or perhaps a new school board. If the community failed to respond, as it often fails to respond now to poor teaching, then, as is consistent with our political principles, it presumably deserves the schools it has. On the other hand, many boards would be hiring *better* people than they now have, if for no

[2] Perry Dunlap Smith, "What and Who Educate Our Educators?" *Independent School Bulletin*, May, 1955, pp. 3-4.

other reason than the vast open market they would have in which to search. And many would get more involved in teacher training than they had ever been before. In view of the low level of teaching that many communities now get with fully certified and licensed teachers, and in view of the tenuous connections between the training that teachers are exposed to and the performance they turn in on the job, a free market for local boards in hiring teachers might on balance be a great gain for public education. Of course, no such thing is going to happen. In fact, the range of choice for school boards is going to get steadily narrower in the future, as we have seen. But it is perhaps useful to speculate about practices that could be an improvement over present ones, whether or not they can be put into effect under existing conditions.

Another such speculation, one that may have a bit more chance of being explored in Education, and that would do much to lead teaching toward the professionalism it so covets, involves some system of qualifying examinations whereby teachers, in order to be licensed, would demonstrate their mastery of the subject they propose to teach. Such a system could operate in a number of different ways, but the principle of *demonstrated mastery* would be paramount whatever the other details. In my view, and I believe in that of most academic and professional people, such a system would be one of the greatest steps that could be taken to advance the education of American teachers and thereby the quality of teaching in public schools. Also, a system of qualifying examinations could open up many new paths to the teaching license in addition to the single, rigid system that now prevails; it could become, that is, the primary requirement for new teachers rather than graduation from an approved school or exposure to some other kind of formal preparation, thus bringing some much needed variety and flexibility into the selection of teachers. Or the system could simply be superimposed on present practices and programs, with graduation from an approved program still mandatory. Either way, though the former would be by far the more preferable, qualifying examinations of real substance could effect great reforms in teacher education.

For experimental purposes such exams might be developed in only one or two academic subjects for secondary teachers and administered voluntarily on a restricted local or state, or even institutional, basis. Their later development might envision the covering of all high school teachers in all subjects, and elementary teachers as well as the movement grows toward specialization in the elementary school and away from the self-contained classroom. Ultimately, the examinations, developed and administered at whatever level — institutional, state, regional, or national (all are possibilities) — would presumably become obligatory for new teachers and, under appropriate circumstances, strongly advisable for those already certified. The exams might well be carried out in two steps, basic and advanced, each of which would yield its particular certificate to successful candidates. Possession of a basic certificate would be needed for regular employment as a public school teacher and would indicate to employers that the individual had demonstrated an adequate knowledge of his teaching field — something that employers assuredly cannot assume now on the basis of one's graduation from an accredited teacher-training program, or certification by the state. The advanced certificate, which might be compared to specialty boards in medicine, would be awarded to candidates who had demonstrated a much deeper knowlege and understanding of their teaching fields than holders of the basic certificate. Possession of the advanced certificate would say to employers that the individual had the greatest degree of mastery of his field that public education at this point in history could reasonably expect of its best teachers.

In whatever way the examinations were carried out, it would be crucial that their preparation be the combined effort of recognized scholars in the subjects involved, appointed perhaps by the learned and academic societies, and public school teachers and educationists. In all probability this would mean an emphasis on the essay and demonstration examination and a de-emphasis on the kind of standardized, machine-scored, multiple-choice examinations which already exist for teachers. Since this is an important point, let me expand it for a moment. The Educational Testing Service has prepared and administered a system of "National Teacher Examinations" each year since 1950. These consist of "Common Examinations" covering pedagogy and professional Education as well as such matters as general cultural development and "non-verbal" reasoning; and "Optional Examinations" covering a number of particular subjects such as English, Social Studies, Biology, etc. In method, these exams greatly resemble the run-of-the-mill standardized intelligence and achievement tests, and they are, to judge from the sample questions available, extremely elementary on the one hand and extremely vague on the other.[3]

---

[3] Almost all of the sample questions from ETS's informational brochures on the National Teacher Examinations seem to suffer either from obviousness or obtuseness. Consider, for example, the simplicity of such questions as these, the first one from the Common Examinations on professional Education, and the second from the Optional Examination for high school specialists in business education:

1. "The most valid argument against using schoolwork as punishment for misbehavior is that

    A. it is not so effective as physical punishment
    B. it may interfere with desirable extracurricular activities
    C. pupils who are disciplinary cases frequently do not need the extra schoolwork
    D. it may make the pupil regard all schoolwork as distasteful
    E. it may take so long to finish that the pupil will not connect it with his misbehavior"

2. "The most valid reason a bookkeeping teacher could have for requiring pupils to bring to the class bookkeeping forms and materials from local businesses is that

    A. students will learn what businesses are located in the community
    B. good public relations will be promoted between the school and the business community
    C. bookkeeping instruction will be kept current and practical
    D. the teacher's instructional procedures will be simplified
    E. these forms and materials will be more easily understood than illustrations in the textbook"

Or consider the grotesque ambiguity of such questions as the following, the first for high school teachers of "social studies," the second for high school teachers

Moreover, they suffer from the fatal handicap of being restricted to testing only what educationists tell ETS they are trying to do in their teacher-training programs. Thus, if what they do in these programs is weak, the exams by definition are the same. It turns out that the people who write the absurd questions of these examinations, including the questions in academic subjects, are mostly people nominated by the NEA

---

of English, and the third for high school teachers of art (an interesting and instructive experience is to be had by anyone who will ask these questions of a number of recognized scholars in the fields involved):

1. "A class in contemporary events finds that two accounts of the same event differ considerably. Which of the following is the best procedure for the teacher to follow?

    A. Tell the class which account to accept, giving the reasons for the decision.
    B. Ask the class to compare the two accounts and accept the details common to both.
    C. Explain that the class has no means of determining which account is most accurate.
    D. Start a discussion about how the reporter's point of view can influence his account.
    E. Suggest that the class find a third version and accept it in place of the other two."

2. "An eleventh grade teacher wishes to develop his students' understanding of the modern novel as a mirror of contemporary society. Which is the best procedure for him to follow?

    A. Select one representative novel which the whole group should study intensively and give brief talks on several other outstanding novels.
    B. Have the whole group study one representative novel intensively and then have each student read one novel of his choice.
    C. Have the whole group study three or four representative novels with the help of prepared study outlines which list specific questions.
    D. Select one representative novel for the whole group to read and then discuss it thoroughly.
    E. Have each student read several novels of his own choice and have informal class discussions based on these readings."

3. "In stimulating students to build mobiles, a teacher might most suitably suggest that they draw their inspiration from

    A. their own emotions
    B. movements in nature
    C. movements of human activity
    D. the rhythms of industry
    E. the rhythms of music"

We are told that the "correct" answers to these questions are "D" "E" and

department that covers the particular field in question, and who go to ETS for a period of three days to confer with one another and do the writing. ETS admits that no systematic data yet exist bearing on the efficacy of these examinations. It only says, not surprisingly, that it has confidence that it can test anything the educationist says he is doing in his teacher-training program. The final shortcoming of the National Teacher Examinations is that the "norms" for them, based on tests given at 31 colleges in 1957, most of them teachers colleges, are bound to be exceedingly low, meaning that a satisfactory score is easily obtained.

In short, the National Teacher Examinations as now constructed would be wholly unsatisfactory in the kind of qualifying examinations system I am discussing. This does not mean that an examination of the same type — standardized exams formulated nationally but administered locally and voluntarily — need be eliminated from consideration; but such exams would have to be much better than the present ones, and the possibility is strong that, if established scholars had the major voice in the preparation of qualifying exams, the emphasis would be on the essay-demonstration type.

The experience of some of our major cities is also relevant in this matter. Cities like New York, Chicago, Los Angeles, and San Francisco have had a mandatory system of screening examinations for new teachers for many years. Some of these systems are very complex, involving not only standardized written tests but interviews, assessment of college work, and many other factors. Yet, these cities are far from notable for

---

"B," whereas the most obvious thing about them, apart from the fact that they could not have been written by anyone who understood the subject, is that the only tenable answer is, "it depends." Yet this kind of typical ETS testing is endemic, wherein the student is forced to choose among prepackaged ambiguities none of which may represent *his* answer but which he must reason his way through to what he supposes the testers may have had in mind in asking the question. If a better instrument than this cannot be developed for examining prospective teachers, perhaps we should abandon the whole idea.

the excellence of their teaching, and they do not find it easy to support in any concrete way the usefulness of their complicated examination procedures. What they do find is that graduates from the teacher-training programs of institutions that enjoy the full accreditation of their regional associations and of the National Council for Accreditation of Teacher Education, and that may have an excellent general reputation, make a very wide range of scores on standardized tests in pedagogy and subject fields. This is merely another evidence of the fact that no common standards of any sort are now defined and met in teacher training. These cities can probably claim, therefore, with some justice that at least the examination system manages to screen out the flagrantly incompetent graduates of teacher education programs, even if it also screens out exceptionally able but unorthodox persons, and even if it fails to assure a real grasp of the teaching subject on the part of successful candidates.

The failure of present examination systems for teachers argues strongly against reliance upon standardized, multiple-choice tests and against the preparation of any examinations in subject matter by groups that do not include established scholars in the subjects being tested. Despite the negative attitude of the Education field, it is safe to say that the overwhelming majority of academicians and their professional associations would see far more virtue than vice in a carefully developed system of qualifying examinations for teachers, and would feel that the exams should be prepared by recognized men in the fields being tested, in collaboration with high school teachers and perhaps other parties. They would also feel, in all probability, that essay-demonstration exams, although expensive to administer, are still the only way to test a person's grasp of most academic disciplines, his ability to reason logically in the field, to organize, relate, synthesize, and give orderly expression to his thoughts. Although examination systems of all kinds tend to be controversial and to develop their particular vices, the bar exams in law and the national medical board exams in medicine, not to mention the specialty medical boards that come later, have the solid support of these professions. A good many medical educators think of the national medical boards, given to all students at the end of medical school, as one of the strongest influences for the maintenance of well-defined standards in medical education. (Whether the standards at any given point are adequate is another question.) And there are state boards, of course, in addition to the national. Teaching is perhaps the only field that claims professional status without having professional qualifying examinations of any kind at any level.

If educationists were willing to accept qualifying exams in principle, a series of experimental exams in subject matter could be developed in a relatively short time through the joint efforts of the major interests involved. They could be given at stipulated times and places each year, the same as other exams of the kind are. If given at the institutional level, they would presumably constitute the final step in the formal training program. Ultimately, if the exams became widely accepted by educationists and school boards, they could constitute a far more effective instrument than accreditation for maintaining standards in the individual institutions. The number of board-certified teachers turned out by an institution would become a far better index to the quality of its teacher-training program than any indexes now available or in prospect. Also, the prestige value of the basic and advanced certificates in school systems would be great. A school system without board-certified teachers would be a little like a hospital without board-certified surgeons or pathologists; the pressures for improvement would become irresistible.

There is much to be said for and against the preparation of such exams at the national level, as there is at any other level. They could be prepared by a national body, as are the ETS exams, thus representing a common national standard, but administered locally and voluntarily by states or school systems or preparing institutions. They could be done wholly at the state or regional level, with the necessarily different standards always involved in such a method. They could even be done — and this might possibly be the most feasible way of all — by the separate institutions. Each college or university could undertake to prepare and administer its own qualifying examinations to teachers before approving them to the state for certification; but in this case, strong safeguards against low standards and poor examinations would be essential, perhaps through supervision or review by outside bodies, and through having the standards well recognized and well publicized. It would be a great mistake to allow each individual school, in the name of institutional autonomy, to control qualifying examinations by itself, for we would then have insured the continuation of precisely what we now have in teacher education, only more of it.

In other words, well-made qualifying examinations for teachers could be developed and administered in a hundred different ways and combinations of ways. But the first and most important step is the acceptance by educationists of the principle itself, at least to the extent of supporting it actively on a trial basis. Without that support, teacher-training programs will continue to suffer from grossly inadequate controls, and the employers of teachers will continue to have no reliable means of assessing the subject-matter qualifications of their staff.

There could possibly be a second component to the exam system we are exploring, covering some kind of examination of the individual's ability to teach. If we raise the banner of *demonstrated ability* in teacher education, we are confronted with the simple fact that mastery of the subject field, however thorough and however well established through qualifying examinations, will not of itself make a teacher. Are not some means needed for the determination of the candidate's ability to teach? All experience to date indicates that teaching ability cannot be determined by written examination or by any other kind of formalized exam, and that it can be determined only hazardously in the usual kind of practice teaching now done in the training programs. This suggests that if teaching ability is to be made part of a qualifying examination system as such, it might have to take the form of an extended apprenticeship or internship organized and supervised by the individual school system, possibly in collaboration with the preparing institution. This would be expensive and complicated and quite possibly unnecessary. It ought to be the employer's responsibility, after all, to determine how well his teachers perform and to create whatever training programs he thinks necessary. He is in a far better position to make this determination than he is to determine his teachers' qualifications in subject matter. Granted, he might reasonably expect graduation from an accredited training program to indicate that the individual had at least been introduced to, and supervised to some undetermined extent in, actual teaching. From that point on, the responsibility ought to be his. Employers in other fields do not assume that graduation from an accredited program or passage of a subject-matter examination guarantees also the individual's capacity to *perform,* which is something that can only be tested on the job. Because the performance of graduates in any field cannot be assured in any other way, employers spend vast sums on extensive training programs for new personnel. Teaching seems to be the only field in which the preparing institutions and the state make bold to say to employers that the license to practice indicates not merely adequate preparation, but also that the individual will perform adequately. Still, there is no reason why a final basic license to teach could not follow an extended apprenticeship or internship, which would be begun at the time of the individual's passing of the basic qualifying examination in his subject, and no reason why it could not be an integral part of the exam system.

I believe that the more modest aim — revolutionary enough in itself! — of effecting an examination system that would enforce clear standards of subject-matter mastery in teaching would be as much as the most sanguine could hope for over the next quarter century. If such exams could open up many new paths to the teaching license, in addition to the usual one of formal college preparation, and open up a vast new source of potential teachers for the public schools, this would be quite enough of a transformation for Education to absorb for a while. But even if such exams were only superimposed on the present system of formal training in accredited establishments, this too would be a giant step forward in the education of American teachers.

Unfortunately, the chances for doing any of this are poor. All major forces at work in teacher education today are moving toward ever greater bureaucratization, greater rigidity, greater formal and prescribed preparation. A few states like West Virginia and Wisconsin and Florida are experimenting in small ways with certification by examination, and a few institutions like Bucknell and Emory and others are experimenting with examinations to take the place of some kinds of formal course work. But most of these experiments have relied on the National Teacher Examinations of the Educational Testing Service as one of the instruments of the program and so have limited severely the possible outcome of the program. Even if these experiments are gloriously successful, they have very little chance of widespread adoption. And there is no chance at all that I can see of a *mandatory* system of qualifying examinations being adopted generally in teacher education. Both educationists and teachers react unfavorably and sometimes violently to any proposal for teacher examinations. They do this, not only because they find it easy to persuade themselves that such exams could not work, but for at least three unacknowledged reasons: First, educationists instinctively oppose licensing teachers by such exams because it seems to denigrate formal preparation, the plain implication of the exams being that people can become good teachers without course work in Education and often without formal preparation in subject fields. As in any bureaucracy of such a size as professional Education, there are extremely large and powerful vested interests, economic and political, to be protected; and the interests are vested in Education and in preparation for teaching as a formalized study expressed mainly in courses. Second, teachers are unenthusiastic about qualifying exams for the same reason that any group faced with a major academic hurdle is. They fear the hurdle of the examinations which, it should be acknowledged, many present teachers could not pass. Third, both teachers and educationists, and many others on the fringes, see entrance by examination as a blow to the professional status they have been striving for. Without a recognized novitiate built upon a rather esoteric body of knowledge and technique, there is nothing, they feel, upon which to found a profession — whereas, in truth, stringent and well-recognized qualifying examinations could perhaps do more than anything else to make teaching truly a profession.

Actually, the fear that an exam system would sideline teacher education programs is hardly warranted. Whatever system of licensing prevails, the great majority of new teachers will undoubtedly continue for the indefinite future to come through organized programs in colleges and universities. An examination system would merely shift the emphasis for admission to teaching from stipulated preparatory programs to demonstrated ability, would afford a possible means of making teaching an open instead of a closed field, and would exert substantial pressure on the formal programs in the direction of high academic standards. Thus it is not hard to understand the opposition of the educationists to a qualifying exam system. The established interests of the field itself, combined with the fears of the teachers themselves, are quite enough to block even the exploration of any such system. To the educationist, "upgrading" teacher education will continue to consist of shuffling and reshuffling the same old blocks of time in the college training programs, examining and re-examining curricula, appointing study commissions, tinkering now and then with state certification requirements, and "re-thinking" admission and retention practices. The one device that could test the efficacy of all these large and small permutations, by testing the people coming out of the programs, will in all probability remain in ill repute.

Recommendations

All that being so, let us turn our attention away from speculative things and toward some of the concrete improvements that might, in fact, be made within the existing framework of teacher education today. Let us recognize that the training of teachers is going to be carried out for the indefinite future through schools and departments of Education, and that Education is going to continue to grow as a discrete field within higher education. Our best hope, therefore, is to effect some improvements in the present structure. Thus I offer the following 13 recommendations as steps that could and should be taken, all of which would not only preserve the basic structure of professional Education as it now exists but would strengthen it.

But first let me make clear once again that all of the strictures of this book are not alone for professional Education, nor do all the needed reforms rest with educationists. The academic departments must accept major responsibility both for the present state of teacher education and for effecting some improvements. Let it be said also that it is the academic departments that have created the educational environment in which the field of professional Education has thrived so mightily. After all, many of the failings of Education are merely aggravated copies of the failings of higher education — low standards, poor teaching, hucksterism, the proliferation of courses, empire-building. Perhaps it is unrealistic for anyone to expect Education to purge itself of sin without some similar activity by, and support from, the academic departments.

Academicians should also recognize that their own teaching is sometimes far from inspired, that it too often is little better than that of Education. The academic classes I visited, although consistently better than those in Education, were often dull and pedestrian performances. In the large institutions, graduate assistants, instead of "assisting" the senior faculty, are frequently full-fledged teachers of freshman and sophomore courses, and they are rarely competent for this job. They simply lack knowledge and experience. They are not yet qualified to lecture in higher education and are wont to employ to excess the same time-killing gadgetry of the Education course: the mushrooming, undirected "discussion," the panel discussion, student reports, field trips. Even the advanced courses in academic areas are much too often needlessly pedantic, dry, and unstimulating, especially for students who do not happen to be majoring in the field involved. Academicians, as everybody knows, are not paid for the quality of their teaching, but chiefly for the quantity of their published research — an evil as widely recognized in the groves of academe as it is ignored. Even so, they have an obligation to teach as well as they can; and they *can* teach, most of them, far better than they do. Although the liberal arts professor has certain teaching advantages over the Education professor, in native ability, in the natural viability of the material, and in the fact that he has students from many fields competing in his classes, he too often fails to make the most of these conditions. Education students consistently regard their academic work as superior to their professional courses, but that in itself should give little reassurance to the liberal arts professor who does less than his teaching best. One should not feel complimented if one's teaching is judged better than that which may represent the worst on the campus.

Apart from the teaching problem, attention should be given by the academic departments to the question of offering special upper-division courses for teachers somewhat different from those taken by regular majors. The standard of performance demanded should be just as high, probably higher, but the emphasis should be different, with attention given less to the minutia of specialization than to fundamental processes and principles of the discipline. Careful attention should also be given to the question of whether the total pattern laid out for the major provides for some of the particular needs of teachers. English teachers, for example, should get work, but usually do not, in advanced composition (not creative writing, journalism, or radio-TV courses), in advanced grammar, in the history of the language, and in the phonetic alphabet. History teachers need some work in historiography and the basic methods of the historian; they badly need to learn to think historically, and to get over their characteristic preoccupation with current events. And they need to be equipped by their history courses to combat the superficiality, not to say the boondoggling, of the ubiquitous "social studies." If the academic departments are fortunate enough to secure additional time, which they should have, for building an adequate major for future teachers, let them set about formulating one with a clear and defensible rationale, and not merely use the time to tack a few more unrelated courses onto an already casual major.

Here are the 13 recommendations that, with the indicated improvements on the academic side, seem to me the most that can be hoped for in the near future in teacher education:

One: The remaining teachers colleges of the United States should be shut down, or converted to general purpose institutions, and those that have already been converted in name should move faster toward conversion in fact. There are now 55 four-year teachers colleges left in the nation that have some type of recognized accreditation, and something over a hundred such schools if unaccredited and two-year institutions are counted. The few advantages that may accrue to future teachers by being trained in a single-purpose establishment are so far outweighed by the disadvantages that the continuance of the teachers college can only be justified on other than academic grounds. There are a great many schools that have changed their name in recent years, removing "Teachers" or "Education" from it. But they have moved much too slowly in strengthening the faculty and in changing the nature of the programs. They remain in effect single-purpose schools, thus misleading students, parents, and the general public.

Let us look at just one highly representative institution that illustrates this important problem: The institution now known as Western Illinois University (Illinois also has a Southern, an Eastern, and a Northern University, all in the pattern of Western) began life in 1899 as a state normal school with one- and two-year training programs for elementary teachers. By 1916 it had begun to move into the training of high school teachers and that year was authorized to give the Bachelor of Science in Education degree, awarding 10 of them by 1920. In 1921 its name was changed to Western Illinois State Teachers College, with three divisions: the Teachers College, which had training programs of one, two, or four years for teachers; the Academy, which was a four-year high school that also served as a demonstration school; and the Elementary School, which served as a demonstration school. It had no admission requirements and had a faculty of 38 persons, including 2 Ph.D.'s and 13 persons who had the master's degree. In 1947 the word "Teachers" was dropped from the name of the school, making it Western Illinois State College and implying that it was a liberal arts or general purpose institution. However, it remained a single-purpose school, graduating almost all of its students as teachers. It still had no admission requirements beyond graduation from high school, had a faculty of 94, at least 70 per cent of whom were in the field of professional Education, many teaching the academic subjects. In 1957 its name was changed once again, this time to Western Illinois University. Although practically all its graduates in 1957 were teachers, the institution was divided into a School of Education, a School of Arts and Sciences, and a School of Graduate Studies; its faculty had grown to 119, and was still 70 per cent educationist. And the school still staffed many of its academic courses with educationists; the English Department, for example, consisted of 12 persons: 5 had the Ph.D. degree (2 with their bachelor's degree in Education), 3 had the Ed.D. degree, and 4 had the master's degree (2 from Teachers College). In short, at least half the English Department was made up of educationists, which was the pattern in other academic departments. The school still had no admission requirements to speak of and was governed by the Teachers College Board of Illinois, as it still is today. Today educationists still constitute about 65 per cent of the faculty of Western Illinois University and still teach many of the academic courses. Admissions procedures still allow any high school graduate to enter. In 1960-1961 the school graduated 470 persons at the bachelor's level, 400 of whom are now certified to teach in Illinois; it graduated 115 persons at the master's level, all of them with the Master of Science in Education degree. In a word, the "University" remains a teachers college.

The cure for this problem is plain enough. Either the states should take seriously the need to train teachers in the atmosphere of a liberal and general-purpose institution, and effect a genuine transformation in the faculty and programs of its teachers colleges to achieve this, or let these schools remain in name what they still are in function. The former course is by far the more preferable.

Two: The regular four-year undergraduate program should

remain the standard preparation for new teachers. The fifth-year programs should by all means be continued, especially the Master of Arts in Teaching programs, and encouraged, but the accelerating movement toward making five years of preparation mandatory for all new teachers is ill advised. If successful, this movement will inflict an enormous and unnecessary burden on graduate schools; it will remove whatever incentives now exist for tightening up the undergraduate programs in teacher education; and it will aggravate a number of the vices presently found in the undergraduate programs. Moreover, the fifth-year programs are frequently overrated, involving nothing more than the piling up of further Education courses with two or three academic ones that might well be at the undergraduate level. In view of the rapid increase of knowledge in many areas, and the gradual academic improvement of public education curricula, a fifth year of preparation may ultimately be needed, but it is not needed now. What is needed now is a tough-minded attack on the waste and weaknesses of the standard undergraduate program in teacher education, where there is sufficient time, especially if future teachers could arrive at college with better high school preparation, for the adequate education of beginning teachers.

Three: Serious academic participation should be secured throughout teacher education. I would emphasize the "serious" and the "throughout." Too often the so-called "institution-wide" approach to teacher education becomes mere window dressing, and too often the academic representation on policy-making bodies is perfunctory and thin. The idea that the education of teachers is an enterprise in which the whole college or university has a vital stake has become one of the clichés of contemporary teacher education. That does not make the idea less valid, but it often lures schools into thinking they have done something when they have appointed an "all-institution committee on teacher education." Academic representation can take many forms, and there is no reason to think that one is better than another. It all depends on the particular institution. What is important — what is indispensable for the education of teachers — is that whatever form the participation of the liberal arts departments may take in a given school, the academic members involved must be willing to devote time and energy to the task, must have substantial, if not majority, representation on the committee or other body, and the committee itself must have substantial power to establish and enforce policy in every phase of the teacher education program. If the representation on the committee is one academic to three or four educationists, if the body meets two or three times a year for "advisory" purposes, if its mandate covers only a few hortatory or inconsequential matters, and if the academicians are bored, bewildered, or uninterested — the teacher education program would be better off without the "all-university" approach. But if genuine institution-wide participation could actually be effected in most schools, it would be one of the greatest gains possible for teacher education. I would also emphasize that the same kind of participation should prevail throughout the *graduate* degree programs in Education, where the ultimate effects of academic representation might possibly be even greater than with the undergraduate teacher-training programs.

Serious academic participation of other kinds, especially in the professional Education courses, is equally important. Joint faculty appointments, for example (the appointees teaching both in Education and in an academic department), serve not only the vital function of keeping the lines of communication open between the Education and academic divisions of the institution, but can be a great impetus to the improvement of the Education courses. Once again, there are as many dangers as virtues. To have much chance of success, joint appointments require highly exceptional persons, who must be acceptable both to the Education division and to the academic departments, and who must combine scholarship in their fields with a knowledge of and an active interest in public education. Because such people are not plentiful, joint appointments, like all-institution committees, are often window dressing. The individual is not fully accepted by either his Education or his academic colleagues, and much too often is a second- or third-rate academic. In a good many of the joint appointments now in effect, a double standard prevails. The man's teaching, his scholarship, and his qualifications for promotion are judged on a different and a lower standard from that of his academic associates. Perhaps first-class joint appointments are still a contradiction in terms, but some have been made and have had a discernible effect on the teacher-training program. One can only hope that the quality of such appointments will be kept high, in which case they are to be strongly recommended.

Four: Grade point averages for admission to, and retention in, the teacher education program should be substantially raised. Although grade averages are very fallible yardsticks and undoubtedly unjust on occasion, they are still the best instrument available for judging the potential of large numbers of students. The best way to predict what groups of students will do academically in the future is to look at what they have done in the past. It seems entirely reasonable, considering the fact that students in teacher education programs are consistently found among the lower academic ranks, to expect that the training programs would be markedly improved if the students themselves were improved. In the state colleges and other institutions that have low or non-existent admission standards, admission to the Education programs might well be restricted to students who have at least a "B" average in their academic work, and retention in the programs might be contingent upon their maintaining the same average. Because grades awarded in Education courses are often unduly high, they should not be regarded in the same light, for purposes of retaining students in the program, as those in academic courses. Schools that admit virtually anyone, but who claim to practice "selective retention" in teacher education by requiring a "C" average or slightly better, are not likely to be turning out high-caliber teachers. Such schools inevitably gear their work in all courses lower than schools with high admission standards, and a "C" average in them is not an impressive requirement for future teachers. For first-class institutions with rigorous entrance requirements and demanding courses for all students, a "C" average has a different meaning and is reasonable enough for admission to the teacher-training program. Whatever letter grade may be appropriate at a given school, which can only be decided on the basis of individual institutions, the aim in teacher training in selecting and retaining students should be substantially higher than it is now. Public schools need not lose those potential teachers who develop late in or out of college or who cannot be admitted for whatever reason to the regular undergraduate training programs; such persons could be licensed to teach, if educationists are sufficiently concerned, through a system of qualifying examinations such as that discussed earlier.

As for the other qualifications, apart from the academic record, that future teachers ought to have, educationists make much of the importance of emotional stability and social adjustment, and much of the importance of screening out of teacher-training programs the psychologically and emotionally unfit. It is very doubtful if this screening can be done by any kind of admissions apparatus, except for catching the obvious misfits, and it is possible, judging from the screening procedures I have seen in operation, that a number of potentially excellent teachers are eliminated from the programs because of the obtuse judgments of those who profess to be screening out incompetents. Nor is it likely that the admissions process can do much about students who have no real desire to teach, who regard it as a second or third choice of ways to make a living, or those who wish to go through the program for obscure reasons. More rigorous grade requirements will catch a good many such people. For the others, one can only wish that they might ponder the hard-headed honesty with which Henry Thoreau once regarded his own teaching experience: "I have thoroughly tried school-keeping, but as I did not teach for the good of my fellow-man, but simply for a livelihood, this was a failure." No system of admissions is going to be without flaws, but that which is based primarily on grades or other evidence of academic ability is the best one now available. Many of its flaws could be neutralized by a less sentimental, less missionary attitude on the part of educationists about students who have been admitted to the program but who are found unable to do satisfactory work. The practice now is to pass such students along anyhow; rarely are any but the most clearly incompetent eliminated once they have been admitted to the program. Retention standards in teacher education ought to be as rigorously enforced as admission standards, and both should be substantially higher than they now are.

Five: Undergraduate majors in Education should be eliminated, and all teachers, including elementary teachers and special school personnel, should be required to major in an academic subject. For secondary teachers, a major of at least 48 semester hours should be required. In a standard 120-semester hour program, this would leave 54 hours for general education outside the major field, and 18 hours for professional Education. For elementary teachers a major of at least 36 semester hours should be required. This would leave 60 semester hours for general education and 24 for professional Education. These majors are far from ideal, but are probably the most that, considering the realities of the Education field, can be hoped for now. If they are well planned by the academic departments and include work that teachers of the subject especially need, and if high standards of performance are maintained, such majors should turn out teachers with a reasonable beginning competence. For both the elementary and secondary teacher, the amount of general education in the above scheme is not far below what they get now in the average program. I would prefer to see it reduced even further for secondary teachers and the time added to the major so that future teachers might spend, say, half of their four years, 60 semester hours, in their teaching subject. If it is objected that this means a shallow general education for the teacher, I answer that his general education is rather shallow as it is and would not be much more so under the above plan, but that the time saved for the major *would* make a significant difference in the teacher's preparation. Depth in the teaching field is always to be preferred, I believe, to a broadened general education that is bound to be superficial and that at best can cover only a fraction of the fields of human knowledge. Better high school preparation would also improve the teacher's general education, permitting him a deeper major in college. Of course, a 60-hour major in one college may not be the equal of a 30-hour major in another, but all things educational must still be measured out in credits and units and hours, at least until we have the kind of qualifying examinations discussed earlier wherein a qualitative rather than a quantitative standard could be defined.

If it is objected that an elementary teacher needs to be a "generalist," I answer that under this proposal she is still getting almost as much general education as she now gets. What she loses is the excessive and redundant work in professional Education, which is frankly aimed at producing technicians instead of educated persons. An elementary teacher is entitled as a human being to at least as good an education as the average undergraduate gets, for she has a life of her own to live in addition to teaching. She needs the intellectual experience of working in an academic field to at least the depth of a weak major; and she also needs to demonstrate to her supervisors in Education her capacity to compete successfully with advanced students in academic fields. Finally, she will be better equipped

with an academic instead of an Education major to participate in the growing movement toward specialization in the
elementary school and away from the self-contained classroom.

Six: The time devoted in teacher-training programs to professional Education should be restricted to state requirements.
This would mean a national average of 18 semester hours in
Education for secondary teachers and 24 for elementary
teachers. As I have amply indicated, I believe these requirements are still too high, but there is not much chance of having
them reduced. The least the training programs could do would
be to avoid exceeding them, as they almost always do now.
The actual national average for elementary teachers, as detailed in Chapter V, is 49 semester hours in pedagogy, more
than twice the state requirement; it is 55 semester hours at
teachers colleges and single-purpose institutions, which still
turn out the majority of elementary teachers. For secondary
teachers, the average is 27 semester hours, and in the single-
purpose institutions is 34. The average state requirement provides more than adequate room for work in those areas thought
by educationists to be essential: for the secondary teacher it
could provide, for example, a course in educational psychology
(which ought to be built on a course in general psychology on
the liberal arts side), a course in the history and philosophy of
education, one in methods, and a full 9 semester hours for
practice teaching. For the elementary teacher, it could provide
6 hours for educational psychology, 6 for methods, 3 for history
and philosophy, and 9 for practice teaching. If these courses
were what they should be, they would constitute more than
ample professional preparation.

Seven: Education courses that are derived directly from academic disciplines — such as those in educational psychology
and in the history and philosophy of education — should be
taught only by persons fully qualified to teach in the appropriate academic department of the same institutions. One should
frankly recognize that this common-sense recommendation

would mean that 90 per cent of the people now teaching such courses would cease to teach them, and so is a bit utopian. But it is at the least a goal toward which professional Education ought to be moving with all deliberate speed. There can be little doubt that courses in educational psychology *not* taught by trained psychologists, or in the history of education not taught by historians, or in the philosophy of education (if such a thing exists) not taught by philosophers, do more harm than good, and in the process steal time that might be used for better purposes. If future teachers cannot be guided in these subjects by competent scholars, they would be better off with no formal work in them at all. I know that it will be a long time before anything significant is done about this problem by educationists — who now teach these courses — but perhaps the academic departments and other agencies can speed the process.

Eight: Conversely, persons whose graduate work has been in professional Education, and who have no recognized qualifications in an academic discipline, should not be allowed to teach academic courses. As we have seen, educationists are frequently found teaching academic courses in teachers colleges and other institutions. This practice can do nothing but harm to future teachers. Academic courses that cannot be staffed with trained persons should be eliminated from the curriculum.

Nine: If competent faculty cannot be secured to teach courses in methods — and most such courses are incompetently taught now — this work should be incorporated into the practice teaching program and formal courses in the subject eliminated. Methods courses are the despair of many an Education student and many a teacher-training program. Subject-matter scholars, who have the deepest understanding of a discipline, usually have no public school teaching experience, have not thought much about the problem of methods at the lower level and have not much interest in the matter; educationists, who may have done some public school teaching at one time, do not have an adequate training in or understanding of the discipline involved. This dilemma suggests that methods work might best be done on the job, as an organized part of the practice teaching program or of the first year of full-time teaching. Failing this, it might be continued as course work if exceptionally able public school teachers could be found to teach it, perhaps with occasional assistance from the academic departments. If methods courses are to continue to be taught by the kinds of people who now teach them, and this is probable, these people at the very least should be required to do two things: 1) do a full semester of public school teaching every three or four years, and 2) regularly *demonstrate* with public school classes the teaching principles and procedures they now only discuss in the sanctuary of the college course; methods courses might then be a bit less vacuous and vague.

Ten: At the graduate level in professional Education, there should be a drastic reduction in the number of specialties and sub-specialties. All specialties that pretend to treat of some limited aspect of such fields as educational administration or psychology or history should be eliminated. There is no defense for doctoral programs in, for example, Elementary School Administration, Curriculum Construction, Human Relations, Audio-Visual Aids, Educational Sociology, Recreation, or many others. There is much to be gained and nothing whatever to be lost by the reduction of graduate Education to a very few specialties; graduates might then be turned out who have the basic equipment to deal themselves with the trivia that is the inescapable part of most educational jobs. If graduate work in Education were available in, say, five specialties — Administration, History of Education, Philosophy of Education, Psychology, and perhaps Comparative Education — it could still encompass all work of any consequence now done in all the graduate programs and at the same time eliminate countless abuses.

Eleven: At least two-thirds of the work for *all* graduate degrees in Education (the Master of Arts in Teaching degree excepted, where it might be about half) should be done in the liberal arts areas. For master's degree candidates this means about 20 semester hours of work in academic subjects and 10 in Education; for doctoral candidates about 60 hours in the liberal arts departments and 30 in Education. Because the greatest deficiencies of all in Education are found at the graduate level, it is here that the greatest changes are needed. This recommended ratio of Education-to-academic courses recovers something of a sane balance, but it is not ideal; it is only an improvement upon the present situation. Graduate Education is desperately in need of a thorough-going overhaul from top to bottom but is not going to get it. The most anyone can hope for is the eventual recognition by educationists of the primacy of the liberal arts in the preparation of people to fill all the jobs now filled by holders of graduate degrees in Education.

Twelve: Dissertation and foreign language requirements should be greatly strengthened in graduate Education. Dissertations are not done most of the time for the Ed.D. degree — a degree that probably should be abolished altogether but that will no doubt continue to grow faster than ever in the future — and very often not for the Ph.D. Those that are done are wretched enough. The only possible answer here, which was covered in recommendation three above, is the substantial participation of the academic faculty on the advisory, reading, and examination committees for the dissertations. Also, control over the graduate degrees, especially the doctorate, should not be lodged with the school of Education but with the graduate school of arts and sciences or its equivalent. Whether with the Ed.D. or the Ph.D., a dissertation should become a standard requirement, as it is in other doctoral programs. If such obvious things as these are not done, there is no reason for anyone to expect improvement in graduate Education or in the dissertations. Likewise, there should be standard foreign language requirements for all doctoral degrees in Education, though I would not want to defend the traditional two languages of the Ph.D. in the way now done, perfunctorily and uselessly. Here the Education field could teach the liberal arts departments a lesson, by requiring real mastery of one foreign language in the doctoral programs, and possibly in the master's programs. Instead, Education has eliminated all languages (including English, I am tempted to say), thereby ensuring not only the prevalence of monolingual educationists but the tragic neglect of foreign languages in teacher-training programs and in public education.

Thirteen: Selection and admission procedures for graduate study in Education should be toughened. *How* this can be done depends on each individual institution, for it is probably useless for anyone to recommend certain grade point averages or other arbitrary qualifications at this level. Whether the determination is made by academic record, interview, observation, demonstration, scores on standardized tests like the Graduate Record Exam or the Miller Analogies Test, or a combination of factors, the point is that the caliber of person accepted by the graduate schools of Education and turned out with degrees must be markedly improved if many of the other improvements we have discussed are ever going to be made in professional Education. Without the recruitment in the graduate programs of persons of greater talent and native ability than are now found there, the limits to which other long-range reforms can be carried in Education will quickly be reached.

What, then, are the prospects for any or all of these recommendations and speculations? Hopeless for some, not good for others, fair for a number. Some improvements in teacher education will be made gradually over the coming years, for there are many forces both inside and outside the Education world working in this direction. The curriculum reform activities of outstanding academicians in the basic subjects of the high school will ultimately have an effect on the preparation of high school teachers, as will the re-training institutes for teachers sponsored by the National Science Foundation and other bodies. The futility of continuing to turn out teachers who must immediately be re-trained in order to handle the improved curricula of the high schools will eventually be realized by those who run the teacher-training programs. Many educationists have shown a willingness in recent years to involve the academic departments in teacher education and to move toward strengthening the admissions procedures of these programs. Pressures will continue to come from many quarters for increasing the liberal-arts content of the training programs, and the field will have to respond to these pressures. There will be, that is, a continuing meliorism evident in teacher education which, ultimately, may put the Education field, and therefore the public schools, into substantially better shape than they are in now.

Whether we can afford this kind of gradualism at this point in our history, and whether we can afford to ignore the more basic changes for which the need is urgent now, are unanswerable questions. We may well *have* to afford these indulgences, for professional Education may not be able to tolerate for a considerable time the really fundamental reforms. The political and economic realities of the field may continue to dictate a future built upon the past. Instead of qualifying examinations for teachers, there may be an ever-greater emphasis on formal preparation measured out in courses and years of study; instead of an "open" occupation, teaching may move more and more toward the exclusionist ideal of the National Council for the Accreditation of Teacher Education; instead of working toward a true professionalism, expressed in mastery of the liberal disciplines, the Education field may put its full force behind a manufactured professionalism, expressed in the completion of a given number of Education courses; instead of making the most of our educational resources and rendering out the fat from the standard four-year preparatory program, Education may move to impose a wholly unjustified fifth year of college work on beginning teachers and on an already overtaxed system of graduate education; instead of at least beginning some of the vast reforms and retrenchments so badly needed in the master's and doctor's programs in Education, the field may move in precisely the opposite direction, toward even more trivial specializations that may be more removed from the liberal arts and pursued by even less qualified candidates. Over all this may reign a steadily growing Establishment, in which an increasing concentration of power over teacher education may be manifest. The few remaining sources, that is, of diversified control, as it has sometimes been exercised by state departments of Education, by local school boards, and by maverick institutions, may cease to function. The future in teacher education may bring centralized control with a vengeance, which in turn may bring a few improvements but which may also bring many more, and many more serious, problems.

On the other hand, the future may not, and certainly need not, be this way. Small numbers of men can often exert a large influence. In this fact lies one of the best hopes of the future in teacher education. A handful of very able men now found among the younger educationists, men who know better than anyone else what is wrong in the field today, may well have an impact far beyond their numbers. They are in the best position of any to raise the standards of professional Education and they are bent on doing so. The academicians, for their part, should constitute a second major force moving in the same direction through active and continuous participation in teacher education; if they fail to do so, and show themselves unwilling to take on their share of responsibility in this most crucial of enterprises, they have no grounds for continuing to complain about its short-comings. A handful of independent-minded school boards in each state could also, through new hiring and salary policies of the kind we have discussed, have far-reaching effects on other boards and ultimately on the training of teachers. The atmosphere in professional Education, despite the persistence of certain debilitating gases, is now more amenable to change than it has been since the triumph of progressivism; and if the many forces working for change and reform in teacher education can begin to complement one another, reinforce one another, and push together with a common purpose, they may indeed find it possible to move professional Education forward rapidly enough to meet the exigencies of our national life. Right now it is a tossup whether the future in teacher education will repeat the past or become a brave new era.

English or Educanto?

The purpose of Newspeak was not only to provide a medium of expression for the world-view and mental habits of the devotees of Ingsoc, but to make all other modes of thought impossible.

— George Orwell's *1984*

No MORE appropriate postscript could be added to our discussion of the present state of teacher training in America than one dealing with the peculiar language of Education. The subject is important, for it has important consequences. The modern educationist has invented a new *lingua franca* that, like Orwell's Newspeak, does indeed provide its devotees with a medium of expression for their world-view and mental habits that comes close to making other modes of thought impossible. Most outsiders who for one reason or another must keep up with educationist literature are able only with the greatest difficulty to tolerate this corrupt and unmistakable argot. The language of modern Education, which has been aptly called "Educanto," can reduce any mildly sensitive layman to a state of helpless fury in a matter of minutes. Even a reader conditioned by long exposure to the syntactical depredations of advertising men, the non-language of politicians, or the learned Choctaw of certain academicians is not ready for Educanto. In the hands of an experienced man, who I suppose must be called an "Educantoid," the language of Education can be practically incomprehensible. It can also induce severe nausea.

The educationist, pen in hand, seems to exhibit by some kind of instinct an almost total insensitivity to the rhythms of the English tongue; and he can at the same time practice in one paragraph all the worst vices to be found in contemporary writing — a considerable achievement. His prose as well as his speech is apt to be marked by an excessive wordiness, by a genuine fondness for platitudes, by an irredeemable addiction to ugly coinages and meaningless jargon, and by a plenitude of strange constructions and original usages. It calls to mind the comment of Daniel Defoe, who in 1702 saw the urgent need for the creation of an English Academy to combat the barbarous writings of the learned world:

> We have seen many great Scholars, meer Learned Men, and Graduates in the Last Degree of Study, whose English has been far from Polite, full of Stiffness and Affectation, hard Words, and long unusual Coupling of Syllables and Sentences, which sound harsh and untuneable to the Ear, and shock the Reader both in Expression and Understanding.

A fair description of the harsh and untunable language of the modern educationist, which Defoe was spared.

Though it is an easy object of ridicule and humor, Educanto is a serious phenomenon with many pernicious effects. It has a great deal to do with the condition of Education as an academic field, for it is both a symptom and a cause of poor academic health. It reflects the educationist's artificial drive to create a profession and has now become an accepted mark of professionalism among educationists. It masks a lack of thought, and in fact makes thought of any important kind extraordinarily difficult. As one who has devoted a large amount of time during this survey of teacher education, and for several years before that, to the writings of educationists, I consider myself rather an expert on Educanto. I not only can read it; I can write it and speak it. And because Educanto constitutes a serious problem in making the field of Education what it is today, I would like to review and illustrate what seem to me its major manifestations encountered everywhere. Although the phenomenon is, as I say, deadly serious in its consequences, perhaps it is best discussed in a somewhat different vein. Jonathan Swift wrote many heated tracts against the political theoreticians of London, but the one best remembered is the short, ironical "A Modest Proposal." One can profit from the lesson, if not duplicate the performance. Imagine, therefore, that a committee of master Educantoids has prepared a short primer for neophytes on the development and principles of Educanto. It might be titled "The Theory and Practice of Educanto," and it might go like this:

THE THEORY AND PRACTICE OF EDUCANTO

As a beginner, you must understand at once that Educanto is chiefly a means for advancing the Revolution. It is the deliberate and premeditated invention of the Party and is meant to serve our political purposes only. No one realizes better than ourselves that Educanto serves and can serve no other useful function. As you know, professional educators were quick to realize many decades ago that so long as dissent — that is, freedom of thought — was permitted in American education, our rise to power would be seriously impeded. We therefore organized the vast underground revolutionary movement into which you have now been initiated, a giant conspiracy to insure our eventual control of the nation's entire educational system, and ultimately, we hope, of a good deal more. One of our means for doing this is the marvelously bold and simple invention of Educanto.

As men of extraordinary intellectual power, we disdain the coarse old ways of revolution. In plotting our own, we realized that little was to be gained by violence and propaganda, or by trying to control the press or the thought and actions of the people. Something far more fundamental, we reasoned in a brilliant extrapolation, was needed to bring the Party to power: the professional educator must control the *means* of thought, from which thought-control itself would naturally follow. We must, that is, control language, without which no thought is possible. He who controls educational language controls educational thought; he who controls educational thought controls much of the present and perhaps all of the future. No mean prize.

The fundamental problem, obviously, was to put a stop to standard English, the instrument that, by making orderly thought possible, holds the Revolution enchained. Some of the best minds among us therefore went to work and invented, through great trial and travail, the language of Educanto — a wholly meaningless patois with which to undermine by imperceptible degrees, and finally to suppress entirely, the English tongue. When that goal is reached, and Educanto is the only language in which educational thought or discussion can take place, then of course all thought and discussion will cease and the Party will be in absolute power. It is a plan as potent as it is simple, the product of genius.

Because the Revolution is making thousands of converts daily, Educanto is being practiced all too imperfectly by the newer members of the Party. There is a widespread felt need among our newcomers for a handbook of usage. It is also felt that the attrition and decay of English under the impact of Educanto have progressed to the point that an overt structuring of certain fundamentals, to insure a persistent goal-oriented behavior in the Party, might be the means of advancing the Revolution by as much as three years. Accordingly, the Party has directed the preparation of this document setting forth briefly the more important principles of Educanto, in the "DO-DON'T" form most useful to beginners. A brief discussion of each principle is also offered, with illustrative examples. It is hoped that this short document, enriched by the criticisms and suggestions of other master Educantoids, will serve as the framework for a full-scale textbook to be developed in the near future.

Principle One: The Enervating Fugue

DO make an effort under all circumstances to see how many needless words and phrases you can use and repeat in a given space. *DON'T* under any circumstances imitate decadent writers and fall into the pit of clarity and economy of expression. Your best help here is the Enervating Fugue, one of the first great principles of Educanto. The Enervating Fugue is a precise contrapuntal exercise in which a theme is stated, preferably an obscure theme obscurely stated, and explored at enervating length, with graceful convolutions and inspired redundancy. Here is a fine example, necessarily a somewhat lengthy one, taken from the mimeographed outline of a course in "Social and Philosophical Foundations of Education," taught by a master of the craft at one of our finest institutions of higher learning:

> Because of these characteristics of the teacher's function — the need of careful choices in action situations, the desirability of consistency in choosing, and the consequences of choices which affect a large number of people in basic ways — we need to cultivate the resources which will enable us to handle better our everyday problems. We need to formulate more adequate principles to guide our choices and to re-examine as critically and carefully as we can the bases of our operation. We should re-create and revise our basic criteria by which we choose one course of action in preference to another. We need to study the important issues concerning which some position will be taken in our choosing. We should cultivate the habits necessary in searching for these issues and stating them clearly so that we may see what is involved in our choosing. We need to become skilled at clarifying the meanings of various statements about what we as educators should do. We should, in short, become better able to think critically and comprehensively about the nature and function of our work as educators.
>
> We have been trying to do these things as best we could while we work at our tasks of everyday existence. We have grown up

with some basis for making choices, we have been operating on some insights into basic issues, we have many resources for conducting education wisely. But we need an opportunity to re-examine our resources, to recreate our criteria, to broaden and enrich our experiences through planned contact with others who are similarly thoughtful. We need a chance to help each other at the tasks of clarifying our values, of developing our habits of critical thinking, of searching for the fundamental assumptions underlying actions and beliefs, of developing the implications of ideas. In short, we need an opportunity to re-examine our existing philosophies of education so that they may be recreated, more thoughtfully held, more adequate in guiding our decisions.

Notice the mild hypnotic coma that is induced when the Enervating Fugue is done really well. Nothing, as you know, establishes more effectively the necessary atmosphere of an Education course; and nothing enfeebles so nicely the ordinary kind of educator's English. But it is not easy to do. Maximally meaningful effort will be necessary before you can make sustained use of this important principle in your work.

Principle Two: The Extended Cliché

DO remember that another of the powerful ways, available to the merest beginner, of decimating the enemy language is to fill your writing and speech with hackneyed thoughts expressed in hackneyed ways. *DON'T* search for a fresh way to discuss tired themes, and *DON'T* ever consider not discussing them at all. Here, for instance, are the opening paragraphs of a textbook in "Social Studies" that is widely used in professional courses for teachers:

The schools of America are dedicated to the preservation and extension of democratic ideals and to the development of the highest type of democratic citizenship on the part of every child. The discharge of this responsibility requires an educational program that will develop each child's potentialities to the fullest and at the same time bring growth in the competencies essential to democratic living. The major emphasis being given to citizenship education at the present time is concrete evidence of the importance accorded this responsibility by American educators.

Every opportunity should be utilized to meet this challenge. Each area of the curriculum, experiences in school and on the playground, activities before and after school, the school-community enterprises should make contributions to the achievement of this goal. Of crucial importance are the social studies, which in many schools serve as the core for developing the social learnings needed in democratic living. Yet the social studies cannot do the job alone. A balanced curriculum must be planned for children and with children, and each area of the curriculum must be pointed toward the development of citizenship. The social studies, however, because of the experiences, content, and materials they encompass, have a unique role to play.[1]

In a splendid follow-through, the author adds to this passage 513 more pages in the same idiom. In 1957 he was awarded the national cup for mastery of the Extended Cliché at a secret meeting of the Party. Good Educanto also abounds with the short cliché sired by the dead figure of speech; but because they are common as dirt and thick as flies throughout educational writings, we can probably pass them by with a general commendation.

Principle Three: The Forward Passive

DO shun the active voice wherever possible, thus obviating any possibility of producing vigorous English. *DON'T* ever be caught dead using the first person singular. It should be remembered that nothing so contributes to the power of Educanto, apart from the native literary talent of the practitioner, as does the imitation of science. In fact, the Revolution must rest squarely, as you know, on our success in persuading the

[1] John U. Michaelis, *Social Studies for Children in a Democracy*, Prentice-Hall, Second Edition, 1956, p. 1.

public that professional education *is* a profession *and* a science. It is therefore indispensable that all written matter, whatever its lack of substance, be suggestive of the scientific method and suggestive of a large body of esoteric scientific knowledge. Important to this end is the passive construction, which permits the scattering of parentless participles and infinitives through any passage, which piles up verbs in an impressive, Germanic fashion, and which gives the desired flavor of ambiguity, lifelessness, and scientific detachment to the written word. All the writer needs for mastery of Principle Three is a proper attitude toward his material. So universal has the Forward Passive become, it is intended by the writers of this document that only a few quite representative samples should be offered. The first is from the printed directions to prospective teachers in a course in educational psychology; the second is from a standard work on educational administration; the third from an educational research report; and the fourth from an institutional publication on "professional laboratory experiences":

1. It is suggested that you claim a seat within the first week. The instructor has no preference where you sit, however, to facilitate the taking of roll a permanent seating chart will be organized after the first week.

2. With the administrator's role defined as educational leadership or statesmanship, it will be the purpose of this volume to contribute as effectively as possible to the realization of this goal.

3. By assuming that teaching involves much problem solving behavior and that teaching problems are composed of segments or tasks, the possibility arose that the problem solving behavior of the teacher might be studied outside the classroom if problems or tasks similar to those encountered in the classroom were constructed. . . . Second, it was assumed that as professional persons, it is desirable that teachers assume and be capable of attaining those objectives asserted as desirable by the leaders of the profession.

4. To help in understanding the children, the student-teacher is encouraged to inquire further into the special services he knows

the school offers. . . . To function effectively, it is necessary for the student teacher to learn as much as possible about the children. . . . It is recognized that public elementary schools differ depending upon the educational needs of their communities and their philosophies of education. . . . It is believed that student teaching experiences in varied situations can broaden the concepts and extend the understandings of student teachers as they prepare to enter the profession of teaching. . . . It is believed that the student teachers can contribute positively to the life of the school if permitted to participate in all activities.

Notice the charming modesty in the first example, the confusion of goals in the second, and the complete lack of any identifiable agent, except "it," doing the actions mentioned in three and four. The possibilities for use of the Forward Passive are clearly limitless. Hoping they will be used by you in the future, it is recommended that some conscious attention to this principle be rendered by you to it.

Principle Four: The Grandiloquent Bromide

DO make a special effort to present even the simplest thought in the most complex manner possible. *DON'T* waste time trying to discuss complicated subjects, in case you have any to deal with, in simple language; the record, fortunately, shows that no Educantoid has ever succeeded. One of the most valuable resources of our language is its infinite capacity for the Grandiloquent Bromide, not to be confused with the Extended Cliché. Principle Four demands, not a cliché necessarily, but simply an inconsequential idea which can then be inflated to scientific profundity. Here is a fine example, taken from a well-known "research" report on the habits of school superintendents:

Another consequence of abandoning the postulate of consensus on role definition that deserves exploration lies in the implications it has for explaining different behaviors of incumbents of the same position. Most students concerned with role phenomena, assuming consensus on role definition, have tried to account for the variability in behavior by invoking such variables as different motivations, attitudes, or personality characteristics. Our research experience suggests that different expectations held for incumbents' behavior and attributes are crucial for an understanding of their different behaviors and characteristics. Theoretical formulations which attempt to explain different behaviors of incumbents of the same position cannot be based on concepts in which the postulate of role consensus is involved.[2]

To appreciate the mastery of Principle Four shown in such a passage, one must consider the raw material with which the writers began. In standard English it would be: "People do not agree on the functions of the school superintendent. Their varying ideas, together with the superintendent's own ideas, affect his performance." But such a naked thought, which in less able hands might not have been worth recording, is wonderfully attenuated and overlaid with scientific grandeur when attacked by established Educantoids. In fact the whole volume, a delightful exercise in Principle Four, is strongly recommended.

Or consider this passage, from a book on school administration used in many graduate Education courses in this vital subject:

Purpose shapes the communication process and is the benchmark against which effectiveness must be measured. The purposes of communicators have different dimensions and can be classified into various categories. For example, is there a single purpose in the communication, or are there multiple purposes? If there are multiple purposes, which is more and which is less important to the communicator? Is the purpose general or specific? Does it apply to one person or to many persons? Is it primarily personal to the communicator, or does it have a social character? Is the communicator clearly or only vaguely aware of

[2] Neal Gross, *et al.*, *Explorations in Role Analysis*, John Wiley, 1958, p. 321.

the purpose? Does the purpose concern itself more with thought or more with action? If the purpose is concerned more with thought, is it designed to produce consensus and agreement, or is it designed to stimulate diversity and difference in viewpoint? Is the purpose immediate and short-term, or is it long-term and future-oriented? Such questions suggest some of the dimensions that relate to the concept of purpose.[3]

Translated from the Educanto into ordinary, decadent English, this says: "If your reasons for writing or speaking are clear to you, you will be more effective than if they are not." This passage is not particularly superior to the remaining 508 pages of the book; thus you can see that the only limit upon the use of the Grandiloquent Bromide, as with the other principles of Educanto, is the talent of the writer.

Principle Five: The Jargonized Pyrotechny

DO try to choose at least every other word of your writing from the magnificent jargon that, with long and devoted effort by innumerable practitioners, has been built into Educanto. *DON'T* allow your meaning, if any, to get in the way of your vocabulary. The ultimate glory of Educanto is in the Jargonized Pyrotechny, without which there could be no science of Education, no profession, no Party, and certainly no Revolution. It is recommended that you devote your nights and days, not to Addison, as Samuel Johnson treacherously advised young writers to do, but to Principle Five and to the spectacular effects you can achieve with it. The first step in its mastery is a little practice in the many ritual words at your command in Educanto, words that serve any purpose with any subject on any occasion. Here are ten to start with: "democracy," "growth," "experiences," "behaviors," "structures," "goals," "learnings," "concepts," "meaningfulness," and "insightfulness." Practice using these nouns in place of any you are now using

[3] Jack A. Culbertson, *et al.*, *Administrative Relationships*, Prentice-Hall, 1960, p. 381.

until they become quite automatic; then practice turning them into adjectives to make phrases. They are all interchangeable. For example, you can say "goal concepts," or "conceptual goals"; "insightful behaviors," or "behaviorial insightfulness"; "learnings structures," or "structured learnings"; "meaningful experiences," or "experiential meanings."

After you have automated a number of ritual words, you are ready to learn the specious substitution — that is, the systematic substitution of a jargonized name or definition for its everyday English equivalent. For example, *DON'T* refer to bright students at all if you can help it, but if you can't, *DO* call them "fortunate deviates." *DON'T* call retarded students retarded, and certainly not stupid; *DO* call them "exceptional pupils." *DON'T* define a teacher in the usual reactionary way, as a person who imparts knowledge to students and in the process tries to develop their ability to think. *DO* say that teachers, as "research" proves, are, among many things, "critical inquirers," "directors of experiences," "adult models," "measurers and recorders," "producers of effects," "communicators," "discussants," "substitute parents," "learning-aids officers," "motivators," "evaluators," "adapters," "structurers of frameworks," "catalytic agents," "discussion dominators" (or preferably "participants"), "co-learners," "creators of learnings environments," or "school situations analyzers."

DON'T say that teachers have several functions to fill in modern schools; *DO* say that they have "role demands," "role performances," and "role-dispositions." [4] *DON'T* say that a teacher is anything as simple as a seeker after truth; *DO* say that he "must reveal a strong interest and a growing competence in truth-checking, truth-finding, truth-compiling, truth-evaluating, truth-organizing, and truth-interpreting within those chosen fields of study." [5] Or describe a teacher in the way that one of the most popular volumes on educational psychology, a glori-

---

[4] Nevitt Sanford, in *The American College*, John Wiley, 1962, p. 52.
[5] Milt Lehr, "Teacher Selection in *One* State College," *Phi Delta Kappan*, March, 1962, p. 246.

ous 710-page triumph of advanced Educanto, does it: ". . . a decision-maker who, on the basis of his evaluation of pupils' readiness for learning or present status in learning, organizes a learning experience which will lead the child on to new differentiations and integrations of behavior." [6]

DON'T use the word "intelligence" as an independent noun. *DO* put one or more of these words ahead of it: "biological," "perceptual," "abstract," "protean," "conative," "effective," "operational," "social," "whole," "latent," "mechanical," "ideational," "cognative," "socio-verbal," or "nonintellective." And *DON'T* use the word "test" as an independent noun. *DO* put one or more of these words in front of it: "situational," "anecdotal," "undimensional," "triangular," "parallel," "unit," "significance," "spiral," "randomized," "refractive," "submatrix," "dualistic," "suppressor," "projective," "extrinsic," "sociometric," "attitudinal," "comparative," "symbol-elaboration," or "life-conceptioned."

With enough practice in the Jargonized Pyrotechny, you will find yourself putting together jawbreaking groups of nouns and adjectives fully as impressive as those of nuclear physicists. You will find yourself saying things like, "the progressive familial subcultural mental retardation," "the cathartic construction projective dimension," "the normative generalization reference cue," "the situation response relationship reinforcement," or "the extrinsic dualistic organization of coordinate administration." And you will find yourself able to write suitably unintelligible passages of ever-increasing length. You will start with single sentences like this one, from a recent report of an NEA "task force" being acclaimed throughout the field as "seminal": "*Significance* for high-quality use is proposed as the central criterion for content selection and organization on the new horizon." [7]

[6] Frederick J. McDonald, *Educational Psychology*, Wadsworth, 1959, p. 27.
[7] Margaret Lindsay, ed., *New Horizons for the Teaching Profession*, National Education Association, 1961, p. 37.

And you will move on to paragraphs, essays, and eventually to whole works. Here is a final example that seems to the Committee to demonstrate competence in all five principles of Educanto at once; you might well use it as a model in your beginning work. It is taken from a report of an expert in educational guidance at one of our most prestigious universities; he is discussing the future of his "discipline":

> Responsibility for being is manifested in the evolving *attitude* toward self in world which each person is affecting. This attitude forms successively in relation with a person's accomplishments of his identities as person, child, friend, boy or girl, student, player, husband, or wife, parent, citizen, and man. Effects of the resolution of these several identity crises are cumulative. Together the resulting identities and the accumulating attitudes toward self in world form the personality of a man. Guidance attempts to maintain productive character in emerging personality.

When you find yourself reading such passages without a pause, recognizing all the words and the Educantoid principles involved, you will be ready for advanced work. You will know that dynamically reinforced growth of your ideational and cross-fertilized learnings has occurred, hopefully through intra-variable autorivalry, enriched need arousal, purposeful goal-oriented behavior, and persistent achievement motivations. Your self-actualization, together with your real-life readiness for situational and refractive testing against Yoakam's Readability Formula will be concretioned. You will be ready to socialize to your peer group, whose modal behaviors as practitioners of Educanto have been randomized within the framework of reference of the contextual analogies of Flannery's Critical Incident Index so that all isolates have been integrated into the appropriate activity constructs — and both over-achievers and fortunate deviates whose role-playing compulsions have excititioned peer wrath and even Ganser's Syndrome are assigned intervisitational field laboratory experiences for greater concomitant learning experiences. In a word, you will be a full-membered Educantoid achieving high for the Revolution — that great day upon which the Party takes over the entire educational establishment, then the nation itself, ultimately the world, perhaps the universe! It is worth achieving for. Educanto is the only way. It is an iron discipline. Work at it!

Appendix A

APPENDIX A

Further Information
from the Transcripts of Credit

As A CHECK against the national sample of transcripts from the 32 schools listed in Chapters V and VI and for comparative purposes generally, I gathered a further sample of 129 transcripts from the Connecticut State Department of Education. These transcripts were selected by Dr. James S. LeSure, Consultant on Teacher Education to the Department, with a view toward adequate diversity and representation among the schools supplying Connecticut with teachers. The sample therefore was not a random, but a selected sample, drawn on the basis of expert knowledge of the population involved. All of the 129 transcripts, representing 89 different preparatory institutions, were for teachers certified in Connecticut, thereby yielding also a check against any significant difference between the records of those who merely complete teacher-training programs and those who actually go on to become certified teachers. In many states, of course, graduation from an accredited institution means automatic certification, but this was not true of the Connecticut sample, since almost all of the transcripts were from out-of-state institutions. Here are the institutions from which the 129 teachers were graduated, plus the classification given them by the United States Office of Education according to the highest degree and the types of program offered; Table VI, following the list of the Connecticut schools, is a reproduction of the system by which the U.S. Office classifies the 2,028 institutions of higher education in the United States:

1.	Albertus Magnus College (Conn.)	II e
2.	Albion College (Mich.)	III e
3.	Allegheny College (Pa.)	III e
4.	Alma College (Mich.)	II e
5.	American International College (Mass.)	III f
6.	Anna Maria College for Women (Mass.)	II e
7.	Annhurst College (Conn.)	II e
8.	Bates College (Maine)	II b
9.	Boston College	IV k
10.	Boston University	IV k
11.	Brooklyn College	III f
12.	Brown University (R.I.)	IV e
13.	Bucknell University (Pa.)	III j
14.	Central Missouri State College	III f
15.	College of Education at Cortland (N.Y.)	III d
16.	College of Education at New Paltz (N.Y.)	III d
17.	College of Education at Plattsburg (N.Y.)	III d
18.	College of New Rochelle (N.Y.)	II e
19.	College of Our Lady of the Elms (Mass.)	II e
20.	College of William and Mary (Va.)	III j
21.	Connecticut College	III b
22.	Davis and Elkins College (W. Va.)	II f
23.	Denison University (Ohio)	II j
24.	East Stroudsburg State College (Pa.)	II d
25.	Elizabethtown College (Pa.)	II e
26.	Fairfield University (Conn.)	III e
27.	Farmington State College (Maine)	II d
28.	Gannon College (Pa.)	II j
29.	Good Counsel College (N.Y.)	II e
30.	Gorham State Teachers College (Maine)	II d
31.	Goucher College (Md.)	III e
32.	Harvard University (Mass.)	IV k

33. Hunter College (N.Y.)   III e
34. Keene Teachers College (N.H.)   III d
35. Lake Erie College (Ohio)   II e
36. Lesley College (Mass.)   III d
37. Lyndon Center State Teachers College (Vt.)   II d
38. MacMurray College (Ill.)   III e
39. Marietta College (Ohio)   II e
40. Mary Washington College (Va.)   II b
41. Marymount College (N.Y.)   II e
42. Maryville College (Tenn.)   II e
43. Michigan State University   IV k
44. Middlebury College (Vt.)   IV e
45. Mills College (Calif.)   II d
46. Mississippi Southern College   IV e
47. Montana State University   IV k
48. Mount St. Mary's College (Md.)   II b
49. Newton College of the Sacred Heart (Mass.)   II b
50. Northwestern University (Ill.)   IV k
51. Ohio Wesleyan University   III e
52. Pennsylvania State University   IV k
53. Providence College (R.I.)   III e
54. Queens College (N.C.)   II e
55. Regis College (Mass.)   II e
56. Rhode Island College of Education   III d
57. St. Joseph's College (Pa.)   III f
58. St. Lawrence University (N.Y.)   III j
59. Seton Hill College (Pa.)   II e
60. Smith College (Mass.)   IV j
61. Southern Methodist University (Texas)   IV k
62. State College at Boston   III d
63. State College at Bridgewater (Mass.)   III d
64. State College at Fitchburg (Mass.)   III d
65. State College at Salem (Mass.)   III d
66. State College at Westfield (Mass.)   II d
67. State College at Worcester (Mass.)   III d

68. Syracuse University (N.Y.)   IV k
69. Tufts University (Mass.)   IV k
70. University of Bridgeport (Conn.)   III k
71. University of Kansas   IV k
72. University of Maine   IV k
73. University of Michigan   IV k
74. University of Rochester (N.Y.)   IV k
75. University of Vermont   IV k
76. University of West Virginia   IV k
77. University of Wisconsin   III j
78. Wagner College (N.Y.)   II e
79. Washington College (Md.)   III b
80. Wells College (N.Y.)   II e
81. West Virginia Wesleyan   III e
82. Wheaton College (Ill.)   III d
83. Wheelock College (Mass.)   II e
84. Whitman College (Wash.)   II f
85. Wilkes College (Pa.)   III e
86. William Smith College (N.Y.)   II e
87. Wilson College (Pa.)   III j
88. Wittenberg University (Ohio)
89. Woman's College of the University
    of North Carolina   III k

The preponderance of eastern institutions is evident, especially those in Massachusetts, New York, and Pennsylvania, as is the preponderance of schools that have strong liberal arts traditions. About 37 per cent of the sample are Type II schools, which are generally undergraduate liberal arts colleges. As noted in Chapter V, such schools do not turn out a large percentage of teachers nationally. Half of all new teachers probably come from teachers colleges or from institutions where the majority of graduates have been through the teacher-training programs; and another large percentage comes from the universities. The Connecticut sample includes only three schools with the name "Teachers" in the title, and only a dozen or so more whose principal business is teacher education. The sample, while it can hardly be considered representative nationally, does afford a broad look at what is happening in a number of liberal arts colleges and a number of state colleges and universities, and it does afford an interesting comparison with the results obtained in the main sample.

Table VII reports the results for the Connecticut sample on 26 items of information tabulated from the transcripts. This Table should be compared with Tables III, IV, and V of Chapter V. These results — judged from an "academic" point of view — are a bit better than those from the main sample, presumably because of the selection of institutions involved. On the whole, however, the results are quite consistent between the two groups.

A third check against the reliability of the main sample of transcripts, though much more limited than the Connecticut group, is the study of college catalogues reported in 1961 by the Institute of Higher Education at Teachers College, and discussed briefly in Chapter V.[1] The study drew a sample of 35 institutions, chosen for geographical distribution and representativeness, and computed certain information about the teacher-training programs from the school catalogues. Although the study does not list the institutions used, the Institute has been good enough to supply me with the list; here it is, with the classification of the U.S. Office added, and arranged according to type of school:

Teachers Colleges

1. Kansas State Teachers College	III f
2. Oregon College of Education	III e
3. Plymouth Teachers College (N.H.)	III d

[1] Earl J. McGrath, and Charles H. Russell, "Are School Teachers Illiberally Educated?" Published for the Institute of Higher Education by the Bureau of Publications, Teachers College, 1961.

TABLE VI

United States Office of Education System of Classification of Institutions of Higher Education, by Type of Program, and by Level of Offering.

Type of program	Total	I 2 but less than 4 years of work beyond 12th grade	II Only the bachelor's and/or first professional degree	III Master's and/or second professional degree	IV Doctor of philosophy and equivalent degree	V Other
		Highest level of offering				
a. Terminal-occupational (below bachelor's degree)	52	51				1
b. Liberal arts and general	130	43	70	14	2	1*
c. Liberal arts and general, and terminal-occupational	308	289	17	1		1
d. Primarily teacher-preparatory	120	32	35	50	2	1
e. Both liberal arts and general and teacher-preparatory	520	42	333	137	6	2
f. Liberal arts and general, terminal-occupational, and teacher preparatory	270	117	108	41	2	2
g. Professional or technical only (not including teacher-preparatory)	195	7	68	69	39	12
h. Professional or technical and teacher preparatory	80	7	21	34	14	4
i. Professional or technical and terminal-occupational	33	5	20	4	1	3
j. Liberal arts and general with 1 or 2 professional schools	147		62	62	19	4
k. Liberal arts and general with 3 or more professional schools	173		5	43	125	
Total	2,028	593	739	455	210	31

* The Institute for Advanced Study, Princeton, N.J.

Source: Higher Education, Part 3, "Education Directory, "1960-1961," U.S. Office of Education (OE-50000-61), p. 9.

TABLE VII

Selected Sample of Certified Teachers in the State of Connecticut, 86% of Whom Received Their Bachelor's Degree in 1960, from 89 institutions, in 24 States. Asterisk indicates items not tabulated.	68 elementary teachers	61 secondary teachers of academic subjects
1. *Mean semester hours in professional Education*	*45.6*	*25.3*
2. *Mean semester hours in academic education*	*78.2*	*107.7*
3. *Per cent of total program devoted to professional Education*	*36.8%*	*19.4%*
4. *Per cent of total program devoted to academic education*	*63.2%*	*80.6%*
5. Per cent of time devoted to Education in an assumed 120-semester-hour program	38.0%	21.0%
6. Per cent of time devoted to academic education in an assumed 120-semester-hour program	65.0%	87.2%
7. Composite grade point average in professional Education	2.98	2.58
8. Composite grade point average in academic education	2.58	2.67
9. Mean semester hours devoted to practice teaching	10	5
10. Mean semester hours devoted to methods of teaching	10	*
11. Mean semester hours devoted to field of English (non-majors)	14	12
12. Mean semester hours devoted to field of mathematics (non-majors)	2	3
13. Mean semester hours devoted to field of science (non-majors)	9	8
14. Mean semester hours devoted to field of foreign languages (non-majors)	4	10
15. Per cent of transcripts showing no advanced work in any academic field(s)	50%	*
16. Per cent of transcripts showing 1-6 semester hours of advanced work in any academic field(s)	27%	*
17. Per cent of transcripts showing 7-12 semester hours of advanced work in any academic field(s)	22%	*
18. Per cent of transcripts showing over 12 semester hours of advanced work in any academic field(s)	1%	*
19. Mean semester hours in English for majors	*	35
20. Mean semester hours in mathematics for majors	*	32
21. Mean semester hours in science for majors	*	27
22. Mean semester hours in science for "general science" majors	*	40
23. Mean semester hours in history for majors	*	33
24. Mean semester hours in "social studies" for majors	*	46
25. Mean semester hours in foreign languages for majors	*	34
26. Mean semester hours in major field for entire sample, including majors in "general science" and "social studies"	*	37

4. Southwest Texas State Teachers College   III f
5. West Chester State Teachers College (Pa.)   III d

State Colleges

6. Adams State College (Colo.)   III f
7. Albany State College (Ga.)   II f
8. Central Michigan College   III k
9. Central Missouri State College   III f
10. Eastern Illinois State College   III e
11. Flagstaff State College (Ariz.)   III e
12. Moorhead State College (Minn.)   III j
13. Morehead State College (Ky.)   III f
14. San Francisco State College   III f
15. State College of Washington   II d
16. Trenton State College (N.J.)   III d
17. Troy State College (Ala.)   III d
18. West Virginia State College   II f

Liberal Arts Colleges

19. Abilene Christian College (Texas)   III e
20. Augustana College (S.D.)   II e
21. High Point College (N.C.)   II e
22. St. Anselm's College (N.H.)   II e
23. Viterbo College (Wisc.)   II e

Universities

24. Hamline University (Minn.)   III j
25. Loyola University (La.)   III k
26. Northwestern University (Ill.)   IV k
27. Rutgers University (N.J.)   IV k
28. State University of Iowa   IV k
29. Temple University (Pa.)   IV k
30. University of Florida   IV k
31. University of Idaho   IV k
32. University of Oklahoma   IV k

33. University of Omaha   IV k
34. University of Vermont   IV k
35. University of Wisconsin   IV k

Using the published catalogues of these institutions, the
authors computed requirements in professional and liberal arts
courses for teachers. Based on an assumed total program of
120 semester hours, the study found that elementary teachers
spend an average of 36 per cent (43 semester hours) of their
time in Education courses, and that secondary teachers spend
an average of 17 per cent (20 semester hours) of their time in
Education courses.[2] While these figures compare reasonably
well with the Connecticut group just discussed, they compare
less well with the national sample described in Chapter V, and
are, I believe, less accurate than the data given there. Several
reasons for the discrepancies suggest themselves: reliance upon
the catalogues instead of the transcripts of credit; differences
in what is called "professional" and what "academic" courses;
and differences in the sample of institutions. Also, about 54 per
cent of the schools in the McGrath-Russell sample, as against
37 per cent of the Connecticut sample, are Type III schools,
whose primary concern is usually teacher training and who
therefore, as we have seen, require considerably more courses
in Education and fewer in liberal arts than do universities or
liberal arts colleges. In other words, the ratio of professional
to academic courses in the McGrath-Russell sample would
probably have been considerably more unfavorable, in view
of the fact that the majority of their institutions are actually
teacher-training establishments, if they had made their tabulations from the transcripts of credit instead of from the published catalogues.

There follow 20 additional case histories, reproduced in the
same manner as in Chapter V. Cases No. 1-8 are for elementary

[2] *Ibid.*, p. 3.

teachers with a bachelor's degree; they are intended to demonstrate the range of course work in the elementary programs, beginning with the most professional and least academic programs and going to the least professional and most academic. Case No. 9 illustrates a fairly typical program of a diminishing specialty, junior high school teaching. Cases No. 10-15 are for secondary teachers of academic subjects; they are intended to demonstrate something of the range of course work of the secondary programs, beginning with the most professional and least academic and going to the least professional and most academic. Cases No. 16-20 are illustrative of various master's degrees in Education; since the course work for these degrees, and certainly for the doctor's degrees, tends to be very much alike on the professional side, despite the fact that graduate degrees are given in a great many different specialties, there seems little point in reproducing many graduate records additional to those of Chapter VI.

CASE NO. 1

Degree of Bachelor of Arts awarded January, 1960.
All work done at a state teachers college.
Major: Elementary Education.

Liberal Arts Courses (47 semester hours)

Expressed in Quarter Hours
Biological Sciences (4)
Human Biology (3)
Economic Problems (5)
English Composition (8)
Fundamentals Speech (4)
Math for General Education (4)
Exploring Music (3)
Governmental Problems (4)
Problems of Society (3)

Ancient Times-Renaissance (4)
Renaissance-French Revolution (4)
The Physical Sciences (5)
World Resources (3)
French Revolution-Present (4)

Expressed in Semester Hours
Man and Materials (2)
Social and Econ. History of U.S. (4)
Introduction to Philosophy (2)

Education Courses (80 semester hours)

Expressed in Quarter Hours
Exploring the Teaching Profession (3)
Fundamentals of Teaching, I (5)
Fundamentals of Teaching, II (5)
Arithmetic Principles and Teaching (5)
Teaching Kindergarten-Primary Curriculum (4)
Early Childhood Education (3)
Reading and Language Arts, I (5)
Library Orientation (1)
Children's Literature (3)

Expressed in Semester Hours
Social Foundations of Education (4)
Lower Elementary Curriculum (3)
Occupational Information (2)
Parent Education (3)
Physical Education Elementary School (2)
Biology for Elementary Grades (2)

Teaching of Arithmetic (2)
Reading and Language Arts, II (2)
Remedial Reading (3)
Personality Growth of Child (2)
Adolescent Psychology (2)
Physically Handicapped (2)
The Exceptional Child (2)
The Retarded Child (2)
Lower Elementary Teaching (4)
Lower Elementary Teaching (4)
Clinical Experience (3)
Speech Correction (2)
Arts for Elementary Grades, I (2)
Arts for Elementary Grades, II (2)
Elementary Grade Music (3)
Literature for Lower Elementary Child (3)
Physical Science for Elementary Grades, II (2)

Further Information:

1. Per cent of total program devoted to Education	63.0%
2. Per cent of total program devoted to liberal arts	37.0%
3. Grade point average in Education	2.21
4. Grade point average in liberal arts	1.84

CASE NO. 2

Degree of Bachelor of Arts awarded June, 1960. All work done at a state teachers college. Major: Elementary Education.

Liberal Arts Courses (55 semester hours)

Expressed in Quarter Hours
English I and II (8)
Fundamentals of Speech (4)
Man and Materials (3)
Human Biology (3)
Exploring Music (3)
Mathematics for General Education (4)
Ancient Times to Renaissance (4)
Renaissance to French Rev. (4)
French Rev. to Present (4)

The Physical Sciences (5)
The Biological Sciences (4)

Expressed in Semester Hours
World Resources (3)
American History since 1877 (3)
History of (state) (2)
Introduction to Philosophy (2)
World Religions (3)
Man in Society (8)
Anglo America (3)

Education Courses (71 semester hours)

Expressed in Semester Hours
Audio-Visual Materials in Education (1)
Teacher and the Child (5)
Social Foundations of Education (4)
Upper Elementary Curriculum, I (4)
Reading and Language Arts, I (4)
Reading and Language Arts, II (2)
Arithmetic Principles and Teaching (3)
Teaching of Arithmetic, II (2)
Remedial Reading (3)
Story Telling (2)
Psychology of Learning (5)
The Exceptional Child (2)
Upper Elementary Teaching (8)

Speech Correction (2)
Children's Literature (2)
Creative Drama for Children (2)
Elementary Grade Music (3)
Arts for Elementary Grades, I (2)
Crafts for Recreation (2)
Arts for Elementary Grades, II (2)
Physical Education for Elementary Grades (2)
Physical Science for Elementary Grades, II (2)
Biological Science for Elementary Grades, II (2)
Group Evaluation Technique (3)
Upper Elementary Curriculum, II (2)

Further Information:

1. Per cent of total program devoted to Education   56.4%
2. Per cent of total program devoted to liberal arts   43.6%
3. Grade point average in Education   3.11
4. Grade point average in liberal arts   2.89

CASE NO. 3

Degree of Bachelor of Science in Education awarded June, 1960.
All work done at a state university. Major: Elementary Education.

Liberal Arts Courses (73 semester hours)

General Botany (5)
Freshman English (6)
American Literature (6)
Intermediate Composition (3)
Fundamentals of Speech (3)
Voice Training (3)
Physical Geography (5)
Conservation (3)
General Geology (5)
U.S. History since 1865 (3)
Ancient Rome (3)

English History to 1688 (3)
History of West (3)
Opera (2)
American Government (3)
American Politics (3)
Man in Society (3)
Social Disorganization (3)
Juvenile Delinquency (3)
Social Psychology (3)
Freshman Forum (2)

Education Courses (55 semester hours)

Introduction to Elementary Education (2)
Identifying Teaching Problems (2)
School and Society (3)
Health Information (3)
Curriculum and Instruction Elementary School (10)
Planning for Teaching (6)
Nature and Direction of Learning (3)

The Child (3)
Mathematics for Elementary Teachers (4)
Introduction Library Materials (2)
Creative Design in Art Education (3)
Integrated Arts (4)
Practice Teaching (10)

Further Information:

1. Per cent of total program devoted to Education   43.0%
2. Per cent of total program devoted to liberal arts   57.0%
3. Grade point average in Education   3.50
4. Grade point average in liberal arts   2.83

CASE NO. 4

Degree of Bachelor of Arts in Elementary Education awarded
January, 1961. All work done at a state college.
Major: Elementary Education.

Liberal Arts Courses (67 semester hours)

Modern Science (3)
General Biology (3)
English Fundamentals (3)
Reading and Composition (6)
English Literature (3)
Voice Training (3)
Physical Geology (3)
Westward Movement (3)
Far East in Modern Times (3)
U.S. to 1865 (3)
Western Civilization, A (3)

Western Civilization, B (3)
U.S. since 1865 (3)
Theory and Structure of Music (6)
History and Appreciation of Music (4)
History of Modern Philosophy (3)
Psychology (3)
Physiological Psychology (3)
Introduction to Sociology (3)
Physical Anthropology (3)

Education Courses (51 semester hours)

School and Community (2)
School Health (3)
Principles of Curriculum and
  Method Elementary Grades (8)
Kindergarten-Primary Education
  (4)
Psychological Foundations of Education (6)
Child Psychology (3)
Directed Teaching (8)

Arithmetic for Elementary Grades
  (3)
Music for Children (4)
Art in the Elementary School (2)
Crafts in the Elementary School
  (2)
Physical Education in the Elementary School (3)
Speech and Dramatic Acting in
  the Elementary School (3)

Further Information:

1. Per cent of total program devoted to Education   43.2%
2. Per cent of total program devoted to liberal arts   56.8%
3. Grade point average in Education   2.51
4. Grade point average in liberal arts   2.01

CASE NO. 5

Degree of Bachelor of Science in Education awarded June, 1961.
All work done at a small liberal arts college.
Major: Elementary Education.

Liberal Arts Courses (74 semester hours)

History and Appreciation of Art (6)

Inorganic Chemistry (4)

Quantitative Analysis (4)

English Composition (6)

U.S. History (6)

European History (6)

Introduction to French (6)

Introduction to Music (3)

Music in Baroque and Viennese Periods (3)

Logic (3)

American Government (3)

General Psychology (3)

Abnormal Psychology (3)

Hebrew Heritage (3)

Christian Heritage (3)

Principles of Sociology (3)

Social Psychology (3)

Survey of English Literature (6)

Education Courses (48 semester hours)

Audio-Visual Education (3)

Introduction to Education (3)

Health and Physical Education in Elementary School (2)

Teaching Elementary School Social Studies (3)

Teaching Elementary School Science (2)

Teaching Elementary School Arithmetic (2)

Teaching Elementary School Reading (3)

Teaching Elementary School English (3)

Children's Literature and Story Telling (3)

Elementary School Curriculum (3)

Educational Psychology (3)

Child Psychology (3)

Student Teaching (6)

Music in the Elementary School (3)

Art in the Elementary School (3)

Tests and Measurements (3)

Further Information:

1. Per cent of total program devoted to Education — 39.3%
2. Per cent of total program devoted to liberal arts — 60.7%
3. Grade point average in Education — 2.52
4. Grade point average in liberal arts — 1.95

CASE NO. 6

ELEMENTARY TEACHER

Degree of Bachelor of Arts awarded June, 1960.
All work done at a liberal arts college.
Major: Elementary Education.

Liberal Arts Courses (82 semester hours)

Introduction to the Visual Arts (7)
Introduction to Astronomy (2)
General Biology (8)
Techniques of Reading-Writing (6)
Introduction to Literature (6)
English Novel (3)
Public Speaking (3)
Intermediate French (6)
Elementary Spanish (10)

Introduction to Music (3)
Problems of Philosophy (3)
American Government (4)
Introduction to Psychology (6)
Introduction to Sociology (4)
The Family (2)
Cultural Anthropology (3)
Life and Teachings of Jesus (3)
Religion and the Bible (3)

Education Courses (36 semester hours)

School and Society (3)
History of Education (3)
Evaluation and Guidance (3)
Social Studies for Children (3)
Reading (3)
Child Development (3)

Human Growth and Development (3)
Student Teaching (6)
Music for Children (3)
Applied Art (3)
Children's Literature (3)

Further Information:

1. Per cent of total program devoted to Education   30.5%
2. Per cent of total program devoted to liberal arts   69.5%
3. Grade point average in Education   2.70
4. Grade point average in liberal arts   2.43

CASE NO. 7

Degree of Bachelor of Arts awarded June, 1961.
All work done at a private university.
Major: Elementary Education.

Liberal Arts Courses (89 semester hours)

20th Century Art (3)
General Biology (6)
English Composition (6)
Masterpieces of Literature (6)
Oral Interpretation of Lit. (3)
Social Geography (3)
Physical Geology (3)
Historical Geology (3)
Elementary Spanish (3)
Functional Spanish (3)
Intermediate Spanish (6)
Fundamentals of Mathematics (3)
Introduction to Music (2)

Elementary Logic (3)
Ethics (3)
Eastern Religion (3)
Western Religion (3)
American Government (3)
General Psychology (6)
Adolescence and Maturity (3)
Introduction Social Psychology (3)
Marriage and Family (3)
History of the American People (3)
History of America (3)
American Revolution to 1801 (3)

Education Courses (31 semester hours)

Introduction to Education (3)
School Health (3)
Principles of Teaching in Elementary School (3)
Teaching Arithmetic (2)
Elementary School Organization (2)
Children's Literature (2)

Reading in the Elementary School (3)
Materials and Methods in Elementary School (3)
Educational Psychology (3)
Student Teaching (5)
Public School Art (2)

Further Information:

1. Per cent of total program devoted to Education   25.8%
2. Per cent of total program devoted to liberal arts   74.2%
3. Grade point average in Education   2.29
4. Grade point average in liberal arts   2.02

CASE NO. 8

Degree of Bachelor of Science in Education awarded June, 1961.
All work done at a private university.
Major: Geography.

Liberal Arts Courses (104 semester hours)

History of Art (1)
Principles of Biology (8)
Freshman English (6)
Appreciation of Literature (6)
Oral Interpretation of Lit. (2)
Geopolitics and World Power (3)
Survey of Africa (3)
Russia—Land of Soviets (3)
U.S. and Canada (3)
Asia—Its Land and Peoples (3)
Europe (3)
The Earth's Landforms (3)
Colonial America (3)
Westward Movement (3)
Western Civilization (6)

Elementary French (8)
Intermediate French (6)
College Algebra (3)
Trigonometry (3)
History of Music (3)
American Government (3)
Logic (3)
Philosophy of Being (3)
Philosophy of Man (3)
Natural Theology (3)
Ethics (3)
Survey of Systematic Philosophy (3)
General Psychology (4)

Education Courses (29 semester hours)

Organization and Management Elementary School (2)
History of Education (3)
Teacher and School Health (2)
Children's Literature (2)
General Techniques of Elementary Teaching (2)
Educational Psychology (3)

Practice Teaching (5)
Foundations in Reading (2)
Music for Elementary Teachers (2)
Art for Elementary Teachers (2)
Physical Education for Elementary Teachers (2)
Arithmetic for Elementary Teachers (2)

Further Information:

1. Per cent of total program devoted to Education   21.8%
2. Per cent of total program devoted to liberal arts   78.2%
3. Grade point average in Education   3.20
4. Grade point average in liberal arts   2.58

CASE NO. 9

Degree of Bachelor of Science in Education awarded June, 1961.
All work done at a state teachers college.
Major: Social Studies and Science.

Liberal Arts Courses (68 semester hours)

Art History and Appreciation (3)
Survey of Astronomy and Geology (3)
Meteorology (3)
College Biology (6)
General Chemistry (8)
Written Expression (3)
English Literature (3)
British and American Lit. (3)

Spoken Expression (3)
World Geography (3)
U.S. History (6)
Civilization in the Americas (3)
History of Western Civilization (3)
Fundamentals of Mathematics (6)
Elements of Physics (3)
Introduction to Social Sciences (6)
U.S. as a World Power (3)

Education Courses (53 semester hours)

History and Philosophy of Education (3)
Human Development and Behavior (6)
Personal and Community Health (3)
Organization and Function of Junior High School (3)
Curriculum Materials: Arithmetic and Social Studies (2)
Curriculum Materials: Reading and Language Arts (2)
Reading Development Junior High School (3)

Science in the Junior High School (3)
Social Science in the Junior High School (3)
Educational Psychology with Tests and Measurements (6)
Adolescent Psychology (3)
Student Teaching (10)
Music in the Junior High School (1)
Art in the Junior High School (2)
History of [state] (3)

Further Information:

1. Per cent of total program devoted to Education — 43.8%
2. Per cent of total program devoted to liberal arts — 56.2%
3. Grade point average in Education — 2.09
4. Grade point average in liberal arts — 2.44

CASE NO. 10

Degree of Bachelor of Science in Secondary Education awarded August, 1961. All work done at a state university.
Major: Social Studies.

Liberal Arts Courses (81 semester hours)

Weather and Man (2)
General Zoology (3)
Essentials of Chemistry (6)
Principles of Economics (3)
Composition and Rhetoric (3)
Exposition (3)
English Grammar (3)
American Literature (6)
History of the English Language (3)
Effective Speech (3)
World Geography (3)

U.S. History (6)
American Military History (3)
Modern European History (6)
Middle Ages (3)
Analytic Geometry (4)
Music Appreciation (3)
Politics in Modern Society (3)
American National Government (3)
State Government (3)
Psychology (3)
Introduction to Sociology (3)
General Anthropology (3)

Education Courses (48 semester hours)

Visual and Other Sense Aids (2)
Education in American Society (3)
Professional Orientation to Teaching (3)
Secondary Education, I (4)
Secondary Education, II (6)
Teaching Social Studies in High School (3)
Reading Problems in the Secondary School (2)

Teaching Secondary School English (3)
Educational Psychology (3)
Student Teaching (9)
Educational Measurements (2)
Elements of Reference Work (3)
Radio and TV in Education (2)
Literature Teaching in Secondary School (3)

Further Information:

1. Per cent of total program devoted to Education   37.2%
2. Per cent of total program devoted to liberal arts   62.8%
3. Grade point average in Education   3.02
4. Grade point average in liberal arts   2.17
5. Total semester hours in major field   39

CASE NO. 11

Degree of Bachelor of Arts awarded June, 1961.
All work done at a private university. Major: Mathematics.

Liberal Arts Courses (91 semester hours)

Expressed in quarter hours
Orientation-Art (3)
Plane Trigonometry (3)
Biology and Hygiene (4)
Principles of Biology (4)
General Chemistry (10)
English Composition (6)
General Literature (9)
Fundamentals of Speech (2)
Speech Analysis (3)
Human Geography (5)
History of Civilization (10)
Intermediate Algebra (5)

College Algebra (5)
Geometry and Calculus (5)
Engineering Problems in Math (6)
Analytic Geometry (10)
Foundations Geometry (3)
Analytics and Calculus (10)
Linear Algebra (3)
Orientation to Music (3)
Engineering Physics (15)
General Psychology (5)
Matter and Energy (4)
Earth and Universe (3)

Education Courses (41 semester hours)

Expressed in quarter hours
Teaching Profession (2)
Philosophy and Curriculum (5)
State School Law (2)
State Government for Teachers (3)
Physical Science Secondary School (3)
Psychology for Teachers (5)
Human Growth and Development (5)

Observation and Teaching (3)
Intermediate Teaching (8)
Materials and Methods Secondary Education (3)
General Mathematics for Secondary Teachers (3)
Advanced Teaching (16)
Evaluation (3)
Library Orientation (1)

Further Information:

1. Per cent of total program devoted to Education   31.1%
2. Per cent of total program devoted to liberal arts   68.9%
3. Grade point average in Education   2.78
4. Grade point average in liberal arts   2.56
5. Total semester hours in major field   32

CASE NO. 12

Degree of Bachelor of Arts awarded June, 1960. All work done at
a private university. Major: English.

Liberal Arts Courses (80 semester hours)

Elements of Composition (6)
History of Civilization (3)
General Psychology (3)
Extemporaneous Speaking (2)
Classical Literature (3)
Music Appreciation (2)
Modern Civilization (3)
Principles of Economics (3)
Survey of English Literature (6)
Survey of American Literature (6)
History of U.S. (6)

Introduction to Sociology (3)
Human Biology (5)
Civil War (3)
Introduction to Citizenship (3)
Modern English Grammar (3)
Eighteenth Century Lit. (3)
World Masterpieces (3)
Physical Science Survey (5)
Introduction to Anthropology (3)
Chaucer (3)
Shakespeare (3)

Education Courses (31 semester hours)

Personal and Community Health (3)
Introduction to Educational Psychology (3)
Human Development (3)
Introduction to Education (3)

Educational Sociology (3)
High School Methods (4)
Visual Aids in Education (3)
Methods in Physical Education (3)
Supervised Teaching (6)

Physical Education Courses (25 semester hours)

Fundamentals of Major Sports (3)
Football Theory (2)
Football [apparently awarded for
playing the sport] (7)
First Aid (2)
Officiating (2)

Play Activities (2)
Basketball (2)
Track and Field (2)
Administration in Physical Education
(3)

Further Information:

1. Per cent of total program devoted to Education   22.8%
2. Per cent of total program devoted to physical education   18.4%
3. Per cent of total program devoted to liberal arts   58.8%
4. Grade point average in Education   2.63
5. Grade point average in physical education   3.64
6. Grade point average in liberal arts   2.10
7. Total semester hours in major field   38

CASE NO. 13

Degree of Bachelor of Arts awarded June, 1961.
Two years of work done at a private college and a state university.
Last two years done at a second state university. Major: Sociology.

Liberal Arts Courses (94 semester hours)

Expressed in quarter hours

Psychology (3)
Algae and Fungi (4)
Liverworts-Mosses-Ferns (4)
Seed Plants (4)
Southern Life and Literature (4)
Ideas in Literature (4)
History of Colonial America (4)
American Community (4)
The Family (4)
Population (4)
Social Psychology (4)
Introduction to Social Thinkers (4)
Lands and Peoples of the World (4)

Introduction to Social Work (4)
General Biology (12)
General Chemistry (8)
Economics (3)
English Composition (9)
English Literature (9)
American History (9)
Basic Mathematics (9)
Introduction to Music (3)
Religion (9)
Sociology (9)
Criminology (3)
Juvenile Delinquency (3)

Education Courses (30 semester hours)

Expressed in quarter hours

History of Education (3)
Secondary School Curriculum (5)
Guidance Secondary School (2)
Teaching Social Studies in Secondary School (4)
Human Growth and Development (3)

Student Teaching (16)
Measurement and Evaluation in Secondary School (2)
Nature Study (4)
Child Psychology (3)
Education (3)

Further Information:

1. Per cent of total program devoted to Education — 24.4%
2. Per cent of total program devoted to liberal arts — 75.6%
3. Grade point average in Education — 3.33
4. Grade point average in liberal arts — 3.15
5. Total semester hours in major field — 26

CASE NO. 14

Degree of Bachelor of Science awarded June, 1960.
All work done at a state university.
Major: Biology.

Liberal Arts Courses (104 semester hours)

General Botany (5)
General Zoology (5)
Advanced Botany (5)
General Morphology (3)
Algae Taxonomy (3)
Heredity (3)
Field Zoology (3)
Morphology Angiosperm (4)
Classification Seed Plants (3)
General Invertebrate Zoology
  (Audited)
Economic Cooperation (3)
Freshman English (6)
Intermediate Composition (3)
Conservation (3)
Recent American History (3)

First Semester Spanish (4)
Second Semester Spanish (4)
Introduction College Algebra (4)
Calculus and Analytical Geometry
  (12)
American Government and Politics
  (3)
Introduction to Psychology (4)
Man in Society (3)
Social Disorganization (3)
Man and Culture (3)
Introduction to Social Psychology
  (3)
Cultural Anthropology (3)
Contemporary Literature (6)

Education Courses (18 semester hours)

Social Issues and Education (3)
Teaching Mathematics (4)
Teaching Social Studies (5)

Nature of Learning (3)
The Child (3)

Further Information:

1. Per cent of total program devoted to Education   14.7%
2. Per cent of total program devoted to liberal arts   85.3%
3. Grade point average in Education   3.66
4. Grade point average in liberal arts   3.22
5. Total semester hours in major field   37

CASE NO. 15

Degree of Bachelor of Arts awarded June, 1960.
One year of work done at a state college, and the last three years at
a private liberal arts college.
Major: Spanish.

Liberal Arts Courses (117 semester hours)

Introduction to Astronomy (4)
Introduction to Biology (4)
Elements of Drawing and Composition (2)
Oils and Painting (2)
Introduction to Chemistry (4)
Freshman English (4)
English Literature (3)
American Literature (2)
Shakespeare (3)
History of the English Language (3)
Expository Writing (2)
Basic Speech (4)
History Colonial America (2)

History American West (2)
The ABC Powers (3)
History of Civilization (24)
Intermediate Spanish (8)
Introduction Spanish Literature (3)
Latin American Novel (3)
Survey Spanish Literature (3)
Modern Spanish Literature (6)
Spanish-American Literature (6)
Government Latin America (3)
Introduction Psychology (3)
Literature of Bible (4)
Indian Culture (2)
Elementary French (8)

Education Courses (18 semester hours)

Scope of the Secondary School (2)
Audio-Visual Instruction (2)
Philosophy of Education (4)
Methods of Teaching Foreign Languages (2)

Educational Psychology (4)
Student Teaching (4)

Further Information:

1. Per cent of total program devoted to Education   13.3%
2. Per cent of total program devoted to liberal arts   86.7%
3. Grade point average in Education   2.76
4. Grade point average in liberal arts   2.84
5. Total semester hours in major field   38

CASE NO. 16

Undergraduate Record — Major: Elementary Education

Liberal Arts Courses (69 semester hours)

History of Western Civilization (3)
American History (6)
Speech Improvement (2)
Western Civilization (3)

Modern Government (3)

Transfer credit: 52 semester hours
from a junior college.

Education Courses (52 semester hours)

Psychology of Learning (3)
Use of Audio-Visual Aids (2)
Personal and Community Hygiene (2)
History and Philosophy of Education (3)
Elementary Education (3)
Teaching of Reading (3)
Social Studies in the Elementary School (3)
Music Methods in the Elementary School (3)

School and Society (3)
Student Teaching (6)
Teaching Language Arts (3)
Methods in Health Education (3)
Methods in Teaching Arithmetic (3)
Art in the Elementary School (3)
Educational Measurements (3)
Student Teaching (6)

Graduate Record

Liberal Arts Courses (3 semester hours)

Abnormal Psychology (3)

Education Courses (33 semester hours)

Guidance in the Elementary School (3)
Child Psychology (3)
Psychology of Personality (3)
Psychological Testing in Guidance (3)
Seminar in Guidance in the Elementary School (3)

Techniques in Guidance (3)
Remedial Reading in the Elementary School (3)
Seminar in Education of the Exceptional Child (3)
Studies in Guidance (3)
Counseling (3)
Measurement of Intelligence (3)

Further Information:

1. Per cent of total college career devoted to Education   54.1%
2. Per cent of total college career devoted to liberal arts   45.9%
3. Grade point average for entire college career in Education   2.69
4. Grade point average for entire college career in liberal arts   2.00

CASE NO. 17

Undergraduate Record — Major: Elementary Education

Liberal Arts Courses (65 semester hours)

Communication Skills (6)
Introduction to Science (3)
Biology (3)
Music Essentials (2)
Introduction to Mathematics (3)
Essentials of Art (2)
American Literature and Composition (6)
General Geography (3)
American Heritage (3)
Europe and the Modern World (3)

Statistics (3)
General Science (6)
Music Literature (2)
Sociology (3)
Speech and Radio (3)
Oral Interpretation of Literature (2)
Marriage and Family (3)
American Government (3)
Social Problems (3)
Major English Writers (3)

Education Courses (55 semester hours)

Child Development (6)
Community Health (2)
Child and the Curriculum (6)
Physical Education for Teachers (2)
Student Teaching (15)
Organization and Administration of Education (3)
Crafts (2)

Family and Child Care (2)
Education Seminar (6)
Children's Theatre (3)
Acting (3)
Science in the Elementary School (3)
Play Production in the Elementary School (2)

Graduate Record

Liberal Arts Courses (0 semester hours)

Education Courses (32 semester hours)

Guidance in Secondary Education (3)
Survey of Approaches to Counseling (2)
Development of the Child from Birth to Six (3)
History of Education (3)
Introduction to Measurement (2)
Curriculum Development (2)
Overview of Public School Administration (2)

Materials and Methods in Education (2)
Teachings in Guidance (3)
Youth Guidance (4)
Activities in College and Secondary School (2)
Study of Occupations (2)
Educational and Community Development (2)

Further Information·

1. Per cent of total college career devoted to Education — 57.3%
2. Per cent of total college career devoted to liberal arts — 42.7%
3. Grade point average for entire college career in Education — 3.10
4. Grade point average for entire college career in liberal arts — 2.36

CASE NO. 18

MASTER'S DEGREE IN ADMINISTRATION, 1961

Undergraduate Record — Major: Elementary Education

Liberal Arts Courses (70 semester hours)

English Composition (6)
Appreciation of Literature (3)
Humanities (6)
Fundamentals of Mathematics (6)
Fundamentals of Geography (3)
Geography North-South America (6)
Physical Science Survey (8)

Public Speaking (3)
Biology (8)
History of Civilization (6)
American History (6)
Sociology (3)
Pan-Pacific History (3)
Principles of Economics (3)

Education Courses (59 semester hours)

Educational Psychology (6)
Language Arts Instruction (6)
Methods and Techniques of Teaching (10)
Evaluation in Guidance (3)
Principles of Elementary Education (3)

Mental Hygiene (3)
Health Education (3)
Children's Literature (3)
Remedial Reading (3)
Current Professional Problems (3)
Student Teaching (16)

Graduate Record

Liberal Arts Courses (0 semester hours)

Education Courses (34 semester hours)

Philosophy of Education (3)
Curriculum Development (3)
Social Foundations of Education (3)
Audio-Visual Aids (3)
Administration of Secondary Schools (3)
Supervision in Schools (3)

Field Services in Physical Science Education (6)
Principles of Guidance (3)
Educational Finance and Business Management (3)
Graduate Project (2)
Advanced Concepts of Arithmetic (2)

Further Information:

1. Per cent of total college career devoted to Education — 57.1%
2. Per cent of total college career devoted to liberal arts — 42.9%
3. Grade point average for entire college career in Education — 3.42
4. Grade point average for entire college career in liberal arts — 2.87

CASE NO. 19

Undergraduate record not available;
student took a Bachelor of Science in Education degree in
1957 from a state teachers college.

Graduate Record

Liberal Arts Courses (0 semester hours)

Education Courses (33 semester hours)

Curriculum Construction in Secondary School (2)

School Administration (4)

Educational and Psychological Measurement (2)

Basic Educational Trends (2)

Community Relations (2)

Organization of the High School (2)

Organization of Extra-Curricular Activities (2)

Driver Education (3)

Methods and Instruction in Research (2)

Seminar in Curriculum Development (2)

Supervision of Instruction in Secondary School (2)

Prevention and Care of Athletic Injury (2)

School Health Services (2)

Core Curriculum in High School (2)

Camping and Outdoor Activities (2)

CASE NO. 20

Undergraduate record not available;
student took a Bachelor of Science in Education degree in 1957,
with a major in social studies, from a private university.

Graduate Record

Liberal Arts Courses (16 semester hours)

History of South America (4)

History of Europe in 20th Century (4)

Socialism (4)

National Government of the U.S. (4)

Education Courses (16 semester hours)

Contemporary Issues in American Education (4)

Introduction to the Philosophy of Education (4)

Social Sciences in the Secondary School (4)

Introduction to Educational Psychology and Measurement (4)

Appendix B

APPENDIX B

Completion of Opinions from One Hundred Graduates

IN THE SECTION of Chapter IV called "Opinions from One Hundred Graduates" are reprinted 20 opinions from recent graduates of teacher-training programs about their college work. The remaining 80 are reprinted below, continuing the numeration begun in Chapter IV. The questionnaire discussed in that chapter is reproduced on pages 333-335. All comments are taken verbatim from the returned questionnaires, chiefly from Item No. 7 of page 1, but occasionally from page 2 also. The 80 teachers represented below were graduated from 26 different colleges or universities in 13 states; they are about equally split between elementary and secondary teachers, but also with a few graduate students in Education:

21. I feel the vast majority of courses taken in the areas I have marked "D" to be superficial and a great deal of "busy work." [So marked were courses in Educational Psychology, History and Philosophy of Education, and Methods.] I believe the elementary teacher (my field) should have a much broader background in fine arts and sciences than the average elem. ed. major allows.

22. [This teacher marks all of the courses listed under Education on page 2 of the questionnaire with an "F" and adds these comments]: Ed Psych — Awkwardness of text, unchallenging; Methods — Read 3 books (3 credit course) one for math, one reading, one literature — nothing but recitation of what we read

— no practical application; Practice Teaching — Scanty, under pressure at same time of school responsibilities and activities, carried 3 other courses at time. Too traditional a critic teacher — no opportunity to even try reading groups; Supervision and Administration — Read 2 chapters in a book, discussed them.

23. The educational program which I went through [physical education] was well organized and presented. It included most of the problems which one could be confronted with in any school system, and also included methods and systems which could be set up to improve classroom situation. I feel that most of the instructors were well qualified, especially in their particular field.

24. My liberal arts courses were of consistently high quality, my education courses were not. . . . My association [with teaching] is as an elementary school librarian. I will not teach until teachers are given more assistance and the menial jobs are eliminated as well as the nonsense from the curriculum.

25. Education courses, except in the philosophy and student teaching areas, seem on the whole useless. They never come down to brass tacks and tell how to impart a *desire* for learning to the child. Nor can this be expected. I think a good teacher can instill this desire into his or her students by infection — almost, instinctively. I find my liberal arts background along with a cooperative guidance dept. is superior in dealing with children than any psychology course I ever took.

26. Three out of four of the 3-credit education courses I took were dull, *completely* useless outside of the reading and relating exercises, and were led by asses. There was *no* training offered, or received in any course which could be of the least use in the real world of education — it was 75% to 100% idealistic horse-feathers and bunk from storybooks of the "once upon a time" variety. Better to throw would be teachers into the teaching situation *directly* with a minimum of so-called "preparation"; but allow them books to refer to as needed, and, also elder educators to chat with if any too-complex situations come up for the shaky neophyte.

QUESTIONNAIRE USED IN SAMPLING
THE OPINIONS OF EDUCATION GRADUATES

As a recent graduate of a training program in the field of education, you are in a position to assist in an important way a study we are engaged in of schools and departments of education in American colleges and universities. This is a two-year study (supported by The Relm Foundation, Ann Arbor, Michigan) focused on the professional aspects of teacher training. We would be most grateful if you would take a few minutes to consider the questions below, relating to your feelings about the college work you did in education and in the liberal arts, and to respond to as many of them as you can. A stamped, addressed envelope is enclosed for your use in returning the form. Many thanks for your help.

1. The anonymity of respondents is, of course, guaranteed, as is customary in such an opinion survey as this. However, if you should wish to see a summary report of the survey results, please give the name and address to which the report should be mailed:

Name: _____

Address: _____

2. Educational background:

   A. Check degree(s) you hold: ☐ Bachelor's   ☐ Master's
      Enter dates received: _____   _____

   B. Semester hours of work done at institutions other than the one granting the degree(s) you hold — work, that is, for which transfer credit was granted:

Transfer credit for *bachelor's degree*	☐ none ☐ 0-15	☐ 16-30 ☐ 31-45	☐ 46-60 ☐ 61-75	☐ 76-90 ☐ over 90
Transfer credit for *master's degree*	☐ none ☐ 0-15	☐ 16-30 ☐ 31-45	☐ 46-60 ☐ all undergraduate work	

3. What program of studies did you complete for each degree you hold?

   Bachelor's Master's
   ☐   ☐   Elementary education
   ☐   ☐   Secondary education, and my major field was: _____
   ☐   ☐   Administration and supervision
   ☐   ☐   Other (please specify): _____

4. For the bachelor's degree, I earned approximately _____ semester hours of credit in education courses, and _____ hours in liberal arts courses.

5. For the master's degree, I earned approximately _____ semester hours of credit in education courses, and _____ hours in liberal arts courses.

6. Are you now teaching or otherwise engaged professionally in the field of education?   ☐ Yes   ☐ No
   If "no," do you plan to be so engaged within five years?   ☐ Yes   ☐ No

(*continued on next page*)

7. Page 2 of this form asks for your reaction to course work in the major subjects of academic and professional education. However, you might also wish to record your general view of your own education. How do you feel, on the whole, about the programs of studies you followed, both in education and in the liberal arts — about their overall quality, relevance to your needs and interests, effectiveness in preparing you for your vocation, etc.? If you were writing your own prescription for the education of teachers, or administrators, what would be the gist of it? Use back of the sheet if necessary.

8. Reversing the usual procedure of professors grading students, the following table asks you to grade, on the usual A-F scale, the course work you have had, both in education and in the liberal arts. The courses are grouped, not by specific offerings, but by broad fields or by departments; if you want to make finer distinctions, please do so under "Explanatory comments." Use the back of the sheet if necessary. The grade you award each of the categories should be a general rating — the grade, everything considered (materials of the courses, quality of the instruction, etc.), that you feel is most appropriate. It is, of course, important that you be completely candid, and enter the grade for each group that you honestly feel it deserves. Please use the following table of values in arriving at each grade you give. (And thanks again!)

"A" For course work that was definitely superior, among the best you had.
"B" For course work that was excellent, but not the best.
"C" For course work that was undistinguished, run-of-the-mill.
"D" For course work that was definitely poor.
"F" For course work that was rock-bottom.

LIBERAL ARTS

Your courses in:	Grade A-F	Explanatory comments — reasons for ratings — other remarks
English — Comp, Literature, Speech, etc.		
Social Sciences — History, Economics, Government, Sociology, etc.		
Foreign Languages		
Religion, Philosophy		
Mathematics		
Physical and Biological Sciences		
All other work — Do not specify unless you wish		

(*continued on next page*)

EDUCATION

Your courses in:	Grade A-F	Explanatory comments — reasons for ratings — other remarks
Educational Psychology — may come under many different names		
History and Phil. of Ed. — School & Society, Social Foundations, etc.		
Methods — General, or specific subjects		
Practice Teaching		
Supervision, Administration, Curriculum Dev., Guidance, etc.		
All other work — Do not specify unless you wish		

(end of questionnaire)

27. Has any professional educator written a textbook which might be classified as interesting? They seem to be caught in a vicious circle of quoting each other.

28. Most courses in education border on the ridiculous and antiquity. Most teachers of the subject matter have been so submerged in reading the educational journals that every other aspect of education per se has been neglected. Most have little or no contact with the everyday, real life situations that exist in the secondary school classrooms of today. The attempt is not to improve the quality of education, but rather to enhance the mediocrity of education. If I had an opportunity to eliminate courses of undergraduate training, the education courses would be the first to go. The only reservations to this would be a realistic worthwhile program of education courses, but I do not forsee this in the near future.

29. Examination questions in education courses were often the most poorly worded of any I have ever seen. If they were not

required for state certification, I would not have taken half of the education courses which I did and, I believe, I would be just as good a teacher without most of them.

30. I feel that the liberal arts courses were mediocre in content and leadership in many areas. Many of the methods courses turned out to be "busy work" and offered little in actual help when I went student teaching. My student teaching experiences were my greatest preparation for teaching. I felt that this preparation was above average compared to many teacher-training programs. I wasn't intellectually stimulated in very many of the liberal arts areas.

31. I feel that the liberal arts background I had was excellent and helped immensely in actual teaching. So far, I have been unable to apply any material from Educ. courses to actual teaching. I feel that all, with the exception of a grad. course in philosophy of education were a waste of time.

32. I believe that many education courses could be combined, leaving more time for liberal arts persuits. Methods of Science, Social Studies, etc. seem to be repeatitious and hence boring. Most of my learning, as far as methods went, was in actual teaching.

33. With the possible exception of student teaching [which she grades "C"; she grades all her other Education courses "F"], I honestly believe that I did not learn one thing in an education course that actually helped me in teaching.

34. I do not feel as adequately prepared to teach as I would like. My general education was probably adequate, but in the area of my major subject I feel unprepared. . . . Education courses were much too repetitious. I could have taken one course and eliminated the other three required without losing any valuable information. I have found that the educational lectures I have attended since graduation were merely reiterations of these courses.

35. I think foreign language should be a requirement for all elementary majors. There are too many kiddy courses and not

enough really solid courses. My best courses were taken with
Science and Social Science majors.

36. In my education courses, I find that the subject matter
overlaps so much that you find the professor just talking about
whatever they may feel like. Although there are bad points about
the way the professors teach, there are also many good points.
I find that some professors are wonderful teachers and do a fine
job in preparing teachers. I feel that to many people are tearing
education apart and writing unfavorable things about it. They
ought to take the other side just once and take a look at all the
good points.

37. The gap between the liberal arts courses and the Ed
courses is very large in regard to intellectual content and challenge. The Ed. courses generally lack substance. Students should
take more liberal arts courses, and a bare minimum of methods
courses.

38. Too much emphasis on "methods" — not enough on content. Many teachers poorly prepared to teach one specific subject. Education courses, on the whole, are a waste of time and
money.

39. Because you had to be registered in a school of education
to be eligible for practice teaching, I was unable to take the English seminars or comprehensive exam for English majors. I would
have preferred more English, Art, Phil., and Government courses
during college, but my schedule was crowded with education
courses. . . . My main cry is more subject matter and less education courses!

40. One day while sleeping through an Education course my
professor droned "You-must-vary-your-teaching techniques." I
guffawed. The preliminary course in Education is "Human Development, Learning and Teaching." This was the most horrible
torture I have ever known. There was nothing to underline in
the text as it said nothing. The professor monotoned his way
through a year of theory and lists of Aims and Benefits and What
Kiddies Do When They're Six Years Old. No wonder a bright

person shudders at the idea of taking such a course. No wonder Phi Beta Kappa overlooks Education majors when selecting its membership — a moron could pass the final exam and I've thought about stealing one and giving it to a 12 year old child and having it graded. . . . Methods. These are the worst. We learned no methods. . . . I am happy that a survey such as this is being taken. I only hope that future generations of college students will proudly say they are Education majors instead of the current trend of being ashamed to be taking "the easy way out of college." Excepting student teaching, all of my Education courses were a waste of time and money and I could have better spent my time learning more about my subject area.

41. I thought that I was wise in doing my graduate work in the field of secondary education because I wanted to have a taste of everything — curriculum study, guidance, supervision, etc. What a mistake I made! If I had it to do again, I would get a master's in my major field of study. To me, educational courses are a waste of time and money.

42. A good education for an elementary-teacher-to-be would be one of fewer methods courses as they are taught today. I believe their should be more liberal arts courses required and less education.

43. The liberal arts courses I have taken [both undergraduate and in a famous Master of Arts in Teaching program] have been of excellent quality and, I am sure, have prepared me quite adequately for teaching secondary school. The course I have taken in education have not been so valuable. Once a prospective teacher is aware of the various methods, etc., the only way he can learn is through experience.

44. The quality of liberal arts courses was to me far superior to those given in education. Education courses to me, for the most part, lacked real substance and/or true subject matter, although some of the better taught courses did have relevance to later teaching situations. . . . From my academic and professional teaching experiences I will give liberal arts courses a considerably higher rating both in quality and in interest.

45. My feelings are adverse to courses in education. The only quality course given in my program was a course in measurement.

46. A teacher, even in the elementary grades, must have, today, more than a superficial knowledge of such subjects as history, english, etc. I took far too many "methods" courses — one would have sufficed — with more emphasis on subject matter. Practice teaching was invaluable — the opportunity to *see* far surpassed hearing and reading about teaching.

47. A strong and varied background in the liberal arts and humanities I feel is the greatest aid to good teaching. The broader the background of the teacher the better he is equipped to teach the fundamentals of learning, and most important of all provide a challenge and inspire a love for learning which his students can develop on their own.

48. The courses I took in education, except for student teaching, were close to useless. . . . I cannot picture anyone understanding how ridiculous and "unhelpful" these have been, unless they, too, have experienced them.

49. I felt more time whould have been spent on study in my field rather than on time consuming education courses. I gained little or nothing from the latter. My other courses were excellent.

50. I would carefully evaluate education courses offered to see that they were not filled with irrelevant material. Too often teachers of education seem ill-prepared and totally unable to pinpoint specific and necessary ideas.

51. I am aghast at the lack of liberal education and the *shallow* values held by many teacher school products. As a school librarian I have found that many teachers do not even know the basic tools (Reference books, important writers in their field) of their profession and are afraid to branch out or try new ideas.

52. I feel that the courses offered at the university I attended were very much redundant. I feel that these educational courses should be reorganized and given in one semester. As it was they were carried over to the next semester. The liberal arts courses were good. I feel that they served my needs and interests very

well. In my major, physical education, the courses were excellent and were taught very well by the professors. In my own personal opinion the courses in physical ed could be better organized. They, as in the case of the education courses, were redundant.

53. Most of the general academic courses especially the sciences were useful, well organized, and well taught. The education courses were too long, poorly organized, the information too simple and too general. The methods courses were the worst.

54. I feel that if more effort were spent in the preparation of one's major and minor fields of study and less on professional courses the beginning teacher would be much more qualified. I do want to say, however, that the course in student teaching is of inestimable worth.

55. The teacher sets the standards for the classes and also inspires a certain feeling for scholarship and love of learning for its own sake. Small classes were the rule rather than the exception in the English courses I was in. Discussions were lively, disciplined and based on preparation both by students and teachers. Sloppy work was graded accordingly. In the majority of education courses, on the other hand, there seemed to be a feeling that we were a "select group" already screened (how I never knew) and therefore no one need worry about failing — B was a standard grade and with a minimum of effort one could obtain an A. Teachers were, in my opinion, poorly prepared even in their lectures.

56. I feel that my program of study in the liberal arts has been invaluable for the most part — I have forty semester hours in English, twenty four hours in History and Government, and numerous other courses in the liberal arts field. The quality of these courses has been high. The fly in the ointment has been in the education courses required. I felt the number of hours required excessive, and the material very repititeous — to the point of being ridiculous. . . . The real meat in the education field was in the observation and student teaching courses. Here one had a chance to learn what was apparently being hidden in

the college education classrooms — what I learned in these hours is my real strength — the other hours are only paper power.

57. Liberal arts at _____ far exceed the education courses in my opinion. . . . They should have a better guidance course than that which is offered now. The history of education is a two semester course which could be covered in one semester. Learning and teaching is another poor course which could use revamping. The only good part is the field trips and hints given for teaching. The textbook is terrible. This too could be put into one semester. A lot of the course is repetitious of educational psychology and child psychology. These courses all potential teachers must take. They are boring and some people drop out of education because of them.

58. I feel that the education courses I had were too repetitive, and had very little "meat" in them. The required courses I had could have been combined into 2 or 3 really stimulating, informative courses.

59. My liberal arts courses were, on the whole, good or better than average. . . . My only regret here is that I did not have a chance to take as many courses in my major field as I would have liked. . . . My education courses were only fair. Much was repetition. I would like to see at least half of the psychology and history of education courses eliminated and replaced by more practice teaching.

60. I feel if the education courses could only be consolidated, and the repetition and overlapping eliminated (the methods and student teaching excepted) then more liberal arts courses could be included in the student's program and all would benefit.

61. My education on the undergraduate level in the liberal arts was excellent. . . . The education courses offered were mediocre and I found little challenge. My actual teaching experience has proven valuable, fascinating and interesting. In all frankness I must say I actually derived very little from the education courses.

62. I feel I was offered an excellent liberal arts background which improved my education a great deal. However, my edu-

cation courses presented little challenge and were not very worthwhile.

63. My first two years was spent in the College of General Education not in the School of Education. We were given an excellent general background in all areas by very qualified instructors. . . . In education received nothing from the educational psychology course. Professor and course was a complete farce. . . . History and philosophy of education course another farce. This time book was written by professor, thus couldn't manage to learn anything except dislike and disgust. . . . Could have condenced methods [course]. More demonstration and observation would be more beneficial.

64. To put my feelings about this in a simple way, I would say that, there is need for greater emphasis on academic training and less education courses. I recognize the need for some training in the field of education, but I feel its direction requires some change. I would like to see more stress placed on practice teaching programs and much less on methods and educational psychology.

65. I feel that much of the educational courses were useless. All could have been combined into 2 or 3 comprehensive courses. I feel my M.A. was most useful because it was taken in a solid subject area.

66. This teacher rates her academic work 3 A's, 1 B, and 1 D. She rates her Education courses as follows; Educational Psychology: "F" — "Mediocre instructors — dull, stupidly simple content." History and Philosophy of Education: "C" — "I can't even remember these courses — except that they were extremely dull and disgustingly easy." Methods: "D" — One methods course in Social Science which I took by correspondence from ———————————————— was superior. All others were rock-bottom." Practice Teaching: "A" — "My high-school critic teacher made this course worthwhile — not my college supervisor." Supervision and Administration: "F" — "Guidance — ugh!"

67. Teaching courses are nebulous, repitious, and in many cases fail to give the teacher a proper base but perhaps more at fault are the student teachers who expect education courses to substitute for experience.

68. I feel that my liberal arts courses prepared me much better for my field of teaching. Many of my "education courses" were merely rehashing of textbooks assigned and did little to prepare me for the practical situations I would meet.

69. These courses [educational psychology, history and philosophy of education] are not worthy even of an "F" [she grades them "X"]. To me, they were completely useless, worthless, and time consuming. Perhaps this is due to poor instruction. At any rate, had these courses been given to me after I had done student teaching I might have understood what was intended. At least I had a chance to catch up on some sleep.

70. One or two solid courses in methods and techniques of education would be more than sufficient to enable a talented person to teach effectively. The teacher learns to teach in the classroom, not within the covers of a book.

71. As a general comment I feel teacher preparation in the United States is at an all time low — it is deplorable to see graduates of Education schools who are not the least scholastically minded teaching children to read the exact way I was tuaght. They are poor scholars themselves — many culturally lacking and are great mimeographers!!

72. It has been my general opinion that "education" courses are of very little value. They are known for their lack of demand on the student. . . . More emphasis on subject matter and less on methods is necessary in teacher-education.

73. My reaction to education courses was primarily negative. Although I had only 12 semester hours of education, both on an undergraduate and graduate level, I found them to be of little practical value. The content of these courses tended to be vague and far too theoretical for practical application. I found my practice teaching experience to be of more concrete help than all of

my education courses combined. All were courses of *poor* quality. Liberal arts courses were, of course, more tangible and in many cases far more exciting than education courses.

74. I believe that while in college the potential teacher should have a course of study which consists of 90% liberal arts and only 10% education. Later on, when teaching, the teacher can take those education courses that she feels she needs for professional improvement.

75. I feel that 21 hours of education is too much and that more time should have been devoted to English, History (my major) and general subjects too. My background in Biology, Sociology is very poor. I feel that the program at my college taught me little if anything in that area.

76. [Graduate of Radcliffe and of a Master of Arts in Teaching program:] My freshman year in Psych taught me more, had a much better reading list and was better presented than course in educational psychology. The Ed Psych was an unspeakable bore, poorly presented, and loaded with fatuous reading assignments. The course in history of ed was one of the very few ed courses worth taking. It had content and was well-presented. About a fourth of the methods course was helpful and informative. The rest was rehash. One course [in administration] had good reading but most of the discussions were a waste of time. The other courses were a complete waste of time.

77. I felt both my educational courses and liberal arts courses were of a great help to me in my teaching profession. I did feel in some courses in the arts that they were too far removed from my choosen subjects [Health and Physical Education] to help me a great deal in my teaching. In some of my education courses too, I felt overlaped too much, and that I was wasteing time, but as a whole, I am sure I need them all.

78. The instruction in practically all education courses was mediocre. In the majority of these courses motivation and interest were definitely absent. The application of a double standard was practiced by most instructors, i. e., "do as I say not as I do."

Some instructors become noticeably indignant at any challenge or constructive criticism of a particular theory or philosophy which they are presenting. The comment frequently made regarding Ed courses, "if the student has one, he has had them all," I disagreed with at first; however, I have now come to accept that as a truism based on my own exposure to Ed courses both as an undergraduate and graduate student.

79. [Graduate of a Master of Arts in Teaching program:] I am very satisfied with my educational program. I would not relinquish one liberal arts hour. A brief, concentrated program in education suited my needs. I would wish now in service training — workshops, conferences, but these are not available in our system. You don't really know what you need to know until you're teaching. I believe teachers need less pre-teaching training (ala State Teachers' Colleges) and more in service training.

80. Practically all the education courses offered some insight into general problems and administration of education. However from the sum total I got very little practical help from most of it. I have been teaching on emergency certificate while getting my degree and I am sorry to have to say that most help comes from experience. There is a great deal of repetition in ed. courses. Much stating and restating of principles in several different ways, but few actual ideas of practical classroom use. Probably half the time spent in ed. courses was a complete waste of time.

81. The liberal arts courses I took were, for the most part, well-conducted, informative, and satisfying. On the other hand the education courses through which I suffered were tedious, repetitious, and tiresome. Generalties prevailed to the extent that one could pass or even make an *A* by hardly reading the text and by using a little horse sense. As an exhausted and frustrated first-year teacher, I recognize the greatest failing as a lack of material transferable from the college classroom to the high school classroom. The teaching of grammar, composition, elocution, etc. in which I find myself involved for half the school year, as do all other English teachers in my state, was an area totally ignored by the curriculum of the state teachers college I attended. My

three hour methods course designed to deal with such was, instead, an aspiring and elevated effort to determine long-range goals for teachers and students. In actual practice though, I find my greatest goal is that of teaching my students not to say "I ain't got none" and teaching them the difference between their and there.

82. More time should be given to subject matter than to education courses. More specifics in education courses and less discussion about generalities should be given in education courses. I had only 6 weeks of student teaching. I think 12 weeks of student teaching and fewer education courses would be far more valuable.

83. Most of the areas in liberal arts are too restrictive in coverage. In the field of English, too many of the required courses are in the field of literature. This is probably why too many students come out of high school deficient in the use of good grammar. Not enough teachers are thoroughly trained to teach it. With a "minor" in English, I had *one* course in English grammar.

In the Social Sciences, too many courses are built around American History. Although this might be considered necessary, there is not enough time left to get well acquainted with Economics, Government, or Sociology. Not very many Social Science majors feel competent in these areas. It must be assumed that most Social Science majors will teach history, but this is not the case.

The liberal arts area could probably be more useful to future teachers, especially secondary school teachers, if it was not so restricted to specific areas.

My only complaint with education courses is that they are too idealistic in their approach to education training. Most courses teach from a standpoint of the "ideal" situation. The graduating teacher does not find this in reality. Practice teaching makes this "painfully" apparent. It is only then that you find that what you have been led to expect just doesn't exist.

84. [Graduate of a Master of Arts in Teaching program:] Old-fashioned supervising teacher drew up lessons, word by word,

and was most pleased when student teacher did not deviate in any way from them. Very stifling atmosphere. "F" to my immediate college supervisor who was aggressively belligerent toward *all* his student teachers, and to *his* supervisor as well. Instead of helping, he would have near tantrums if his badly given instructions were not understood and asked to be repeated. "A" to his most understanding supervisor, a faculty member, who tried to ameliorate the difficulties he sparked.

85. The gist of my prescription would be fewer courses in education and more in liberal arts. In the latter one generally can expect to find content which is much more vital and penetrating, and instruction on a much higher plane. When one finally become a classroom teacher, he quickly finds that his courses in education and methods are of little value. I would be far more effective as a teacher if I had had more training in my subject area and additional courses in literature, philosophy, and the arts. I am a human being first and a teacher second!

86. For the most part the education courses that I had were of very little help to me when I entered the teaching field. The courses I had in Home Economics and the liberal Arts were the most help to me.

87. As far as my own experiences were concerned I feel that my four years of college were a total waste. I was prepared for a very small school and started teaching science only in a very large system and found out very soon that I did not have enough depth in the subject. Also the pupils were nothing like those we have in training school because their environment was much different, and because none of my courses taught us how to handle these children, I seem to have a very difficult year.

88. General education was satisfactory. Education courses — much too little is offered that is useful. Too much time wasted on busy work which teaches nothing and bores greatly. Too much emphasis placed on the *nobleness* of the teaching profession (?!) and too little on the actual carrying out of the job.

89. I feel that I wasted my time in most all of my education

courses. I should have had the opportunity to take more liberal arts courses in their place.

90. With a good liberal arts background (no education courses there) a few weeks of *methods* in your field and several months of practice-teaching (and doing as much and as much variety as possible) I think you are ready to teach at the secondary level. The practice-teaching will help weed out most people whose personality is unsuited. All other education courses are of no use in teaching. Some statistics is necessary, but can be gotten in a liberal arts course.

91. The course of studies I followed was a good one; I feel, however, that there should have been more emphasis on education courses. Classroom management is an area that needs much discussion. . . . On the whole the majority of the liberal arts courses were good; there was much "room" left in the curriculum for elective courses.

92. My reaction to my academic and professional education is positive. I felt that I was educated by excellent professors; however, I feel that the idea of complete lecture for a full semester should be challenged. I believe there should be more group work, oral reports, films and other activities of participation by the students. This would draw more interest within the student and create more learning in the classroom itself. Also, the humdrum of routine set up by the teacher would be lessened, and he would be learning once again as well as teaching at the same time.

93. The program of studies that I followed was on the whole excellent. The only weaknesses were in the area of method courses where the actual class situation was discussed. My program for [elementary] teacher preparation would be as follows: Two years of liberal arts — no courses in education. Two years of educational courses plus the opportunity of concentrating in the area of personal choice. One year internship — On the job training — Close supervision.

94. There was and is an overall opinion that all education

courses are dull, but I think this comes from persons in fields other than education as I know I had some very interesting courses in methods and philosophy of education. It was merely courses in history of education and introduction to teaching which would have been difficult to make interesting because of their vague or general subjects covered.

95. I feel that my preparation for teaching was completely satisfactory. Education courses were helpful and constituted a proper balance in relation to courses in other areas [student reports 18 hours in Education and 108 in liberal arts]. Philosophy of education was stressed in my program, and I feel that this was one of the most valuable parts of my preparation for teaching and should be emphasized in any teacher's program of education.

96. I believe that all liberal arts courses, on the whole, were very interesting and worthwhile. I believe that my education courses which stressed theory and methods were too repititous. However, I did enjoy my education courses which provided me with practical experience. I think a few of my education courses could have been combined into one semesters work.

97. My liberal arts education was extensive and excellent. My education within my major field (Physical Education) was outstanding. I felt a very definite lack in other "pure" education courses. The caliber of instructors was low though the material was valuable. I feel fully qualified in physical education, perhaps even more qualified than some teachers I saw during my observation period.

98. I felt that the study needed to train a high school teacher could be accomplished in one or two years. Many of the courses (required) were only for the purpose of keeping students in school for four years or to take up time. The education I received in my major and minor field (Social Science) was average. In education it was above average. In other courses it was about average. Very few instructors tried to show us how to teach but merely taught us subject matter. I would think it more effective if subject and methods were combined.

99. The training I had was very good. The minute I enroll in the school I was looked upon as a future teacher. They always took the problems we would face and help us get the best possible answer to it, as a *teacher*. If you are looked upon as a teacher or future teacher while attending a college, you will feel more prepare when you actually on the job.

100. I believe the courses I took were all necessary for a well informed teacher. She (he) needs a wealth of information at her fingertips to do a good job. . . . I also believe that some of my education courses overlapped each other. These could probably be condensed to make fewer courses and perhaps better courses leaving room for such things as a longer period for seminar of education, psychology and methods.

Index

Index

SICK CITIES

Mitchell Gordon

In 1980, over 90% of all Americans will live in urban areas, as compared with 51% in 1920. This phenomenally rapid growth of our nation's cities has left in its wake critical problems which endanger the health, the safety, and the human spirit of all urban dwellers. Amassing material from studies and tours of 70 U.S. cities, Mitchell Gordon presents a fast-paced survey of deterioration—air pollution, water contamination, lack of recreational facilities, decay of downtown areas, crime, noise, traffic congestion, poor schools, insufficient police protection, inadequate rubbish collection. He defines the nature of the new disease of *metropolitanization*, warns of its consequences, and proposes some possible cures.

"Mr. Gordon dispassionately reports enough sheer horror to make any lay reader instantly and passionately concerned with questions of his own survival."

—The New York Times

"One of the most comprehensive presentations ever to appear in print on the mid-20th century growing pains of the nation's large cities and their expanding suburban areas."

—Chicago Tribune

"Superbly researched volume."

—Los Angeles Times

THE ARMED SOCIETY
Militarism in Modern America

Tristram Coffin

"There is no evidence that we [Americans] are peace-loving or ever have been. We have taken what we wanted by force if need be, sometimes muttering a proper prayer over the vanquished." With these words Washington political writer-novelist Tristram Coffin launches a daring indictment of the American military establishment and the American spirit. In witty, hard-hitting language he describes the military hierarchy, the outmoded reactionary ideals of the military mind, the dangerous hold the military has on the public imagination as well as on the public purse strings.

"Tristram Coffin . . . pulls out the pins and flips hand grenades down the corridors of the Pentagon."
—*The New York Times*

"A serious work, well done, and somewhat frightening."
—*Houston Chronicle*

SOUTH EAST ASIA IN TURMOIL

Brian Crozier

For years South East Asia has been the political fisherman's paradise. Its troubled waters have seen western imperialism, eastern nationalism, comintern agitation, Japanese occupation, Sino-Soviet conflict, American intervention, and the explosive ambitions of the local boy, Dr. Sukarno. To the eye of the non-specialist the whole area presents a bewildering blur.

Brian Crozier has managed to assemble the myriad pieces of this jig-saw puzzle—Laos, Vietnam, Sarawak, Brunei; Hatta, Sihanouk, Ho Chi Minh, Bao Dai, and all the others—into a continuous and coherent narrative. In *South East Asia in Turmoil* he examines Soviet, Chinese, American, British, and French policies, explains where they went wrong, and suggests future courses of action.

South East Asia is a political volcano today. Any reader who is looking for a thread through the labyrinth of violent news from there will do well to read this book, which lays out clearly who has done what . . . where . . . and why.

IN DEFENCE OF POLITICS

Bernard Crick

"Original and profound. It is hard to think of anyone interested in politics at any level who would not benefit by reading it."
—Max Beloff

At a time of brittle cynicism about the activities of politicians, this book makes "an attempt to justify politics in plain words by saying what it is." In a civilized community, which is no mere tribe, the establishment among rival groups and interests of political order – of agreed rules for the game – marks the birth of freedom. In spite of the compromises, deals, half-measures, and bargains which prompt impatient idealists to regard politics as a dirty word – indeed, because of them – the negotiating processes of politics remain the only tested alternative to government by outright coercion.

UNITED NATIONS
Piety, Myth, and Truth

Andrew Boyd

The UN has evolved in unforeseen ways and many people are entirely ignorant of its true nature. This volume presents a behind-the-scenes look at its development and present structure. The off-stage debates, the emergence of executive power, the probable future of the organization are among the points dealt with by Mr. Boyd, who is on the editorial staff of the *Economist*.

THE OTHER AMERICA
Poverty in the United States

Michael Harrington

The book credited with sparking the government's War on Poverty. Michael Harrington gives a vivid description of America's poor – the unskilled workers, the aged, the minorities, and the other rejects of the affluent society. He analyzes the nature and causes of the Other America and warns that in the U.S. today poverty is becoming a self-perpetuating culture, a way of life. He calls for an integrated and comprehensive program to conquer it. The government has responded with the War on Poverty.

"It impressed Jack Kennedy . . . it is clear that [this] book contributed to Johnson's new drive."
                                        —*Time*

"THE OTHER AMERICA has been credited with helping to open the Administration drive on poverty. . . ."
                                        —*The New York Times*

"It is an excellent book – and a most important one."
                                        —*The New Yorker*